Learning Robotics
Using Python

Design, simulate, program, and prototype an interactive autonomous mobile robot from scratch with the help of Python, ROS, and Open-CV!

Lentin Joseph

[PACKT] open source ✳
PUBLISHING   community experience distilled

BIRMINGHAM - MUMBAI

Learning Robotics Using Python

First published: May 2015

Production reference: 1250515

Published by Packt Publishing Ltd.
Livery Place
35 Livery Street
Birmingham B3 2PB, UK.

ISBN 978-1-78328-753-6

www.packtpub.com

Cover image by Jarek Blaminsky (milak6@wp.pl)

Credits

Author
Lentin Joseph

Reviewers
Avkash Chauhan
Vladimir Iakovlev
Blagoj Petrushev
Marek Suppa

Commissioning Editor
Rebecca Youé

Acquisition Editor
Rebecca Youé

Content Development Editor
Athira Laji

Technical Editors
Ankur Ghiye
Manali Gonsalves

Copy Editors
Pranjali Chury
Relin Hedly
Merilyn Pereira
Adithi Shetty

Project Coordinator
Harshal Ved

Proofreaders
Stephen Copestake
Safis Editing

Indexer
Priya Sane

Graphics
Sheetal Aute

Production Coordinator
Nitesh Thakur

Cover Work
Nitesh Thakur

About the Author

Lentin Joseph is an electronics engineer, robotics enthusiast, machine vision expert, embedded programmer, and the founder and CEO of Qbotics Labs (`http://www.qboticslabs.com`) in India. He got his bachelor's degree in electronics and communication engineering at the Federal Institute of Science and Technology (FISAT), Kerala. In his final year engineering project, he created a social robot, which can interact with people. The project was a huge success and got mentioned in visual and print media. The main feature of this robot was that it could communicate with people and reply intelligently. It also has some image-processing capabilities, such as face, motion, and color detection. The entire project was implemented using the Python programming language. His interest in robotics, image processing, and Python began this project.

After graduation, he worked at a start-up company based on robotics and image processing for 3 years. In the meantime, he learned famous robotic software platforms—such as Robot Operating system (ROS), V-REP, and Actin (a robotic simulation tool)—and image processing libraries, such as OpenCV, OpenNI, and PCL. He also knows about robot 3D designing, embedded programming on Arduino, and Stellaris Launchpad.

After 3 years of work experience, he started a new company called Qbotics Labs, which is mainly focused on research to build great products in domains such as wearable technology, robotics, machine vision, green technology, and online education. He maintains a personal website (`http://www.lentinjoseph.com`) and a technology blog called technolabsz (`http://www.technolabsz.com`). He publishes his works on his tech blog. He was a speaker at PyCon2013 India, and he spoke on the topic of learning robotics using Python.

I would like to dedicate this book to my parents because they gave me the inspiration to write it. I would also like to convey my regards to my friends who helped and inspired me to write this book.

I would like to thank Marek Suppa for his valuable contribution in writing *Chapter 1, Introduction to Robotics*, in addition to reviewing this book.

About the Reviewers

Avkash Chauhan is currently leading a team of engineers at a start-up based in San Francisco, where his team is building a big data monitoring platform using machine learning and new age methods to improve business continuity and gain maximum advantage from the platform itself. He is the founder and principal of Big Data Perspective, with a vision to make the Hadoop platform accessible to mainstream enterprises by simplifying its adoption, customization, management, and support. Before Big Data Perspective, he worked at Platfora Inc., building big data analytics software running natively on Hadoop. Previously, he worked for 8 years at Microsoft, building cloud and big data products and providing assistance to enterprise partners worldwide. Avkash has over 15 years of software development experience in cloud and big data disciplines. He is a programmer at heart in full-stack discipline and has the business acumen to work with enterprises, meeting their needs. He is passionate about technology and enjoys sharing his knowledge with others through various social media. He has also written a few books on big data discipline and is very active in the tech social space. He is an accomplished author, blogger, technical speaker, and he loves the outdoors.

Vladimir Iakovlev is a software developer. Most of the time, he develops web applications using Python, Clojure, and JavaScript. He's the owner of a few semi-popular open source projects. He was a speaker at a few Python-related conferences.

In his free time, Vladimir likes to play with electronic devices, such as Arduino and PyBoard, and image-processing devices, such as Leap Motion. He has tried to build some robots. He has already built a robotic arm.

Currently, Vladimir works at Upwork, where he develops web applications, mostly with Python.

Blagoj Petrushev is a software engineer and consultant based in Skopje, Macedonia. His work revolves mainly around backends, datastores, and network applications. Among his interests are machine learning, NLP, data analysis, modeling and databases, and distributed programming.

Marek Suppa has been playing with (kind of) smart machines for the past few years, which are pretentiously called robots in some parts of the world. Right now, he leads a robotic football team, building tools to help others start with robots and setting off on a new venture to see how far the current technology will let us move toward the goal of creating a robot as it was first defined.

I would like to thank everyone who supported the creation of this book, whoever and wherever they might be.

www.PacktPub.com

Support files, eBooks, discount offers, and more

For support files and downloads related to your book, please visit
www.PacktPub.com.

Did you know that Packt offers eBook versions of every book published, with PDF
and ePub files available? You can upgrade to the eBook version at www.PacktPub.
com and as a print book customer, you are entitled to a discount on the eBook copy.
Get in touch with us at service@packtpub.com for more details.

At www.PacktPub.com, you can also read a collection of free technical articles,
sign up for a range of free newsletters and receive exclusive discounts and offers
on Packt books and eBooks.

https://www2.packtpub.com/books/subscription/packtlib

Do you need instant solutions to your IT questions? PacktLib is Packt's online digital
book library. Here, you can search, access, and read Packt's entire library of books.

Why subscribe?

- Fully searchable across every book published by Packt
- Copy and paste, print, and bookmark content
- On demand and accessible via a web browser

Free access for Packt account holders

If you have an account with Packt at www.PacktPub.com, you can use this to access
PacktLib today and view 9 entirely free books. Simply use your login credentials for
immediate access.

Table of Contents

Preface

Learning Robotics with Python contains twelve chapters that mainly aims at how to build an autonomous mobile robot from scratch and how to program it using Python. The robot mentioned in this book is a service robot, which can be used to serve food at home, hotels, and restaurants. From the beginning to end, this book discusses the step-by-step procedure on how to build this robot. The book starts with the basic concepts of robotics and then moves on to the 3D modeling and simulation of the robot. After the successful simulation of the robot, it discusses the hardware components required to build the robot prototype in order to complete the robot navigation.

The software part of this robot is mainly implemented using the Python programming language and software frameworks, such as Robot Operating System (ROS), Open-CV, and so on. You will understand the application of Python from the aspects of designing the robot to the robot's user interface. The Gazebo simulator is used to simulate the robot and machine vision libraries, such as Open-CV and OpenNI. PCL is used to process the 2D and 3D image data of the robot. Each chapter is presented with an adequate theory to understand the application aspect. The book is reviewed by experts in this field who are passionate about robotics.

What this book covers

Chapter 1, Introduction to Robotics, contains basic concepts and terminologies of robotics. This chapter is a must for beginners who are just starting with robotics.

Chapter 2, Mechanical Design of a Service Robot, discusses the 2D and 3D CAD designing aspect of the robot using LibreCAD and Blender (free software). This chapter also demonstrates how to use Blender Python APIs in order to build the 3D model.

Chapter 3, Working with Robot Simulation Using ROS and Gazebo, takes you through the simulation of the service robot using Gazebo and ROS.

Chapter 4, Designing ChefBot Hardware, explains the hardware designing of the robot, including block diagram and hardware components required to build ChefBot.

Chapter 5, Working with Robotic Actuators and Wheel Encoders, covers interfacing of robotic actuators and wheel encoders using Tiva C LaunchPad. It also mentions high-end smart actuators like dynamixel.

Chapter 6, Working with Robotic Sensors, discusses interfacing of ultrasonic distance sensors, IR proximity sensors, and IMU using Tiva C LaunchPad.

Chapter 7, Programming Vision Sensors Using Python and ROS, talks about the introduction to Open-CV, OpenNI, and PCL libraries and interfacing these to ROS and programming using Python.

Chapter 8, Working with Speech Recognition and Synthesis Using Python and ROS, discusses speech recognition and synthesis using various libraries and interfacing it to ROS programming using Python.

Chapter 9, Applying Artificial Intelligence to ChefBot Using Python, covers tutorials to build a ChatterBot. This can be used to make the robot interactive.

Chapter 10, Integration of ChefBot Hardware and Interfacing it into ROS, Using Python, explores tutorials to integrate the complete hardware and essential software section. It mainly discusses autonomous navigation of the service robot and how to program it using ROS and Python.

Chapter 11, Designing a GUI for a Robot Using Qt and Python, covers tutorials on how to build a GUI for the user who operates the robot in a typical restaurant. The GUI is built using Qt and the PyQt Python wrapper.

Chapter 12, The Calibration and Testing of ChefBot, explores tutorials on how to calibrate and test the robot for the final run.

What you need for this book

The book is all about how to build a robot. To start with this book, you should have some hardware. The robot can be built from scratch, or you can buy a differential-drive configuration robot with an encoder feedback. You should buy a controller board, such as Texas Instruments Launchpad, for embedded processing. You should have at least a laptop/net book for the entire robot process. In this book, we will use Intel NUC for robot processing. It's very compact in size and delivers high performance. For the 3D vision, you should have 3D sensors, such as laser scanner, Kinect, and Asus Xtion Pro.

In the software section, you should have a good understanding on how to work with GNU/Linux commands. You should also have a good knowledge of Python. You should install Ubuntu 14.04.2 LTS to work with the examples. If you have knowledge about ROS, OpenCV, OpenNI, and PCL, it will be a great add-on. You have to install ROS Indigo to test these examples.

Who this book is for

Learning Robotics with Python is a good companion for entrepreneurs who want to explore the service robotics domain, professionals who want to implement more features to their robots, researchers who want to explore more about robotics, and hobbyist or students who want to learn robotics. The book follows a step-by-step guide that can be easily understood by anyone.

Conventions

In this book, you will find a number of styles of text that distinguish between different kinds of information. Here are some examples of these styles, and an explanation of their meaning.

Code words in text, database table names, folder names, filenames, file extensions, pathnames, dummy URLs, user input, and Twitter handles are shown as follows: " The first procedure is to create a world file and save it with the .world file extension."

A block of code is set as follows:

```
<xacro:include filename="$(find
  chefbot_description)/urdf/chefbot_gazebo.urdf.xacro"/>
<xacro:include filename="$(find
  chefbot_description)/urdf/chefbot_properties.urdf.xacro"/>
```

Any command-line input or output is written as follows:

```
$ roslaunch chefbot_gazebo chefbot_empty_world.launch
```

New terms and **important words** are shown in bold. Words that you see on the screen, in menus or dialog boxes for example, appear in the text like this: " we can command the robot to navigate to some position on the map using the **2D Nav Goal** button".

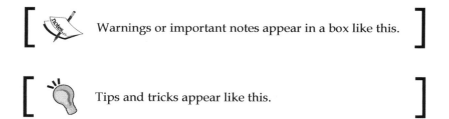

> Warnings or important notes appear in a box like this.

> Tips and tricks appear like this.

Reader feedback

Feedback from our readers is always welcome. Let us know what you think about this book—what you liked or may have disliked. Reader feedback is important for us to develop titles that you really get the most out of.

To send us general feedback, simply send an e-mail to feedback@packtpub.com, and mention the book title via the subject of your message.

If there is a topic that you have expertise in and you are interested in either writing or contributing to a book, see our author guide on www.packtpub.com/authors.

Customer support

Now that you are the proud owner of a Packt book, we have a number of things to help you to get the most from your purchase.

Downloading the example code

You can download the example code files for all Packt books you have purchased from your account at http://www.packtpub.com. If you purchased this book elsewhere, you can visit http://www.packtpub.com/support and register to have the files e-mailed directly to you.

Downloading the color images of this book

We also provide you a PDF file that has color images of the screenshots/diagrams used in this book. The color images will help you better understand the changes in the output. You can download this file from: `https://www.packtpub.com/sites/default/files/downloads/7536OS_ImageBundle.pdf`.

Errata

Although we have taken every care to ensure the accuracy of our content, mistakes do happen. If you find a mistake in one of our books—maybe a mistake in the text or the code—we would be grateful if you would report this to us. By doing so, you can save other readers from frustration and help us improve subsequent versions of this book. If you find any errata, please report them by visiting `http://www.packtpub.com/submit-errata`, selecting your book, clicking on the **errata submission form** link, and entering the details of your errata. Once your errata are verified, your submission will be accepted and the errata will be uploaded on our website, or added to any list of existing errata, under the Errata section of that title. Any existing errata can be viewed by selecting your title from `http://www.packtpub.com/support`.

Piracy

Piracy of copyright material on the Internet is an ongoing problem across all media. At Packt, we take the protection of our copyright and licenses very seriously. If you come across any illegal copies of our works, in any form, on the Internet, please provide us with the location address or website name immediately so that we can pursue a remedy.

Please contact us at `copyright@packtpub.com` with a link to the suspected pirated material.

We appreciate your help in protecting our authors, and our ability to bring you valuable content.

Questions

You can contact us at `questions@packtpub.com` if you are having a problem with any aspect of the book, and we will do our best to address it.

1
Introduction to Robotics

If you read an introductory chapter in any technical book, you may have noticed that it pretty much always follows the same structure. It begins by describing how awesome the topic is, what a good decision it is to start reading the book, and how you should keep on reading because there are many exciting things awaiting you in its further chapters.

This chapter is no such chapter. It starts with the following quote:

Robotics is an art.

Although, such a strong statement does probably deserve some explanation, we believe that after you finish reading this book (and building your own robots!), no further explanation will be needed.

So if robotics is an art, how does one learn it? To put it differently, what are the differences between learning to play a musical instrument, learning to paint, learning to write, and learning robotics? We believe that there are not too many of them. Just as musicians need to play on their instruments, painters need to produce paintings, and writers need to write their texts, roboticists (the term we use to describe people who build robotics) need to build their robots. Just as musicians, painters, and writers need to learn the jargon used in their trades, roboticists need to familiarize themselves with a few basic terms that they might run into while reading tutorials, researching scientific literature, and talking to other robotics enthusiasts. Also, just as any artist needs to know at least a little bit about the history of their respective art, so does any good roboticist need to know a thing or two about the history of robotics. That's why in this chapter, we will cover:

- What is a robot?
- Where do robots come from?
- What can we find in a robot?
- How do we build robots?

What is a robot?

Rather than defining what a robot is right away, let's pause for a moment and discuss whether we need to answer a question like this after all. Everybody knows that a robot is some sort of a machine that can move around and depending on what movie you saw or which book you read, it can either help humans in their day-to-day life or mean the end of humanity.

It's clear that there is some controversy and lots of misunderstandings about robots and their role in the past, present, and the future. In order to better understand the situation, let's first examine closely the term "robot" itself. Then, we will try to define it a bit more formally to prevent any misunderstanding or controversy.

History of the term robot

The term "robot" was used for the first time by Karel Čapek, a Czech writer in his play **Rossum's Universal Robots (R.U.R)** that he wrote in 1920, to denote an artificial human made out of synthetic organic matter. These robots (*roboti* in Czech) were made in factories and their purpose was to replace human workers. While they were very efficient and executed orders they were given perfectly, they lacked any emotion. It seemed that humans would not need to work at all because robots seemed to be happy to work for them. This changed after a while and a robot revolt resulted in extinction of the human race.

R.U.R is quite dark and disturbing, but it does not leave the future hopeless. It was considered quite a success back in the day and we certainly do recommend you to read it. As its copyright had already expired in many countries at the time of writing this book, it should not be a problem to find a version online, which is in the public domain.

> *"When he (Young Rossum) took a look at human anatomy he saw immediately that it was too complex and that a good engineer could simplify it. So he undertook to redesign anatomy, experimenting with what would lend itself to omission or simplification. Robots have a phenomenal memory. If you were to read them a twenty-volume encyclopedia they could repeat the contents in order, but they never think up anything original. They'd make fine university professors."*
>
> *– Karel Capek, R.U.R. (Rossum's Universal Robots), 1920*

While many attribute the term robot to Karel Čapek as he wrote the play in which it appeared for the first time, there are sources suggesting that it was actually Čapek's brother Josef who came up with the term (it seems that there was an article in Czech daily print written by Karel Čapek himself, in which he wants to set the record straight by telling this story). Karel wanted to use the term *labori* (from Latin labor, work), but he did not like it. It seemed too artificial to him, so he asked his brother for advice. Josef suggested *roboti* and that was what Karel used in the end.

Now that we know when the term *robot* was used for the first time and who actually created it, let's find out where does it come from. The explanation that many use is that it comes from the Czech words *robota* and *robotník*, which literally means "work" and "worker" respectively. However, the word *robota* also means "work" or "serf labor" in Slovak. Also, we should take into account that some sources suggest that by the time Karel was writing R.U.R, he and his brother often visited his father in a small Slovak spa town called Trenčianske Teplice. Therefore, it might very well be that the term robot was inspired by the usage of the word "robota" in Slovak language, which is coincidentally, the native language of one of the authors of this book.

Whether the term robot comes from Czech or Slovak, the word robota might be a matter of national pride, but it does not concern us too much. In both cases, the literal meaning is "work", "labor", or "hard work" and it was the purpose of the Čapek's robots. However, robots have evolved dramatically over the past hundred years. To say that they are all about doing hard work would probably be an understatement.

So, let's try to define the notion of a robot as we perceive it today.

Modern definition of a robot

When we try to find a precise definition of some term, our first stop is usually some sort of encyclopedia or a dictionary. Let's try to do this for the term robot.

Our first stop will be *Encyclopedia Britannica*. Its definition of a robot is as follows:

> *"Any automatically operated machine that replaces human effort, though it might not resemble human beings in appearance or preform functions in a humanlike manner."*

This is quite a nice definition, but there are quite a few problems with it.

First of all, it's a bit too broad. By this definition, a washing machine should also be considered a robot. It does operate automatically (well, most of them do), it does replace human effort (although not by changing the same tasks a human would do), and it certainly does not resemble a human.

Secondly, it's quite difficult to imagine what a robot actually is after reading this definition. With such a broad definition, there are way too many things that can be considered a robot and this definition does not provide us with any specific features.

It turns out that while Encyclopedia Britannica's definition of a robot does not fit our needs well enough, it's actually one of the best ones that one can find. For example, The Free Dictionary defines a robot as "*A mechanical device that sometimes resembles a human and is capable of performing a variety of often complex human tasks on command or by being programmed in advance.*" This is even worse than what we had and it seems that a washing machine should still be considered a robot.

The inherent problem with these definitions is that they try to capture vast amount of machines that we call robots these days. The result is that it's very difficult, if not impossible, to come up with a definition that will be comprehensive enough and not include a washing machine at the same time. John Engelberger, founder of the world's first robotics company and industrial robotics (as we know it today) once famously said, "*I can't define a robot, but I know one when I see one.*"

So, is it even possible to define a robot? Maybe not in general. However, if we limit ourselves just to the scope of this book, there may be a definition that will suit our needs. In her very nice introductory book on the subject of robotics called *The Robotics Primer* (which we also highly recommend), *Maja J. Mataric* uses the following definition:

> *"A robot is an autonomous system which exists in the physical world, can sense its environment, and can act on it to achieve some goals."*

At first sight, it might not seem like a vast improvement over what we have so far, but let's dissect it part by part to see whether it meets our needs.

The first part says, "A robot is an **autonomous** system". By autonomous, we mean that a robot makes decisions on its own—it's not controlled by a human. This already seems to be an improvement as it weeds out any machine that's controlled by someone (such as our famous washing machine). Robots that we will talk about throughout this book may sometimes have some sort of a remote function, which allows a human to control it remotely, but this functionality is usually built-in as sort of a safety measure so that if something goes wrong and the robot's autonomous systems fails to behave as we would expect them to, it's still possible to get the robot to safety and diagnose its problems afterwards. However, the main goal still stays the same, that is, to build robots that can take some direction from humans and are able to act and function on their own.

However, just being an autonomous system will certainly not be enough for a robot in this book. For instance, we can find many computer programs that we can call autonomous systems (they are not controlled by an individual and make decisions on their own) and yet we do not consider them to be robots.

To get around this obstacle, we need the other part of the sentence that says, "which exists in the **physical** world".

Given the recent advances in the fields of artificial intelligence and machine learning, there is no shortage of computer systems that act on their own and perform some work for us, which is what robots should be for. As a quite notorious example, let's consider **spam** filters. These are computer programs that read every e-mail that reaches your e-mail address and decides whether you may want to read it (and that the e-mail is indeed legitimate) or whether it's yet another example of an unwanted e-mail.

There is no doubt that such a system is helpful (if you disagree, try to read some of the e-mails in your Spam folder—I am pretty sure it will be a boring read). It's estimated that over 60 percent of all e-mail traffic in 2014 can be attributed to spam e-mails. Being able to automatically filter them can save us a lot of reading time. Also, as there is a no human involved in the decision process (although, we can help it by marking an e-mail as spam), we can call such a system as autonomous. Still, we will not call it a true robot. Rather, we call them "software robots" or just "bots" (the fact that their name is shorter may come from the fact that they are short of the physical parts of true robots).

While software robots are definitely an interesting group on its own, it's the physical world in which robots operate that makes the process of creating them so exciting and difficult at the same time. When creating a software robot, you can count on the fact that the environment it will run in (usually the operating system) will be quite stable (as in, not too many things may change unexpectedly). However, when you are creating a real robot, you can never be sure.

This is why a real robot needs to know what is happening in the environment in which it operates. Also, this is why the next part of the definition says, "can *sense* its environment".

Sensing what is happening around a real robot is arguably its most important feature. To sense their surrounding environments, robots usually have sensors. These are devices that measure physical characteristics of the environment and provide this information back to the robot so that it can, for instance, react to sudden changes of temperature, humidity, or pressure. This is quite a big difference from software robots. While they just get the information they need in order to operate somewhat magically, real robots need to have a subsystem or subsystems that take care of obtaining this information. If we look at the differences between robots and humans, we will not find many (in our very high-level view, of course). We can think of sensoring subsystems as artificial replacements for human organs that provide this sort of information to the brain.

One important consequence of this definition is that anything that does not sense its environment cannot be called a robot. This includes any devices that just "drive blind" or move in a random fashion because they do not have any information from the environment to base their behavior on.

Any roboticist will tell you that robots are very exciting machines. Many will also argue that what makes them so exciting is actually their ability to interact with the outside world (which is to move or otherwise change the environment they are in). Without this, they are just another static machine that might be useful, but rather unexciting.

Our definition of a robot reflects this in its last part when it says, "can *act on it* to *achieve* some *goals*".

Acting on the environment might sound like a very complex task for a robot, but in this case, it just means changing the world in some (even very slight) way. We call these parts of robots that perform this as *effectors*. If we look at our robot vs human comparison, effectors are the artificial equivalents of hands, legs, and other body parts that allow it to move. Effectors make use of some lower-level systems such as motors or muscles that actually carry out the movement. We call them *actuators*. Although, the artificial ones may seem to function similar to the biological ones, a closer look will reveal that they are actually quite different.

You may have noticed that this part is not only about acting on the robot's environment, but also about achieving some goals. While many hobby roboticists build robots just for the fun of it, most robots are built in order to carry out (or, should we rather say, to help with) some tasks, such as moving heavy parts in a factory or locating victims in areas affected by natural disasters.

As we said before, a system or a machine that behaves randomly and does not use information from its environment cannot really be considered a robot. However, how can it use these information somehow? The easiest thing to do is to do something useful, which we can rephrase as trying to reach some goal that we consider useful, which in turn brings us back to our definition. A goal of a robot does not necessarily need to be something as complex and ambitious as "hard labor for human". It can easily be something simple, such as "do not bump into obstacles" or "turn the light switch on".

Now, as we have at least a slight idea of what a robot is, we can move on to briefly discuss where robots come from, in other words, the history of robotics.

Where do robots come from?

As the title suggests, this part of the chapter should be about the history of robots. We already know a few quite important facts, such as the term robot was coined by a Czech author Karel Čapek in 1920. As it turns out, there are many more interesting events that happened over the years, other than this one. In order to keep things organized, let's start from the beginning.

It's quite difficult to pinpoint a precise date in history, which we can mark as the date of birth of the first robot. For one, we have established quite a restrictive definition of a robot previously; thus, we will have to wait until the 20th century to actually see a robot in the proper sense of the word. Until then, let's at least discuss the honorable mentions.

The first one that comes close to a robot is a mechanical bird called "The Pigeon". This was postulated by a Greek mathematician Archytas of Tarentum in the 4th century BC and was supposed to be propelled by steam. It cannot not be considered a robot by our definition (not being able to sense its environment already disqualifies it), but it comes pretty close for its age. Over the following centuries, there were many attempts to create automatic machines, such as clocks measuring time using the flow of water, life-sized mechanical figures, or even first programmable humanoid robots (it was actually a boat with four automatic musicians on it). The problem with all these is that they are very disputable as there is very little (or none) historically trustworthy information available about these machines.

It would have stayed like this for quite some time if it was not for Leonardo Da Vinci's notebooks that were rediscovered in 1950s. They contain a complete drawing of a 1945 humanoid (a fancy word for a mechanical device that resemble humans), which looks like an armored knight. It seems that it was designed so that it could sit up, wave its arms, move its head, and most importantly, amuse royalty. In the 18th century, following the amusement line, Jacques de Vaucanson created three automata: a flute player that could play twelve songs, a tambourine player, and the most famous one, "The Digesting Duck". This duck was capable of moving, quacking, flapping wings, or even eating and digesting food (not in a way you will probably think — it just released matter stored in a hidden compartment). It was an example of "moving anatomy" — modeling human or animal anatomy using mechanics.

Our list will not be complete if we omitted these robot-like devices that came about in the following century. Many of them were radio-controlled, such as Nikola Tesla's boat, which he showcased at Madison Square Garden in New York. You could command it to go forward, stop, turn left or right, turn its lights on or off, and even submerge. All of this did not seem too impressive at that time because the press reports attributed it to "mind control".

At this point, we have once again reached the time when the term **robot** was used for the first time. As we said many times before, it was in 1920 when Karel Čapek used it in his play, R.U.R. Two decades later, another very important term was coined. Issac Asimov used the term **robotics** for the first time in his story "Runaround" in 1942. Asimov wrote many other stories about robots and is considered to be a prominent sci-fi author of his time.

However, in the world of robotics, he is known for his three laws of robotics:

- **First law**: A robot may not injure a human being or through inaction allow a human being to come to harm.
- **Second Law**: A robot must obey the orders given to it by human beings, except where such orders would conflict with the first law.
- **Third law**: A robot must protect its own existence, as long as such protection does not conflict with the first or second law.

After a while, he added a zeroth law:

- **Zeroth law**: A robot may not harm humanity or by inaction allow humanity to come to harm.

These laws somehow reflect the feelings people had about machines they called robots at that time. Seeing enslavement by some sort of intelligent machine as a real possibility, these laws were supposed to be some sort of guiding principles one should at least keep in mind, if not directly follow, when designing a new intelligent machine. Also, while many were afraid of the robot apocalypse, time has shown that it's still yet to come. In order for it to take place, machines will need to get some sort of intelligence, some ability to think, and act based on their thoughts. Also, while we can see that over the course of history, the mechanical side of robots went through some development, the intelligence simply was not there yet.

This was part of the reason why in the summer of 1956, a group of very wise gentlemen (which included Marvin Minsky, John McCarthy, Herbert Simon, and Allan Newell) were later called to be the founding fathers of the newly founded field of Artificial Intelligence. It was at this very event where they got together to discuss creating intelligence in machines (thus, the term artificial intelligence).

Although, their goals were very ambitious (some sources even mention that their idea was to build this whole machine intelligence during that summer), it took quite a while until some interesting results could be presented.

One such example is **Shakey**, a robot built by the **Stanford Research Institute (SRI)** in 1966. It was the first robot (in our modern sense of the word) capable to reason its own actions. The robots built before this usually had all the actions they could execute preprogrammed. On the other hand, Shakey was able to analyze a more complex command and split it into smaller problems on his own. The following image of Shakey is taken from `https://en.wikipedia.org/wiki/File:ShakeyLivesHere.jpg`:

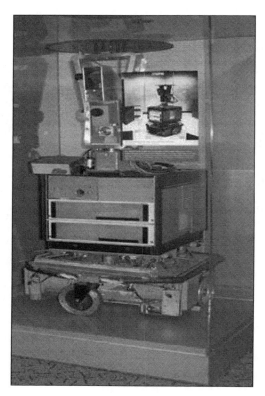

Shakey, resting in the Computer History Museum in Mountain View, California

His hardware was quite advanced too. He had collision detectors, sonar range finders, and a television camera. He operated in a small closed environment of rooms, which were usually filled with obstacles of many kinds. In order to navigate around these obstacles, it was necessary to find a way around these obstacles while not bumping into something. Shakey did it in a very straightforward way.

At first, he carefully planned his moves around these obstacles and slowly (the technology was not as advanced back then) tried to move around them. Of course, getting from a stable position to movement wouldn't be possible without some shakey moves. The problem was that Shakey's movements were mostly of this shakey nature, so he could not be called anything other than Shakey.

The lessons learned by the researchers who were trying to teach Shakey how to navigate in his environment turned out to be very important. It comes as no surprise that one of the results of the research on Shakey is the **A*** search algorithm (an algorithm that can very efficiently find the best path between two goals). This is considered to be one of the most fundamental building blocks not only in the field of robotics or artificial intelligence, but also in the field of computer science as a whole.

Our discussion on the history of robotics can go on and on for a very long time. Although one can definitely write a book on this topic (as it's a very interesting one), it's not this book; we shall try to get back to the question we tried to answer, which was: where do robots come from?

In a nutshell, robots evolved from the very basic mechanical automation through remotely-controlled objects to devices or systems that can act (or even adapt) on their own in order to achieve some goal. If this sounds way too complicated, do not worry. The truth is that to build your own robot, you do not really need to deeply understand any of this. The vast majority of robots you will encounter are built from simple parts that are not difficult to understand when you see the big picture.

So, let's figure out how we will build our own robot. Let's find out what are the robots made of.

What can we find in a robot?

In the very first part of this chapter, we tried to come up with a good (modern) definition of a robot. It turns out that the definition we came up with does not only describe a robot as we know it (or would like to know it), but also gives us some great pointers as to what parts can we most definitely find in (or on) a robot. Let's see our definition again:

"A robot is an autonomous system which exists in the physical world, can sense its environment, and can act on it to achieve some goals."

So, what will these most important parts be? Here is what we think should be on this list.

The physical body

It will be hard for a robot to exist in the physical world without a physical body. While this obviously has its advantages (having a real world robot you can play with is much more exciting than having a computer simulation), there is also some price to be paid. For instance, a physical robot can only be at one place at a time, cannot really change its shape, and its functions are quite limited by how its body looks. As its environment will be the physical world, it's safe to assume that the robot will not be the only object in it. This already poses some challenges, such as making sure that the robot won't run into some wall, object, human, or even another robot. Also, in order to do this, the robot needs to be able, as the definition says, to sense its environment.

Sensors

We already discussed in quite some depth about how important a robot's sensors are because without them, he would be just lost. A good question to ask might be, "So, what does a robot actually sense?". As in many other places (in science and technology), it depends on what the robot's purpose and goal in a given environment is, the design of the robot, and the amount of power it consumes, and so on. A good robot designer and programmer tries to take all these dependencies into account so that in the end, the final robot can have the right amount of information about its environment to fulfill its purpose and reach its goals.

One important notion with regards to sensing is that of a state. A state of a robot basically means a description of all its parameters at any given time. For instance, if we consider a robot to have some sound sensors (thanks to which it could measure the noise level in its environment), but no way of figuring out how much battery power does it have left, we can call its state *partially-observable*. On the other hand, if it had a sensor for every output of the robot and every physical characteristic of the environment the robot resides in, we can call such a state *fully observable*.

Now that we know the state of the robot in the environment, our robot needs something that can be used to leave some effect on its environment. Something like an effector.

Effectors

We already touched (albeit briefly) on the topic of effectors when we were trying to decipher parts of our definition of a robot, so we already know that effectors let the robot do physical things and the small subparts of them, actuators, are actually those that do the heavy lifting.

What we did not mention was that, historically, there are two main activities effectors can help with: **locomotion** and **manipulation**.

In general, locomotion means moving around: going from point A to point B. This is of great interest in a subfield of robotics, which is called mobile robotics. This area of research is concerned with all sorts of robots that move in the air, underwater, or just on the ground.

By manipulation, we mean a process of moving an object from one place to another. This process is of huge interest to manipulator robotics, which is concerned mostly with all sorts of robotic arms that in the vast majority of cases, are used in industry.

Just for the sake of completeness, what are the different effectors our robots can make use of? Among the most basic ones, it will definitely be motors of all sorts along with some wheels that will allow the robot to move around.

Once we have data from the environment, we can also act on it. There is just one piece missing here: the link between them.

Controllers

After all, we finally came to the conclusion of this whole system. If it was not for controllers, a robot could never ever be fully autonomous. This is to use data from sensors to decide what to do next and then execute some actions using effectors. This may look like a simple description, but in the end, it turns out that controllers are quite difficult to get right, especially when you are playing with them for the first time.

For most mobile robots and vast majority of hobby robots, controllers are usually microprocessors that are programmed in some low-level programming language. It's also not uncommon for a robot to use multiple controllers. However, while it definitely helps to have a backup controller ready in case your main one brakes down and great to have a modular system in which everything is its own module (and has its own controller), you do not get this for free. The price you have to pay is the communication between controllers, which requires a good deal of expertise.

Now that we have all the building blocks for a robot ready, we should at least briefly discuss the ways in which they can be organized. This might not seem important, but it turns out that having a good design up front can save us a lot of effort, energy, and resources. So, let's dive into how we can put a robot together architecturally.

How do we build a robot?

If we try to look at the parts of a robot from the previous part of this chapter in an abstract fashion, there are essentially three processes taking place: sensing (done by sensors), acting (done by effectors), and then planning (if there is any, it's done by controllers). Depending on how we put these three processes together (as they are the building blocks they are also called primitives), we can get different architectures with different properties. Let's at least say something about the three very basic architectures (also called paradigms).

Reactive control

Reactive control is probably the simplest architecture (or paradigm) one can put together with the primitives described previously. In this paradigm, as we can see in the following figure, there is no planning process involved. There is a direct connection between sensing and acting, which means that as soon as some sensory data comes in, the effectors act on the environment in some predefined way:

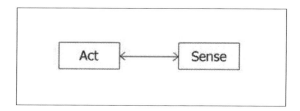

Just as the reflexes in your body do not send the information about something happening all the way up to the brain (which would be quite slow), but rather just to the nearest spinal cord so that the response could be fast, a reactively-controlled robot will not have any complex computation, but fast, precomputed actions that will be stored somewhere.

Hierarchical (deliberative) control

Suppose you were programming a chess playing robot with the rules of ordinary chess, it would be your robot's turn, then your robot's opponent's, and so on. It's obvious that in a setting like this, your robot does not really need to be extremely fast. However, it will be great if it did some planning about the future so that it can anticipate the future opponent's turns and then adjust its strategy, based on the opponent's current turn.

A set up like this will be perfect for hierarchical (or deliberative) control paradigm. As you can see in the following figure, the loop of planning, acting, and sensing is closed. Thus, the system can actively move towards its goal, whatever that might be:

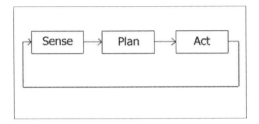

Hybrid control

So far, we discussed control paradigms that was either fast but not very flexible, or smart but quite slow. What we will really need in many cases is something in between. Also, this is precisely what a hybrid control paradigm tries to offer.

How can we use this in a real-life robot? Suppose we want to build a robotic waiter that would serve drinks in a coffee shop (coincidentally, that is what most of this book is about). Such a waiter would definitely need to have its own internal representation of the coffee shop (where are the tables and chairs located, and so on). Once it's given a task of delivering a cup of coffee to a given customer, it will have to plan its path and then move alongside that path. As we can expect this coffee shop to be quite a good one, there maybe other guests inside too. We cannot let our robot bump into any chair or a table, let alone colliding with a customer randomly while it's trying to deliver coffee. For this, we need a well tuned reactive controller.

The following figure shows the schematics of the hybrid control paradigm. We can see that the robot at first plans its task, but breaks it down it into series of actions that can be executed by the reactive paradigm. One interesting thing to note here is the fact that the sensory data is available to aid the planning (as it needs to do some planning) and the acting (as it does the reactive control) parts of the system:

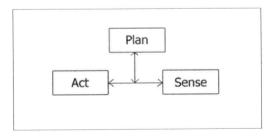

That's about it! Now, you know what a robot is, what makes it a robot, where it came from, the parts needed to create a robot, and how you can architecturally put it together. It's about time you build one yourself!

Summary

In this chapter, you learned what a robot actually is and where this term came from. We did our best to define a robot as an autonomous machine that exists in a physical world, can sense its environment, and can act on it to achieve some goals. We also went through a brief history of the field of robotics and discovered that many interesting machines were built prior to the era of real robots (from our definition). Later on, we discussed the basic building blocks of a robot, that is, effectors, sensors, and controllers, which can be combined in numerous ways. Finally, we dug a bit deeper into the architecture of control systems that are useful to keep in mind when designing a robot.

In the next chapter, we will finally see some real robots along with a real programming language.

2
Mechanical Design of a Service Robot

The main purpose of this book is to learn robotics by designing and building robots and programming it using Python. To learn robotics, we will first look at how to mechanically design a robot from scratch. The robot that we are going to build is used as a service robot in hotels and restaurants to serve food and drinks.

In this chapter, we can see various mechanical components used in this robot. Also, we can see how to assemble its components. We can design and assemble the parts using CAD tool and also build a 3D model of robot for simulating the robot.

The actual robot deployed in hotels may be big, but here we are intending to build a miniature version of it only for testing our technology. If you are interested to build a robot from scratch, this chapter is for you. If you are not interested to build the robot, you can choose some robotic platforms already available on the market to work with this book.

To build the robot body, we first need to know the requirements of designing the robot; after getting the requirements, we can design it and draw the model in 2D CAD tools to manufacture the robot parts. We can also discuss the 3D model to simulate the robot for the next chapter.

The Requirements of a service robot

Before designing any robotic system, the first procedure is to identify its requirements. The following are a set of hardware requirements to be met by this robot:

- The robot should have a provision to carry food
- The robot should be able to carry a maximum payload of 5 kg
- The robot should travel at a speed between 0.25 m/s and 1 m/s
- The ground clearance of the robot should be greater than 3 cm
- The robot must be able to work for 2 hours continuously
- The robot should be able to move and supply food to any table avoiding obstacles
- The robot height should be between 40 cm and 1 meter
- The robot should be of low cost

Now, we can identify the mechanical design requirements such as payload, moving speed, ground clearance, robot height, and the cost of the robot. We will design the body and select components accordingly. Let's discuss the robot mechanism we can use to match these requirements.

Robot drive mechanism

One of the cost effective solution for mobile robot navigation is differential drive systems. It's one of the simplest drive mechanisms for a mobile robot that is mainly indented for indoor navigation. The **differential drive robot** consists of two wheels mounted on a common axis controlled by two separate motors. There are two supporting wheels called caster wheels. It ensures stability and weight distribution of the robot. The following diagram shows a typical differential drive system:

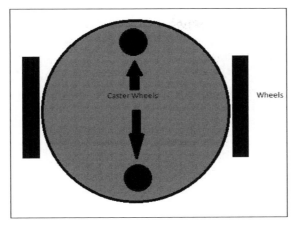

Differential drive system

The next step is to select the mechanical components of this robot drive system, that is, mainly motors, wheels, and robot chassis. Based on the requirements, we will first discuss how to select the motor.

Selection of motors and wheels

Motors are selected after looking at their specifications. Some of the important parameters for motor selection are torque and RPM. We can compute these values from the given requirements.

Calculation of RPM of motors

Assume the required robot's speed as 0.35 m/s. We saw the speed of robot must be within 0.25 m/s to 1 m/s, as per the requirement. Take the diameter of the wheel as 9 cm because according to the requirement, the ground clearance should be greater than 3 cm. Using the following equation, we can calculate the RPM of motors:

RPM = ((60 * Speed /(3.14 * Diameter of Wheel)

RPM = (60 * 0.35)/(3.14 * 0.09) = 21 / 0.2826 = 74 RPM

[You can also take a look at http://www.robotshop.com/
blog/en/vehicle-speed-rpm-and-wheel-diameter-
finder-9786 for computation.]

The calculated RPM with 9 cm diameter wheel and 0.35 m/s speed is 74 RPM. We can consider 80 RPM as the standard value.

Calculation of motor torque

Let's calculate the torque required to move the robot:

1. No of wheels = Four wheels including two caster wheels.
2. No of motors = Two.
3. Let's assume the coefficient of friction is 0.6 and radius of wheel is 4.5 cm.
4. Take total weight of robot = weight of robot + payload = (W = mg) = (~ 100 N + ~ 50 N) W= ~ 150 N, whereas total mass = 15 Kg
5. The weight acting on the four wheels can be written as 2 * N1 + 2 * N2 = W, that is, N1 is the weight acting on each caster wheel and N2 on each motor wheel.
6. Assume that the robot is stationary. The maximum torque is required when the robot starts moving. It should also overcome friction.
7. We can write the frictional force as robot torque = 0 until the robot moves. If we get the robot torque in this condition, we get the maximum torque as follows:

   $\mu * N * r - T = 0$, where μ is the coefficient of friction, N is the average weight acting on each wheel, r is the radius of wheels, and T is the torque.

   $N = W/4$ (assuming that the weight of the robot is equally distributed on all the four wheels)

   Therefore, we get:

   $0.6 * (150/4) * 0.045 - T = 0$

   Hence, T = 1.0125 N-m or 10.32 Kg-cm

The design summary

After design, we calculated the following values:

- Motor RPM = 80
- Motor Torque = 10.32 kg-cm
- Wheel diameter = 9 cm

Robot chassis design

After computing the robot's motor and wheel parameters, we can design the robot chassis or robot body. As required, the robot chassis should have a provision to hold food, it should be able to withstand up to 5 kg payload, the ground clearance of the robot should be greater than 3 cm and it should be low in cost. Apart from this, the robot should have a provision to place electronics components such as **Personal Computer** (PC), sensors, and battery.

One of the easiest designs to satisfy these requirements is a table-like design. The TurtleBot (http://www.turtlebot.com/) design is a kind of table-like design. It has three layers in the chassis. A robot platform called **Roomba** is the drive mechanism of this platform. The Roomba platform has motors and sensors inbuilt, so no need to worry about the designing of robot hardware. The following figure shows the **TurtleBot** robot chassis design:

TurtleBot Robot

We will design a robot similar to TurtleBot with our own moving platform and components. Our design will also have a three layer architecture. Let's see what all tools we want before we start designing.

Before we start designing the robot chassis, we need to know about **Computer-aided design (CAD)** tools. The popular tools available for CAD are:

- SolidWorks (http://www.solidworks.com/default.htm)
- AutoCAD (http://www.autodesk.com/products/autocad/overview)
- Maya (http://www.autodesk.com/products/maya/overview)
- Inventor (http://www.autodesk.com/products/inventor/overview)
- Google SketchUp (http://www.sketchup.com/)
- Blender (http://www.blender.org/download/)
- LibreCAD (http://librecad.org/cms/home.html)

The chassis design can be designed using any software you are comfortable with. Here, we will demonstrate the 2D model in **LibreCAD** and the 3D model in **Blender**. One of the highlights of these applications is that they are free and available for all OS platforms. We will use a 3D mesh viewing tool called **MeshLab** to view and check the 3D model design and use Ubuntu as the main operating system. Also, we can see the installation procedures of these applications in Ubuntu 14.04.2 to start the designing process. We will provide tutorial links to install applications in other platforms too.

Installing LibreCAD, Blender, and MeshLab

LibreCAD is a free, open source 2D CAD application for Windows, OS X, and Linux. **Blender** is a free, open source 3D computer graphics software used to create 3D models, animation, and video games. It comes with a GPL license as per which users can share, modify, and distribute the application. **MeshLab** is an open source, portable, and extensible system to process and edit unstructured 3D triangular meshes.

The following are the links to install LibreCAD in Windows, Linux, and OS X:

- Visit `http://librecad.org/cms/home.html` to download LibreCAD
- Visit `http://librecad.org/cms/home/from-source/linux.html` to build LibreCAD from source
- Visit `http://librecad.org/cms/home/installation/linux.html` to install LibreCAD in Debian/Ubuntu
- Visit `http://librecad.org/cms/home/installation/rpm-packages.html` to install LibreCAD in Fedora
- Visit `http://librecad.org/cms/home/installation/osx.html` to install LibreCAD in OS X

- Visit `http://librecad.org/cms/home/installation/windows.html` to install LibreCAD in Windows

 We can find the documentation on LibreCAD at the following link: `http://wiki.librecad.org/index.php/Main_Page`.

Installing LibreCAD

The installation procedure for all operating systems is provided. If you are an Ubuntu user, you can simply install it from the Ubuntu Software Centre as well.

Installing Blender

Visit the following download page to install Blender for your OS platform: `http://www.blender.org/download/`. You can find the latest version of Blender here. Also, you can find the latest documentation on Blender at `http://wiki.blender.org/`.

If you are using Ubuntu/Linux, you can simply install Blender via Ubuntu Software Centre.

Installing MeshLab

MeshLab is available for all OS platforms. The following link will provide you the download links of prebuilt binaries and source code of MeshLab:

`http://meshlab.sourceforge.net/`

If you are an Ubuntu user, you can install **MeshLab** from an apt package manager using the following command:

```
$sudo apt-get install meshlab
```

Creating a 2D CAD drawing of the robot using LibreCAD

We can take a look at the basic interface of LibreCAD. The following screenshot shows the interface of LibreCAD:

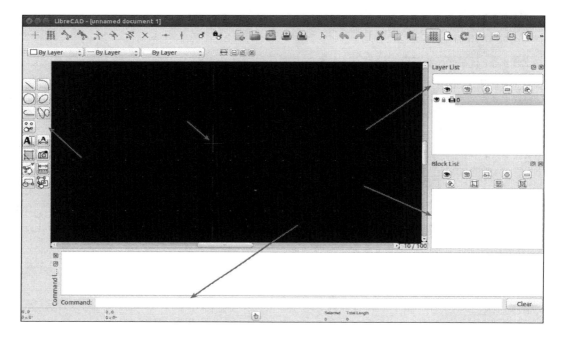

A CAD toolbar has the necessary components to draw a model. The following screenshot shows the detailed overview of the CAD toolbar:

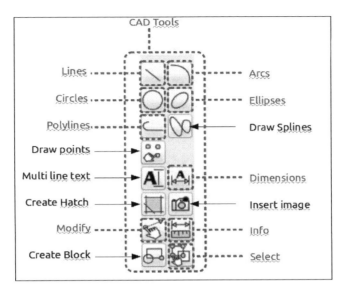

A detailed description of LibreCAD tools is available at the following link:

`http://wiki.librecad.org/index.php/LibreCAD_users_Manual`.

- **Command Box**: This is used to draw figures by only using commands. We can draw diagrams without touching any toolbar. A detailed explanation about the usage of the command box can be found at:

  `http://wiki.librecad.org/index.php/A_short_manual_for_use_from_the_command_line`.

- **Layer List**: This will have layers used in the current drawing. A basic concept in computer-aided drafting is the use of layers to organize a drawing. A detailed explanation of layers can be found at:

  `http://wiki.librecad.org/index.php/Layers`.

- **Block**: This is a group of entities and can be inserted in the same drawing more than once with different attributes at different locations, different scale, and rotation angle. A detailed explanation of Blocks can be found at the following link:

  `http://wiki.librecad.org/index.php/Blocks`.

- **Absolute Zero**: This is the origin of the drawing (0,0).

Now, start sketching by setting the unit of drawing. Set the drawing unit to centimeter. Open LibreCAD, navigate to **Edit | Application Preference**. Set **Unit** as **Centimeters**, as shown in the following screenshot:

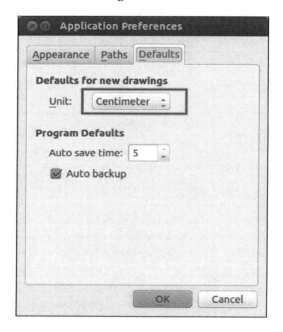

Let's start with the base plate design. The base plate has provisions to connect motors, place battery, and control board.

The base plate design

The following figure shows the robot's base plate. This plate provides provisions for two motors for differential drive and each caster wheel on the front and back of the base plate. Motors are mentioned as **M1** and **M2** in the diagram and caster wheels are represented as **C1** and **C2**. It also holds four poles to connect to the next plates. Poles are represented as **P1-1**, **P1-2**, **P1-3**, and **P1-4**. The screws are indicated as **S** and we will use the same screws here. There is a hole at the center to bring the wires from the motor to the top of the plate. The plate is cut on the left-hand side and the right-hand side so that the wheels can be attached to the motor. The distance from the center to caster wheels is mentioned as **12.5** cm and the distance from the center to motors is mentioned as **5.5** cm. The center of poles is at **9** cm in length and **9** cm in height from the center. The holes of all the plates follow the same dimensions:

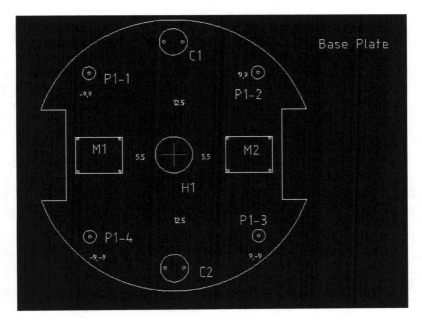

The dimensions are not marked on the diagram; instead, it's mentioned in the following table:

Parts	Dimension(cm)(Length x Height)(radius)
M1 and **M2**	5 x 4
C1 and **C2**	Radius = 1.5
S(Screw)	0.15
P1-1, P1-2, P1-3, P1-4	Outer radius 0.7, Height 3.5
Left and Right Wheel Sections	2.5 x 10
Base plate	Radius = 15

We can discuss more about motor dimensions and clamp dimensions later.

Base plate pole design

The base plate has four poles to extend to the next layer. The poles are **3.5** cm in length with a radius of **0.7** cm. We can extend to the next plate by attaching hollow tubes to the poles. At the top of the hollow tube, we will insert a hard plastic to make a screw hole. This hole will be useful to extend to the top layer. The base plate pole and the hollow tubes on each pole is shown in the following figure. Each hollow tube a radius of **0.75** cm and length of **15** cm:

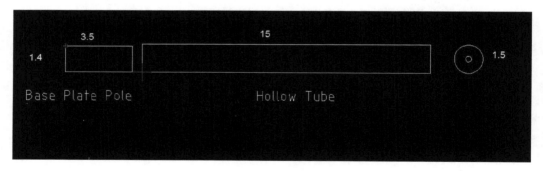

Wheel, motor, and motor clamp design

We have to decide the diameter of the wheel and compute motor requirements. Here, we are using a typical motor and wheel that we can use if the design is successful:

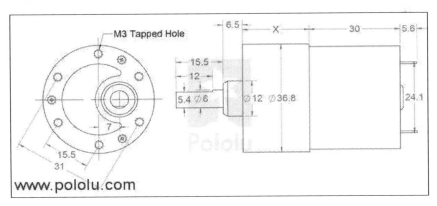

The motor design can vary according to the motor selection; if necessary, this motor can be taken as per the design and can be changed after simulation. The **X** value in the motor diagram can vary according to the speed and torque of motors. This is the gear assembly of motor.

The following figure shows a typical wheel that we can use with a diameter of **90** cm. The wheel with a diameter of **86.5** mm will become **90** mm after placing the grip.

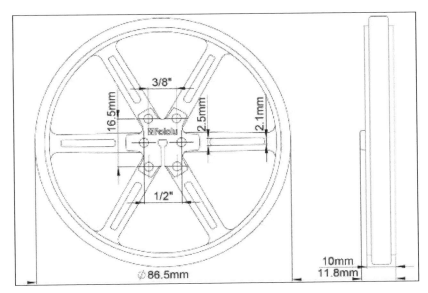

The motor needs to be mounted on the base plate; to mount, we need a clamp which can be screwed onto the plate and also connect the motor to the clamp. The following figure shows a typical clamp we can use for this purpose. It's an L-shaped clamp, with which we can mount the motor on one side and fit another side to the plate:

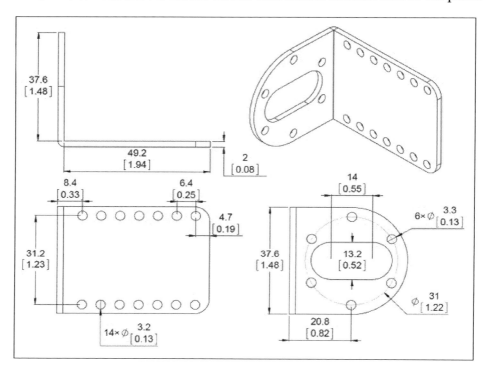

Caster wheel design

Caster wheels need not have a special design; we can use any caster wheel that can touch the ground similar to the wheels. The following link has a collection of caster wheels that we can use for this design:

http://www.pololu.com/category/45/pololu-ball-casters

Middle plate design

The dimension of this plate is same as the base plate, and the screw size is also similar:

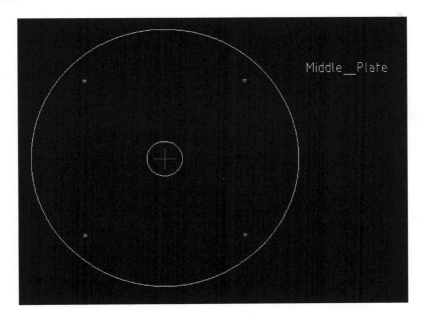

The middle plate can be held above the hollow tubes from the base plate. This arrangement is connected using another hollow tube that extends from the middle plate. The tube from the middle plate will have a screw at the bottom to fix the tube from the base plate to the middle plate, and a hollow end to connect the top plate. The top and side view of the tube extending from the middle plate is shown in the following figure:

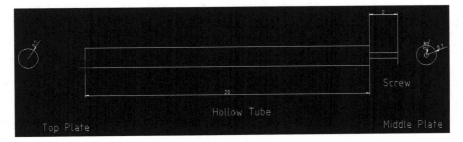

This tube will connect the middle plate to the base plate and at the same time provide a provision to connect the top plate.

Top plate design

The top plate is similar to other plates; it has four small poles of 3 cm, similar to the base plate. These poles can be placed on the hollow tubes from the middle plate. The four poles are connected to the plate, shown as follows:

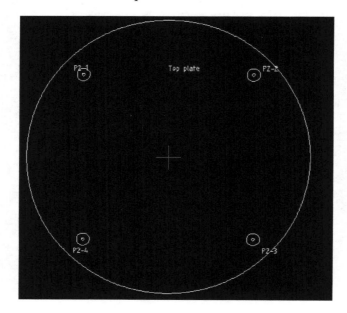

After the top plate design, the robot chassis design is almost finished; let's see the 3D model building of this robot using Blender. The 3D model is built for simulation purpose and the 2D design we build is mainly for manufacturing purpose.

Working with a 3D model of the robot using Blender

In this section, we will design a 3D model of the robot. The 3D model is mainly used for simulation purpose. The modeling will be done using Blender. The version must be greater than 2.6 because we only tested the tutorials on these versions.

The following screenshot shows the blender workspace and tools that can be used to work with 3D models:

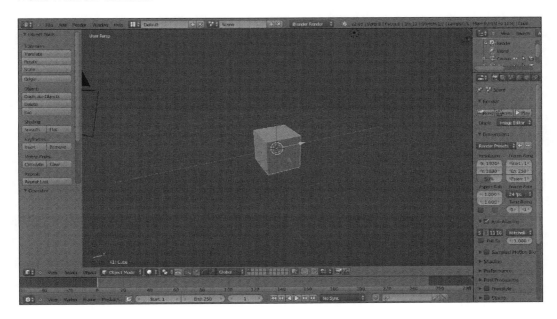

The main reason why we are using Blender here is so that we can model the robot using Python scripts. Blender has an inbuilt Python interpreter and a Python script editor for coding purpose. We are not discussing about the user interface of Blender here. We can find a good tutorial of Blender on its website. Refer to the following link to learn about Blender's user interface:

`http://www.blender.org/support/tutorials/`

Let's start coding in Blender using Python.

Python scripting in Blender

Blender is mainly written in C, C++, and Python. Users can write their own Python script and access all the functionalities of Blender. If you are an expert in Blender Python APIs, you can model the entire robot using a Python script instead of manual modeling.

Blender uses Python 3.x. Blender. Python API is generally stable, but some areas are still being added to and improved. Refer to `http://www.blender.org/documentation/blender_python_api_2_69_7/` for the documentation on Blender Python API.

Let's discuss Blender Python APIs that we will use in our robot model script.

Introduction to Blender Python APIs

Python APIs in Blender can do most of the functionalities of Blender. The main jobs that can be done by these APIs are as follows:

- Edit any data inside Blender, such as scenes, meshes, particles, and so on
- Modify user preference, key maps, and themes
- Create new Blender tools
- Draw the 3D view using OpenGL commands from Python

Blender provides the **bpy** module to the Python interpreter. This module can be imported in a script and gives access to blender data, classes, and functions; scripts that deal with Blender data will need to import this module. The main Python modules we will use in bpy are:

- **Context Access**: This provides access to Blender user interface functions from the (`bpy.context`) script.
- **Data Access**: This provides access to the Blender internal data (`bpy.data`).
- **Operators**: This provides Python access to calling operators, which includes operators written in C, Python, or Macros (`bpy.ops`).

For switching to scripting in Blender, we need to change the screen layout of Blender. The following screenshot shows the option that helps you to switch to **Scripting** layout:

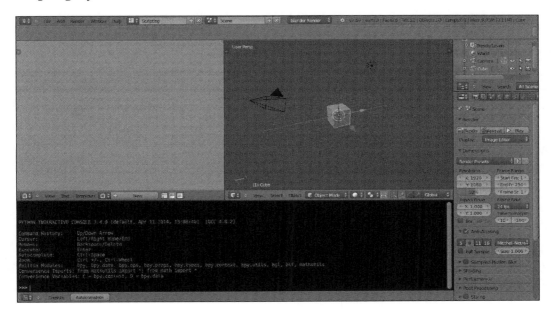

After selecting the **Scripting** tab, we can see a text editor and Python console window in Blender. In the text editor, we can code using Blender APIs and also try Python commands via the Python console. Click on the **New** button to create a new Python script and name it robot.py. Now, we can design the 3D model of robot using only Python scripts. The upcoming section has the complete script to design our robot model. We can discuss the code before running it. We hope you have read the Python APIs of Blender from their site. The code in the upcoming section is split into six Python functions to draw three robot plates, draw motors and wheels, draw four support tubes, and export into the **STereoLithography** (STL) 3D file format for simulation.

Python script of the robot model

The following is the Python script of the robot model that we will design:.

1. Before starting Python script in Blender, we must import the `bpy` module. The `bpy` module contains all the functionalities of Blender and it can only be accessed from inside the Blender application:

```
import bpy
```

2. This following function will draw the base plate of the robot. This function will draw a cylinder with a radius of 5 cm and cut a portion from the opposite sides so that motors can be connected using the `Boolean` modifier inside Blender:

```
#This function will draw base plate
def Draw_Base_Plate():
```

3. The following two commands will create two cubes with a radius of 0.05 meter on either side of the base plate. The purpose of these cubes is to create a modifier that subtracts the cubes from the base plate. So in effect, we will get a base plate with two cuts. After cutting the two sides, we will delete the cubes:

```
bpy.ops.mesh.primitive_cube_add(radius=0.05,
  location=(0.175,0,0.09))
bpy.ops.mesh.primitive_cube_add(radius=0.05,
  location=(-0.175,0,0.09))


####################################################
####################################################

#Adding base plate
bpy.ops.mesh.primitive_cylinder_add(radius=0.15,
  depth=0.005, location=(0,0,0.09))

#Adding boolean difference modifier from first cube

bpy.ops.object.modifier_add(type='BOOLEAN')
bpy.context.object.modifiers["Boolean"].operation =
  'DIFFERENCE'
bpy.context.object.modifiers["Boolean"].object =
  bpy.data.objects["Cube"]
bpy.ops.object.modifier_apply(modifier="Boolean")
```

```
#########################################################
#########################################################

#Adding boolean difference modifier from second cube

bpy.ops.object.modifier_add(type='BOOLEAN')
bpy.context.object.modifiers["Boolean"].operation =
   'DIFFERENCE'
bpy.context.object.modifiers["Boolean"].object =
   bpy.data.objects["Cube.001"]
bpy.ops.object.modifier_apply(modifier="Boolean")


#########################################################
#########################################################

#Deselect cylinder and delete cubes
bpy.ops.object.select_pattern(pattern="Cube")
bpy.ops.object.select_pattern(pattern="Cube.001")
bpy.data.objects['Cylinder'].select = False
bpy.ops.object.delete(use_global=False)
```

4. The following function will draw the motors and wheels attached to the base plate:

```
#This function will draw motors and wheels
def Draw_Motors_Wheels():
```

5. The following commands will draw a cylinder with a radius of 0.045 and 0.01 meter in depth for the wheels. After creating the wheels, it will be rotated and translated into the cut portion of the base plate:

```
#Create first Wheel

bpy.ops.mesh.primitive_cylinder_add(radius=0.045,
   depth=0.01, location=(0,0,0.07))
#Rotate
bpy.context.object.rotation_euler[1] = 1.5708
#Transalation
bpy.context.object.location[0] = 0.135
```

```
#Create second wheel
bpy.ops.mesh.primitive_cylinder_add(radius=0.045,
  depth=0.01, location=(0,0,0.07))
#Rotate
bpy.context.object.rotation_euler[1] = 1.5708
#Transalation
bpy.context.object.location[0] = -0.135
```

6. The following code will add two dummy motors to the base plate. The dimensions of motors are mentioned in the 2D design. The motor is basically a cylinder and it will be rotated and placed in the base plate:

```
#Adding motors

bpy.ops.mesh.primitive_cylinder_add(radius=0.018,
  depth=0.06, location=(0.075,0,0.075))
bpy.context.object.rotation_euler[1] = 1.5708

bpy.ops.mesh.primitive_cylinder_add(radius=0.018,
  depth=0.06, location=(-0.075,0,0.075))
bpy.context.object.rotation_euler[1] = 1.5708
```

7. The following code will add a shaft to the motors, similar to the motor model; the shaft is also a cylinder and it will be rotated and inserted into the motor model:

```
#Adding motor shaft
bpy.ops.mesh.primitive_cylinder_add(radius=0.006,
  depth=0.04, location=(0.12,0,0.075))
bpy.context.object.rotation_euler[1] = 1.5708

bpy.ops.mesh.primitive_cylinder_add(radius=0.006,
  depth=0.04, location=(-0.12,0,0.075))
bpy.context.object.rotation_euler[1] = 1.5708


#######################################################
#######################################################
```

8. The following code will add two caster wheels on the base plate. Currently, we are adding a cylinder as wheel. In the simulation, we can assign it as a wheel:

```
#Adding Caster Wheel

bpy.ops.mesh.primitive_cylinder_add(radius=0.015,
  depth=0.05, location=(0,0.125,0.065))
bpy.ops.mesh.primitive_cylinder_add(radius=0.015,
  depth=0.05, location=(0,-0.125,0.065))
```

9. The following code will add a dummy Kinect sensor:

```
#Adding Kinect

bpy.ops.mesh.primitive_cube_add(radius=0.04,
    location=(0,0,0.26))
```

10. This function will draw the middle plate of the robot:

```
#Draw middle plate
def Draw_Middle_Plate():
    bpy.ops.mesh.primitive_cylinder_add(radius=0.15,
        depth=0.005, location=(0,0,0.22))


#Adding top plate
def Draw_Top_Plate():
    bpy.ops.mesh.primitive_cylinder_add(radius=0.15,
        depth=0.005, location=(0,0,0.37))
```

11. This function will draw all the four supporting hollow tubes for all the three plates:

```
#Adding support tubes
def Draw_Support_Tubes():
###################################################################
############################

    #Cylinders
    bpy.ops.mesh.primitive_cylinder_add(radius=0.007,
        depth=0.30, location=(0.09,0.09,0.23))
    bpy.ops.mesh.primitive_cylinder_add(radius=0.007,
        depth=0.30, location=(-0.09,0.09,0.23))
    bpy.ops.mesh.primitive_cylinder_add(radius=0.007,
        depth=0.30, location=(-0.09,-0.09,0.23))
    bpy.ops.mesh.primitive_cylinder_add(radius=0.007,
        depth=0.30, location=(0.09,-0.09,0.23))
```

12. This function will export the designed robot to STL. We have to change the STL file path before executing the script:

```python
#Exporting into STL
def Save_to_STL():
    bpy.ops.object.select_all(action='SELECT')
#    bpy.ops.mesh.select_all(action='TOGGLE')
    bpy.ops.export_mesh.stl(check_existing=True,
        filepath="/home/lentin/Desktop/exported.stl",
        filter_glob="*.stl", ascii=False,
        use_mesh_modifiers=True, axis_forward='Y',
        axis_up='Z', global_scale=1.0)

#Main code

if __name__ == "__main__":
    Draw_Base_Plate()
    Draw_Motors_Wheels()
    Draw_Middle_Plate()
    Draw_Top_Plate()
    Draw_Support_Tubes()
    Save_to_STL()
```

13. After entering the code in the text editor, execute the script by pressing the **Run Script** button, as shown in the following screenshot. The output 3D model will be shown on the 3D view of Blender. Also, if we check the desktop, we can see the exported.stl file for the simulation purposes:

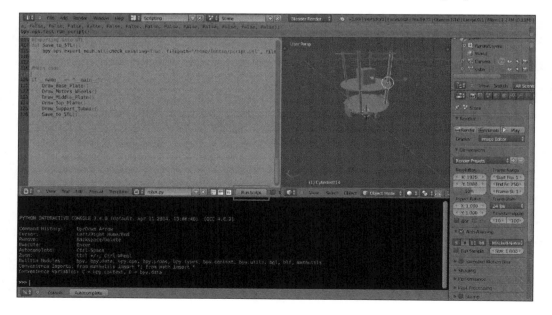

The `exported.stl` file can be opened with MeshLab and the following is a screenshot of MeshLab:

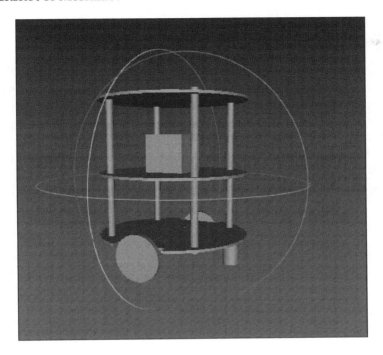

Downloading the example code

You can download the example code files for all Packt books you have purchased from your account at `http://www.packtpub.com`. If you purchased this book elsewhere, you can visit `http://www.packtpub.com/support` and register to have the files e-mailed directly to you.

Questions

1. What is robot modeling and what are its uses?
2. What is the aim of 2D robot model?
3. What is the aim of 3D robot model?
4. What is the advantage of Python scripting over manual modeling?

Summary

This chapter was mainly aimed at robot mechanical designing. It also included the robot parameter calculation and robot chassis design. In robot designing, we first need to have the prerequisites ready. Once it's ready, we can calculate the requirements of the components to be used in the robot. After the component requirements are met, we design the robot chassis according to the given requirements. The robot chassis design involves 2D design of all the parts required to build the robot. After 2D designing, we saw how to build the 3D robot model using Blender and Python script. The 3D model was built using the dimensions that we used in 2D drawing. We also covered the Blender Python script to build the entire 3D model. In this chapter, we got the design of the robot that can be used to manufacture it, and also developed a 3D model for simulation. In the next chapter, we will discuss the simulation of this robot model and some popular simulation tools.

3
Working with Robot Simulation Using ROS and Gazebo

In the last chapter, we looked at the mechanical designing of our robot and designed its 2D and 3D models. In this chapter, we will simulate the robot that we designed. Before diving into simulation, we will look at the uses of robot simulation, advantages, disadvantages, and various robotic software simulation tools.

We will also discuss kinematics and the dynamic parameters of the robot that will help you to understand the functioning of the robot. After discussing these concepts, we will discuss the software platforms that are used for this simulation. We are planning to perform this simulation using **Gazebo** with the help of **Robot Operating System (ROS)**. After we discuss the basic concepts of ROS and Gazebo, we will implement the robot kinematic and dynamic model of the robot according to the Gazebo descriptions. Finally, we will simulate the robot in a typical hotel environment and test the autonomous navigation ability of the robot to serve food.

Understanding robotic simulation

In general, robotic simulation is a process of developing a virtual model capable of emulating the real-world process. Through simulation, we can create a virtual model of the robot and test its design and programming code.

One of the definitions of simulation according to *Systems Simulation: The Art and Science, Robert E. Shannon, Prentice Hall* is:

> *It is the process of designing a model of a real system and conducting experiments with this model for the purpose of understanding the behavior of the system and for evaluating various strategies for the operation of the system. Thus it is critical that the mode be designed in such a way that the model behavior mimics the response behavior of the real system to events that take place over time.*

> *The term's model and system are key components of our definition of simulation. By a model we mean a representation of a group of objects or ideas in some form other than that of the entity itself. By a system we mean a group or collection of interrelated elements that cooperate to accomplish some stated objective.*

Robotic simulators are software applications that can model the robot and render the virtual environment that mimics the real environment of the robot. In our case, the environment is a typical hotel/restaurant with tables and chairs. We have to make this same arrangement in simulators to test its working.

The following figure shows a robot simulator called Gazebo. It also shows a robot called TurtleBot, along with some random objects. You will learn more about Gazebo and TurtleBot in the upcoming sections of this chapter.

Robot simulator Gazebo

We looked at the requirements to build the robot and the mechanical design of the robot. The next step is to simulate the design process. It allows developers to test the programming code and validate the mechanical design of the robot according to the design proposal request. The virtual model of the robot can be modified without any additional costs.

One of the main advantages of performing the simulation process is that we can build a virtual prototype of a complex robot with less cost that behaves similar to the actual design of the robot, and test the virtual robot until it meets the specifications. The disadvantage is that, using simulators, we cannot cover the entire scenario that may occur in the real world.

The advantages of simulation are:

- Low cost to build a robot from scratch
- The actual robot code can be tested with the simulated robot
- The design of the robot can be modified without any cost
- Any part of the robot can be tested
- If it's a complex project, then the robot can be simulated in stages
- A complete simulation can determine whether the robot meets the specifications
- Almost all simulation software are compatible with a wide range of programming languages

Some of the disadvantage are:

- In the real world, there may be more parameters than the virtual world; we can't model all these parameters in simulation
- All simulation programs simulate what they are programmed to simulate

Let's take a look at some of the latest robotic simulator applications:

- **Gazebo**: This is a multirobot simulator with support for many sensors. The software is compatible with ROS. It's a free and open source simulator used extensively for robotic research. The official website of Gazebo is www.gazebosim.org.

- **V-REP**: This is one of the most advanced 3D simulators for industrial robots designed by Coppelia Robotics. This tool offers support for a wide range of programming languages, including C/C++, Python, Java, Lua, Matlab, and Urbi. This simulator has built-in support to develop algorithms in order to simulate automation scenarios. The platform is used in education as well by engineers. The official website of V-REP is http://www.coppeliarobotics.com/.

- **Webots**: This is a 3D simulation platform developed by Cyberbotics and is used in service and industrial robot simulations. This tool offers support for Windows, Linux, and Apple platforms. It's one of the most common simulation software used in education or for research purposes. Any robot can be modeled, programmed, and simulated in C, C++, Java, Python, Matlab, or URBI. This software is compatible with external libraries such as **Open Source Computer Vision (OpenCV)**.

- **RoboLogix**: This is a 3D industrial simulation software developed by Logic Design. The **RoboLogix** platform was designed to emulate real-world robotics applications with five-axis industrial robot. The program installed on the robot can be developed and tested in a wide range of practical applications. The platform offers support for a wide range of industrial robots, including ABB, Fanuc, and Kawasaki.

Before performing the simulation, let's check how the robot works and what is the math behind this.

Mathematical modeling of the robot

The important part of a mobile robot is its steering system. This will help the robot to navigate in the environment. We will use the differential drive model to reduce the complexity, cost, and size of the robot. A differential-drive robot consists of two main wheels mounted on a common axis controlled by separate motors. A differential drive system/steering system is a nonholonomic system, which means it has constraints on the pose change. A car is an example of a nonholonomic system, as it cannot change its position without changing its pose. Let's look at how our robot works and how we model the robot in terms of its mathematics.

Introduction to the differential steering system and robot kinematics

Robot kinematics is the study of the mathematics of motion without considering the forces that affect motion. It mainly deals with the geometric relationships that govern the system. **Robot dynamics** is the study of motion in which all the forces are modeled.

A mobile robot or vehicle has six **degrees of freedom (DOF)** expressed by the pose (x, y, z, roll, pitch, and yaw). It consists of position (x, y, z) and attitude (roll, pitch, and yaw). **Roll** refers to sidewise rotation, **pitch** refers to forward and backward rotation, and **yaw** (called the heading or orientation) refers to the direction in which the robot moves in the x-y plane. The differential-drive robot moves from x-y in the plane, so the 2D pose consists mainly of x, y, and θ, where θ is the head of the robot that points in the forward direction of the robot. This much information is sufficient to describe a differential robot pose.

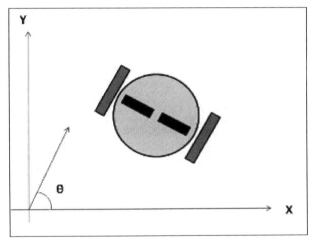

The pose of the robot in x, y, and θ in the global coordinate system

In a differential-drive robot, the motion can be controlled by adjusting the velocity of two independently controlled motors on the left-hand side and the right-hand side, that is, V-left and V-right respectively. The following figure shows a couple of popular differential drive robots available on the market:

iRobot, Roomba, and Pioneer 3DX

The forward kinematics equations for a robot with a differential-drive system are used to solve the following problem:

If robot is standing in a position (x, y, θ) at time t, determine the pose (x', y', θ') at $t + \delta t$ given the control parameters V-left and V-right.

This technique can be used in the robot to follow a particular trajectory.

Explaining of the forward kinematics equation

We can start by formulating a solution for forward kinematics. The following figure is an illustration of one of the wheels of the robot:

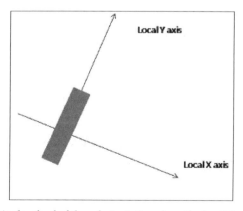

A single wheel of the robot rotating along the local Y axis

The motion around the **y axis** is known as roll; everything else can be considered as slip. Let's assume that no slip occurs in this case. When the wheel completes one full rotation, the canter moves at a distance of $2\pi\, r$, where r is the radius of the wheel. We will assume that the movement is two-dimensional. This means that the surface is flat and even.

When the robot is about to perform a rolling motion, the robot must rotate around a point that lies along its common left and right wheel axes. The point that the robot rotates around is known as **ICC- Instantaneous Center of Curvature (ICC)**. The following diagram shows the wheel configuration of differential-drive with ICC:

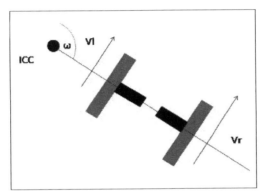

Wheel configuration for a robot with differential-drive

The central concept for the derivation of the kinematic equation is the ω angular velocity of the robot. Each wheel on the robot rotates around ICC along a circle with a wheel radius of r.

The speed of the wheel is $v = 2\,\pi r\,/\,T$, where T is the time taken to complete one full turn around ICC. The ω angular velocity is defined as $2\,\pi\,/\,T$ and typically has the unit radians (or degrees) per second. Combining the equations for v and w yields $\omega = 2\,\pi\,/\,T$.

$$v = r\,\omega \tag{1}$$

A detailed model of the differential-drive system is shown in the following figure:

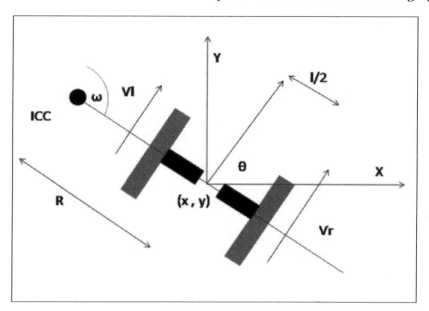

If we apply the previous equation in both wheels, the result will be the same, that is, ω:

$$\omega(R+l/2)=Vr \qquad (2)$$
$$\omega(R+l/2)=Vl \qquad (3)$$

Where, R is the distance between ICC and the midpoint of the wheel axis and l is the length of the wheel axis. After solving ω and R, we get the following result:

$$R=l/2(Vl+Vr)/(Vr-Vl) \qquad (4)$$
$$\omega=(Vr-Vl)/l \qquad (5)$$

The previous equation is useful for solving the forward kinematics problem. Suppose the robot moves with an angular velocity of ω for δt seconds, it can change the robot's orientation or where it is heading to:

$$\theta' = \omega\,\delta t + \theta \tag{6}$$

Where, the center of ICC rotation is given by basic trigonometry as:

$$ICC = \left[ICC_x, ICC_y \right] = \left[x - R\sin\theta, y + R\cos\theta \right] \tag{7}$$

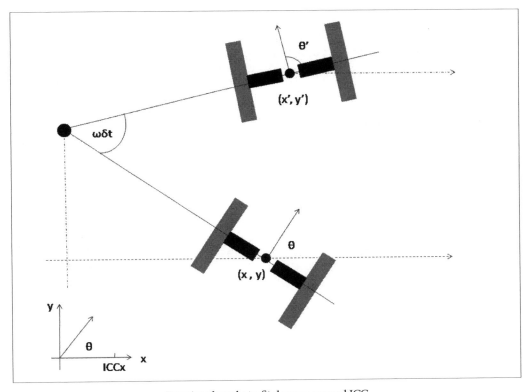

Rotating the robot $\omega\delta t$ degrees around ICC

Given a starting position (x, y), the new position (x', y') can be computed using the 2D rotation matrix. The rotation around ICC with angular velocity ω for δt seconds yields the following position at $t + \delta t$ time:

$$\begin{pmatrix} x' \\ y' \end{pmatrix} = \begin{pmatrix} cos(\omega\delta t) & -sin(\omega\delta t) \\ sin(\omega\delta t) & cos(\omega\delta t) \end{pmatrix} \begin{pmatrix} x - ICC_x \\ y - ICC_y \end{pmatrix} + \begin{pmatrix} ICC_x \\ ICC_y \end{pmatrix} \qquad (8)$$

The new pose $(x', y',$ and $\theta')$ can be computed from equations (6) and (8), given ω, δt, and R.

ω can be computed from equation (5); Vr and Vl are often difficult to measure accurately. Instead of measuring the velocity, the rotation of each wheel can be measured using a sensor called **wheel encoders**. The data from the wheel encoders is the robot's **odometry** values. These sensors are mounted on the wheel axes and deliver binary signals for each step the wheel rotates (each step may be in the order of 0.1 mm). These signals are fed to a counter such that $v\delta t$ is the distance travelled from time t to $t + \delta t$. We can write:

$n * step = v\delta t$

From this, we can compute v:

$$v = n * step / \delta t \qquad (9)$$

If we insert equation (9) in equations (3) and (4), we get the following result:

$$R = l / 2 (Vl + Vr) / (Vr - Vl) = l / 2 (nl + nr) / (nr - nl) \qquad (10)$$
$$w\delta t = (Vr - Vl) \delta t / l = (nr - nl) * step / l \qquad (11)$$

Here, nl and nr are the encoder counts of the left and right wheels. Vl and Vr are the speed of the left and right wheels respectively. Thus, the robot stands in pose (x, y, θ) and moves nl and nr counts during a time step δt; the new pose (x', y', θ') is given by:

$$\begin{pmatrix} x' \\ y' \\ \theta' \end{pmatrix} = \begin{pmatrix} cos(\omega\delta t) & -sin(\omega\delta t) & 0 \\ sin(\omega\delta t) & cos(\omega\delta t) & 0 \\ 0 & 0 & 1 \end{pmatrix} \begin{pmatrix} x\text{-}ICC_x \\ y\text{-}ICC_y \\ \theta \end{pmatrix} + \begin{pmatrix} ICC_x \\ ICC_y \\ \omega\delta t \end{pmatrix} \qquad (12)$$

where,

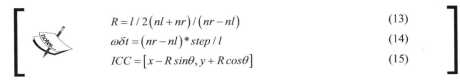

$$R = l/2(nl + nr)/(nr - nl) \qquad (13)$$

$$\omega\delta t = (nr - nl) * step/l \qquad (14)$$

$$ICC = [x - R\sin\theta, y + R\cos\theta] \qquad (15)$$

The derived kinematic equation depends mainly on the design and geometry of the robot. Different designs can lead to different equations.

Inverse kinematics

The forward kinematics equation provides an updated pose at a given wheel speed. We can now think about the inverse problem.

Stand in pose (x, y, θ) at time t and determine the *V-left* and *V-right* control parameters such that the pose at time $t + \delta t$ is (x', y', θ').

In differential-drive, this problem may not have a solution because this kind of robot can't be moved to any pose by simply setting the wheel velocity. It's because of the robot constraints called nonholonomic robots that this problem can be solved, because these kinds of robots can move to any pose.

In nonholonomic robots, there are some ways to increase the constrained mobility if we allow a different sequence (*V-left*, *V-right*). If we insert values from equations (12) to (15), we can identify some special cases of control:

- If *V-right* = *V-left* => $nr = nl$ => $R = \infty$, $\omega\delta T = 0$ =>: This means the robot moves in a straight line and θ remains the same

- If *V-right* = *-V-left* => $nr = -nl$ => $R=0$, $\omega\delta t = 2nl * step/l$ and $ICC = [ICC_x, ICC_y] = [x, y]$ => $x' = x, y' = y, \theta' = \theta + \omega\delta t$ =>: This means the robot rotates in the position around ICC, that is, any θ is reachable, while (x, y) remains unchanged

Combining these operations, the following algorithm can be used to reach any target pose from the starting pose:

1. Rotate until the robot's orientation coincides with the line from the starting position to the target position, *V-right* = *-V-left* = *V-rot*.

2. Drive straight until the robot's position coincides with the target position, *V-right* = *V-left* = *V-ahead*.

3. Rotate until the robot's orientation coincides with the target orientation, *V-right = -V-left = V-rot*.

where, *V-rot* and *V-ahead* can be chosen arbitrarily.

> Refer to `http://www8.cs.umu.se/~thomash/reports/` `KinematicsEquationsForDifferentialDriveAnd` `ArticulatedSteeringUMINF-11.19.pdf` for more information on kinematics equations.

We can switch to the details of tools we are using to simulate this robot. Understanding the kinematics of the robot will help you to build the simulation of the robot. It also helps you to write the software for the robot. The tools we will use for the simulation are:

- Robot Operating System (ROS)
- Gazebo

These are some of the popular tools available for robotics programming and simulation. Let's look at the features and a short introduction of ROS and Gazebo. Later, we will discuss how to perform simulation using these tools.

Introduction to ROS and Gazebo

ROS is a software framework for writing robot software. The main aim of ROS is to reuse the robotic software across the globe. ROS consists of a collection of tools, libraries, and conventions that aim to simplify the task of creating complex and robust robot behavior across a wide variety of robotic platforms.

The official definition of ROS is:

> *ROS is an open-source, meta-operating system for your robot. It provides the services you would expect from an operating system, including hardware abstraction, low-level device control, implementation of commonly-used functionality, message-passing between processes, and package management. It also provides tools and libraries for obtaining, building, writing, and running code across multiple computers. ROS is similar in some respects to 'robot frameworks, such as Player, YARP, Orocos, CARMEN, Orca, MOOS, and Microsoft Robotics Studio.*

> Refer to `http://wiki.ros.org/ROS/Introduction` for more information on ROS.

Some of the main features of ROS are:

- **Distributed Framework**: ROS is a distributed framework that can run on multiple machines, so the computation of the robot can be divided over different machines. It can reduce the on board processing of the robot.

- **Code reuse**: The main goal of ROS is to reuse code. Code reuse enables the growth of a good research and development community around the world. ROS executables are called nodes. These executables can be grouped into a single entity called ROS packages. A group of packages is called a stack and these stacks can be shared and distributed.

- **Language independence**: The ROS framework can be programmed using popular languages (such as Python, C++, and Lisp). The nodes can be written in any language and can communicate through ROS without any issues.

- **Easy testing**: ROS has a built-in unit/integration test framework called **rostest** to test ROS packages.

- **Scaling**: ROS is appropriate for large runtime systems and for large development processes.

- **Free and Open Source**: The source code of ROS is open and it's absolutely free to use. The core part of ROS is licensed under BSD license and it can be reused in commercial and closed source products.

Some of the main concepts of ROS are discussed in the upcoming section.

ROS Concepts

There are mainly three levels of ROS:

- The ROS file system
- The ROS Computation Graph
- The ROS community

The ROS filesystem

The ROS filesystem mainly covers how ROS files are organized on the disk. The main terms we have to understand are:

- **Packages**: ROS packages are the main unit of an ROS software framework. A ROS package may contain executables, ROS-dependent library, configuration files, and so on. ROS packages can be reused and shared.

- **Package Manifests**: The manifests (`package.xml`) file will have all the details of the packages, including name, description, license, and dependencies.

- **Message (msg) types**: Message descriptions are stored in the msg folder in a package. ROS messages are data structures for sending data through ROS. Message definitions are stored in a file with the .msg extension.

- **Service (srv) types**: Service descriptions are stored in the srv folder with the .srv extension. The srv files define the request and response data structure for service in ROS.

The ROS Computation Graph

The ROS Computation Graph is the peer-to-peer network of the ROS process that processes data together. The basic concepts of ROS Computation Graph are nodes, ROS Master, parameter server, messages, and services.

- **Nodes**: These are processes that perform computation. For example, one node of a robot publishes the odometry data of the robot, another node publishes the laser scanner data, and so on. An ROS node is written with the help of an ROS client library (such as *roscpp* and *rospy*). We will look at this library during the sample node creation.

- **ROS Master**: This provides name registration and a lookup for the rest of the Computation Graph. Without starting the master, nodes will not find each other nor send messages.

- **Parameter server**: This allows data to be stored in a central location.

- **Messages**: Nodes communicate with each other by passing messages. A message is simply a data structure comprising of typed fields. This will support data types, such as integer, floating point, Boolean, and so on.

- **Topics**: Nodes exchange data in the form of messages via ROS transport system with a specific name called **topics**. Topic is the name used to identify the content of the message. A node interested in a certain kind of data will subscribe to the appropriate topic. In general, publishers and subscribers are not aware of each other's existence. The idea is to decouple the production of information from its consumption. Logically, one can think of a topic as a strongly typed message bus. Each bus has a name and anyone can connect to the bus to send or receive messages as long as they are the right type.

- **Services**: The publish/subscribe model is a very flexible communication paradigm, but its many-to-many, one-way transport is not appropriate for request/reply interactions, which are often required in a distributed system. Request/reply is done via services, which are defined by a pair of message structures: one for the request and one for the reply. A providing node offers a service under a name and a client uses the service by sending the request message and awaiting the reply. ROS client libraries generally present this interaction to the programmer as if it were a remote procedure call.

- **Bags**: These are formats to save and play back the ROS message data. Bags are an important mechanism to store data (such as sensor data) that can be difficult to collect, but it's necessary to develop and test algorithms.

The ROS Master acts as a name service in the ROS Computation Graph. It stores topics and services registration information for ROS nodes. Nodes communicate with the Master to report their registration information. As these nodes communicate with the Master, they can receive information about other registered nodes and make connections as appropriate. The master will also make call backs to these nodes when this registration information changes, which allows nodes to dynamically create connections as new nodes are run.

Nodes connect to other nodes directly; the Master only provides the lookup information, much like a DNS server. Nodes that subscribe to a topic will request connections from nodes that publish that topic and will establish that connection over an agreed upon connection protocol. The most common protocol used in an ROS is called TCPROS, which uses standard TCP/IP sockets.

The following figure shows how topics and service works between nodes and Master:

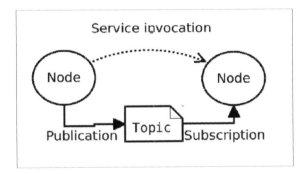

The ROS community level

The ROS community level concepts are ROS resources that enable separate communities to exchange software and knowledge. These resources include:

- **Distributions**: ROS Distributions are collections of versioned stacks that you can install. Distributions play a similar role to Linux distributions: they make it easier to install software and maintain consistent versions of it.

- **Repositories**: ROS relies on a federated network of code repositories, where different institutions can develop and release their own robot software components.

- **The ROS Wiki**: This is the main forum to document information about ROS. Anyone can sign up for an account and contribute their own documentation, provide corrections or updates, write tutorials, and so on.

- **Mailing Lists**: The **ros-users** mailing list is the primary communication channel about new updates to ROS. This is also a forum to ask questions about the ROS software.

There are enough concepts to be discussed about ROS; you can refer to the ROS official website at www.ros.org for more information. Now, we will look at the installation procedure of ROS.

Installing ROS Indigo on Ubuntu 14.04.2

As per our previous discussion, we know that ROS is a meta operating system to be installed on a host system. ROS is completely supported on Ubuntu/Linux and in the experimental stages on Windows and OS X. Some of the latest ROS distributions are:

Distribution	Released Date
ROS Indigo Igloo	July 22, 2014
ROS Hydro Medusa	September 4, 2013
ROS Groovy Galapagos	December 31, 2012

We will discuss the installation procedure of the latest distribution of ROS called Indigo Igloo on Ubuntu 14.04.2 LTS. ROS Indigo Igloo will be primarily targeted at the Ubuntu 14.04 LTS. If you are a Windows or OS X user, you can preferably install Ubuntu in a VirtualBox application and install ROS on it. The link to download VirtualBox is https://www.virtualbox.org/wiki/Downloads.

The installation instructions are as follows:

1. Configure your Ubuntu repositories to allow **restricted, universe,** and **multiverse** downloadable. We can configure it using Ubuntu's **Software & Update** tool. We can get this by tool by simply searching on the Ubuntu Unity search menu and tick the following options, as shown in the following screenshot:

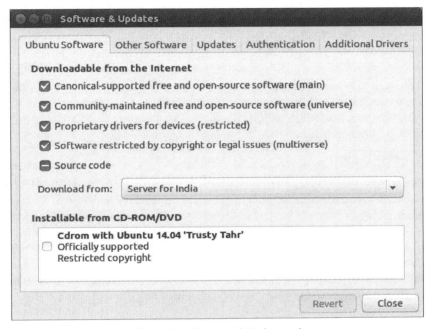

Ubuntu's Software and Update tool

2. Set up your system to accept ROS packages from `packages.ros.org`. ROS Indigo is supported only on Ubuntu 13.10 and Ubuntu 14.04. The following command will store `packages.ros.org` to Ubuntu's `apt` repository list:

    ```
    $ sudo sh -c 'echo "deb http://packages.ros.org/ros/ubuntu
    trusty main" > /etc/apt/sources.list.d/ros-latest.list'
    ```

3. Next, we have to add apt-keys. The **apt-key** is used to manage the list of keys used by apt to authenticate the packages. Packages that have been authenticated using these keys will be considered trusted. The following command will add apt-keys for ROS packages:

    ```
    $ wget https://raw.githubusercontent.com/ros/rosdistro/master/
    ros.key -O - | sudo apt-key add -
    ```

4. After adding apt-keys, we have to update the Ubuntu package index. The following command will add and update the ROS packages along with the Ubuntu packages:

```
$ sudo apt-get update
```

5. After updating the ROS packages, we can install the packages. The following command will install the necessary tools and libraries of ROS:

```
$ sudo apt-get install ros-indigo-desktop-full
```

6. We may need to install additional packages even after the desktop-full installation; each additional installation will be mentioned in the appropriate section. The desktop-full install will take some time. After the installation of ROS, you are almost done. The next step is to initialize **rosdep**, which enables you to easily install the system dependencies for ROS source packages you want to compile and is required to run some core components in ROS:

```
$ sudo rosdep init
```

```
$ rosdep update
```

7. To access the ROS tools and commands on the current bash shell, we can add ROS environmental variables to the .bashrc file. This will execute in the beginning of each bash session. The following is a command to add the ROS variable to .bashrc:

```
echo "source /opt/ros/indigo/setup.bash" >> ~/.bashrc
```

The following command will execute the .bashrc script on the current shell to generate the change in the current shell:

```
source ~/.bashrc
```

8. One of the useful tools to install is rosinstall. This tool has to be installed separately. It enables you to easily download many source trees for the ROS package with one command:

```
$ sudo apt-get install python-rosinstall
```

After the installation of ROS, we will discuss how to create a sample package in ROS. Before creating a package, we have to build an ROS workspace. The packages are created in the ROS workspace. We will use the catkin build system, a set of tools to build packages in ROS. The catkin build system generates executable or shared libraries from the source code. ROS Indigo uses the catkin build system to build packages. Let's see what catkin is.

Introducing catkin

Catkin is the official build system of ROS. Before catkin, ROS used the rosbuild system to build packages. Its replacement is catkin on the latest ROS version. Catkin combines CMake macros and Python scripts to provide the same CMake normal workflow. Catkin provides a better distribution of packages, better cross-compilation, and better portability than the rosbuild system. For more information, refer to wiki.ros.org/catkin.

Catkin workspace is a folder where you can modify, build, and install catkin packages.

Let's check how to create an ROS catkin workspace.

The following command will create a parent directory called catkin_ws and a subfolder called src:

```
$ mkdir -p ~/catkin_ws/src
```

Switch directory to the src folder using the following command. We will create our packages in the src folder:

```
$ cd ~/catkin_ws/src
```

Initialize the catkin workspace using the following command:

```
$catkin_init_workspace
```

After you initialize the catkin workspace, you can simply build the package (even if there is no source file) using the following command:

```
$ cd ~/catkin_ws/
$catkin_make
```

The catkin_make command is used to build packages inside the src directory. After building the packages, we will see a build and devel folder in catkin_ws. The executables are stored in the build folder and in the devel folder, there are shell script files to add to the workspace on the ROS environment.

Creating an ROS package

In this section, we will see how to create a sample package that contains two Python nodes. One of the nodes is used to publish a **Hello World** message on a topic, and the other node will subscribe to this topic.

A catkin ROS package can be created using the `catkin_create_pkg` command in ROS.

The package is created inside the `src` folder that we created during the creation of workspace. Before creating packages, switch to the `src` folder using the following command:

```
$ cd ~/catkin_ws/src
```

The following command will create a `hello_world` package with `std_msgs` dependencies, which contain standard message definitions.The `rospy` is the Python client library for ROS:

```
$ catkin_create_pkg hello_world std_msgs rospy
```

This is the message we get after the successful creation:

```
Created file hello_world/package.xml
Created file hello_world/CMakeLists.txt
Created folder hello_world/src
Successfully created files in /home/lentin/catkin_ws/src/hello_world.
Please adjust the values in package.xml.
```

After the successful creation of the `hello_world` package, we need to add two Python nodes or scripts to demonstrate the subscribing and publishing of topics.

First, create a folder named `scripts` in the `hello_world` package using the following command:

```
$ mkdir scripts
```

Switch to the `scripts` folder and create a script named `hello_world_publisher.py` and another script called `hello_world_subscriber.py` to publish and subscribe to the **hello world** message. The following section covers the code and explanation of these scripts or nodes:

Hello_world_publisher.py

The `hello_world_publisher.py` node basically publishes a greeting message called **hello world** to a topic `/hello_pub`. The greeting message is published to the topic at the rate of 10 Hz.

The step by step explanation of this code is as follows:

1. We need to import `rospy` if we are writing an ROS Python node. It contains Python API's to interact with ROS topics, services, and so on.

2. To send the **hello world** message, we have to import a `String` data type from the `std_msgs` package. It has a message definition for standard data types. We can import using the following command:

```python
#!/usr/bin/env python

import rospy

from std_msgs.msg import String
```

3. The following line of code creates a publisher object to a topic called `hello_pub`. The data type is `String` and `queue_size` is `10`. If the subscriber is not fast enough to receive the data, we can use the `queue_size` option to adjust it:

```python
def talker():
    pub = rospy.Publisher('hello_pub', String, queue_size=10)
```

4. The following line of code is mandatory for all ROS Python nodes. It initializes and assigns a name to the node. The node cannot be launched until it gets a name. It can communicate with other nodes using its name. If two nodes are running with the same node name, one will shut down. If we want to run both nodes, use the `anonymous=True` flag as shown here:

```python
rospy.init_node('hello_world_publisher', anonymous=True)
```

5. The following line creates a rate object called `r`. Using a `sleep()` method in the `Rate` object, we can update the loop in a desired rate. Here, we are given at rate `10`:

```python
r = rospy.Rate(10) # 10hz
```

6. The following loop will check whether `rospy` constructs the `rospy.is_shutdown()` flag. Then, it executes the loop. If we click on *Ctr + C*, this loop will exit.

   Inside the loop, a **hello world** message is printed on the terminal and published on the `hello_pub` topic with a rate of 10 Hz:

```python
    while not rospy.is_shutdown():
        str = "hello world %s"%rospy.get_time()
        rospy.loginfo(str)
        pub.publish(str)
        r.sleep()
```

7. In addition to the standard Python __main__ check, the following code catches a rospy.ROSInterruptException exception, which can be thrown by the rospy.sleep() method, and the rospy.Rate.sleep() method, when *Ctrl + C* is clicked on or your node is otherwise shutdown. The reason this exception is raised is so that you don't accidentally continue executing code after the sleep() method:

```
if __name__ == '__main__':
    try:
        talker()
    except rospy.ROSInterruptException: pass
```

After publishing the topic, we will see how to subscribe it. The following section covers the code to subscribe the hello_pub topic.

Hello_world_subscriber.py

The subscriber code is as follows:

```
#!/usr/bin/env python
import rospy
from std_msgs.msg import String
```

The following code is a callback function that is executed when a message reaches the hello_pub topic. The **data** variable contains the message from the topic and it will print using rospy.loginfo():

```
def callback(data):
    rospy.loginfo(rospy.get_caller_id()+"I heard %s",data.data)
```

The following section will start the node with a **hello_world_subscriber** name and start subscribing to the /hello_pub topic.

1. The data type of the message is String and when a message arrives on this topic, a method called callback will be called:

```
def listener():
    rospy.init_node('hello_world_subscriber',
      anonymous=True)
    rospy.Subscriber("hello_pub", String, callback)
```

2. This will keep your node from exiting until the node is shutdown:

```
rospy.spin()
```

3. The following is the main check of the Python code. The main section will call the `listener()` method, which will subscribe to the /hello_pub topic:

```
if __name__ == '__main__':
    listener()
```

4. After saving two Python nodes, you need to change the permission to executable using the chmod commands:

```
chmod +x hello_world_publisher.py
```

```
chmod +x hello_world_subscriber.py
```

5. After changing the file permission, build the package using the catkin_make command:

```
cd ~/catkin_ws
```

```
catkin_make
```

6. Following command adds the current ROS workspace path in all terminal so that we can access the ROS packages inside this workspace:

```
echo "source ~/catkin_ws/devel/setup.bash" >> ~/.bashrc
```

```
source ~/.bashrc
```

The following is the output of the subscriber and publisher nodes:

1. First, we need to run roscore before starting the nodes. The roscore command or ROS master is needed to communicate between nodes. So, the first command is:

```
$ roscore
```

2. After executing roscore, run each node using the following commands.

3. The following command will run the publisher:

```
$ rosrun hello_world hello_world_publisher.py
```

4. The following command will run the subscriber node. This node subscribes to the `hello_pub` topic, as shown in the following screenshot:

```
$ rosrun hello_world hello_world_subscriber.py
```

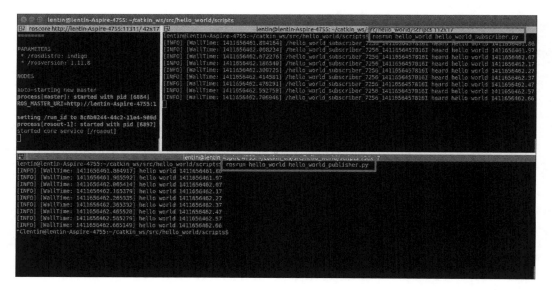

We covered some basics of ROS. Now, we will see what is Gazebo is and how we can work with Gazebo using ROS.

Introducing Gazebo

Gazebo is a free and open source robot simulator in which we can test algorithms, design robots, and perform regression testing using realistic scenarios. Gazebo can accurately and efficiently simulate a population of robots in complex indoor and outdoor environments. Gazebo is built in a robust physics engine with high quality graphics and a convenient programmatic and graphical interface.

The features of Gazebo are as follows:

- **Dynamic simulation**: Gazebo can simulate dynamics of a robot using a physics engine such as **Open Dynamics Engine** (**ODE**). (http://opende. sourceforge.net/), Bullet (http://bulletphysics.org/wordpress/), Simbody (https://simtk.org/home/simbody/), and DART (http://dartsim.github.io/).

- **Advanced 3D Graphics**: Gazebo provides high quality rendering, lighting, shadows, and texturing using the OGRE framework (http://www.ogre3d.org/).

- **Sensors support**: Gazebo supports a wide range of sensors, including laser range finders, kinect style sensors, 2D/3D camera, and so on. We can simulate either with noise or without noise.

- **Plug-in**: We can develop custom plugins for the robot, sensor, and environmental control. Plugins can access Gazebo's API.

- **Robot Models**: Gazebo provides models for popular robots, such as PR2, Pioneer 2 DX, iRobot Create, and TurtleBot. We can also build custom models of robots.

- **TCP//IP Transport**: We can run simulation on a remote machine and a Gazebo interface through a socket-based message passing service.

- **Cloud Simulation**: We can run simulation on the Cloud server using the CloudSim framework (http://cloudsim.io/).

- **Command Line Tools**: Extensive command-line tools are used to check and log simulation.

Installing Gazebo

Gazebo can be installed as a standalone application or an integrated application along with ROS. In this chapter, we will use Gazebo along with ROS for simulation and to test our written code using the ROS framework.

If you want to try the latest Gazebo simulator independently, you can follow the procedure given at http://gazebosim.org/download.

To work with Gazebo and ROS, we don't need to install it separately because Gazebo is built-in along with the ROS desktop-full installation.

The ROS package integrates Gazebo with ROS named gazebo_ros_pkgs, which has created wrappers around a standalone Gazebo. This package provides the necessary interface to simulate a robot in Gazebo using ROS message services.

The complete Gazebo_ros_pkgs can be installed in ROS Indigo using the following command:

```
$ sudo apt-get install ros-indigo-gazebo-ros-pkgs ros-indigo-
  gazebo-ros-control
```

Testing Gazebo with the ROS interface

Assuming that the ROS environment is properly set up, we can start `roscore` before starting Gazebo using the following command:

```
$ roscore
```

The following command will run Gazebo using ROS:

```
$ rosrun gazebo_ros gazebo
```

Gazebo is running as two executables, that is, the Gazebo server and the Gazebo client. The Gazebo server will execute the simulation process and the Gazebo client can be the Gazebo GUI. Using the previous command, the Gazebo client and server will run in parallel.

The Gazebo GUI is shown in the following screenshot:

After starting Gazebo, we will see the following topics generated. Using the `rostopic` command, we will find the following list of topics:

```
$ rostopic list
/gazebo/link_states
```

```
/gazebo/model_states
/gazebo/parameter_descriptions
/gazebo/parameter_updates
/gazebo/set_link_state
/gazebo/set_model_state
```

We can run the server and client separately using the following command:

- Run the Gazebo server using the following command:

  ```
  $ rosrun gazebo_ros gzserver
  ```

- Run the Gazebo client using the following command:

  ```
  $ rosrun gazebo_ros gzclient
  ```

We have installed the basic packages of Gazebo in ROS. If you are not planning to build the hardware for this robot, the alternative plan is to buy another robot called TurtleBot (http://store.clearpathrobotics.com/products/turtlebot-2). Now, we will see how to install the TurtleBot stack on ROS.

Installing TurtleBot Robot packages on ROS Indigo

The TurtleBot installation procedure from its source is mentioned at http://wiki.ros.org/Robots/TurtleBot.

The following is a quick procedure to install the TurtleBot stack and its dependencies from the apt package manager:

1. First, you need to install the synaptic package manager using the following command. Synaptic is a graphical package management program for apt. It provides the same features as the apt-get command-line utility with a GUI frontend based on **GTK+**:

   ```
   $sudo apt-get install synaptic
   ```

2. After the installation of the synaptic package manager, open it and filter its searches using the ros-indigo-rocon keyword.

3. Install all the packages listed on synaptic, as shown in the following screenshot:

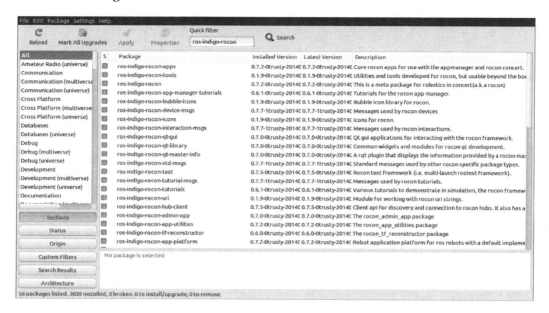

Rocon, also known as robotics in concert, is a dependency of the TurtleBot stack. This package mainly aims to bring ROS to multirobot device tablets. You can read more about rocon at `http://wiki.ros.org/rocon`.

After the installation of `rocon`, we need to install another dependency called the `kobuki` package. Kobuki is a similar robotic mobile platform from Yujin Robots (`http://wiki.ros.org/kobuki`). TurtleBot packages are dependent on these packages.

The `ros-indigo-kobuki` package can be installed using synaptic, such as the rocon package. The following is a screenshot of the installation:

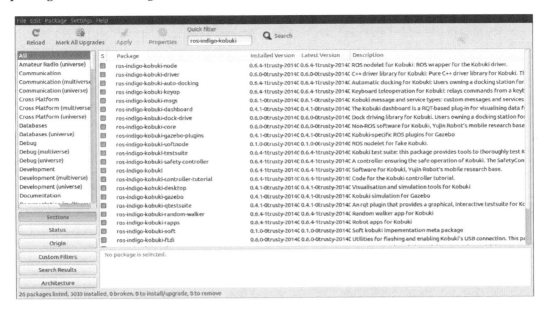

Following is the step by step procedure to build and install TurtleBot's latest ROS packages from the source code in ROS Indigo. The dependencies for installing these packages are already met in the previous procedure.

1. Create a folder called `turtlebot` in the `home` folder using the following command:

   ```
   $ mkdir ~/turtlebot
   ```

2. Switch the directory to `turtlebot` using the following command:

   ```
   $ cd ~/turtlebot
   ```

3. Download the latest source code of TurtleBot using the following command:

```
$ wstool init src -j5
```

```
https://raw.github.com/yujinrobot/yujin_tools/master/
  rosinstalls/indigo/turtlebot.rosinstall
```

4. Install all the dependencies of the source code using the following command:

```
$ rosdep install --from-paths src -i -y
```

5. Build the source code using:

```
$ catkin_make
```

6. To access TurtleBot packages from all terminals, we have to add source ~/ turtlebot/devel/setup.bash command to the .bashrc file. The following command will do this job:

```
$ echo "source ~/turtlebot/devel/setup.bash" >> ~/.bashrc
```

7. This command will execute the .bashrc file:

```
$ source ~/.bashrc
```

Installing TurtleBot ROS packages using the apt package manager in Ubuntu

If you want to install TurtleBot packages without compiling source code, we can use apt package manager. The following is the command to install TurtleBot packages in ROS:

```
$ sudo apt-get install ros-indigo-turtlebot ros-indigo-turtlebot-apps
  ros-indigo-turtlebot-interactions ros-indigo-turtlebot-simulator
  ros-indigo-kobuki-ftdi ros-indigo-rocon-remocon
```

Let's check how to simulate TurtleBot in Gazebo and move the robot on an empty environment.

Simulating TurtleBot using Gazebo and ROS

The TurtleBot simulator package contains the turtlebot_gazebo packages to simulate TurtleBot on Gazebo.

After the successful installation of the TurtleBot package, we can enter the following command to bring up the TurtleBot simulation using ROS and Gazebo:

```
$ roslaunch turtlebot_gazebo turtlebot_empty_world.launch
```

On another terminal, run the following command. This will execute a Python script to control TurtleBot using a keyboard; this is called keyboard teleoperation:

```
$ roslaunch turtlebot_teleop keyboard_teleop.launch
```

Following is the screenshot of the output:

The top-left terminal executes the simulation command and the bottom-left window executes the `teleop` command.

We can move around the robot with keyboard teleoperation using the keys mentioned on the screen. We can also monitor the values from the model using the `rostopics` command. We can view the current topics using the following command:

```
$ rostopic list
```

It publishes all the values from the sensors, such as the kinect sensor, the odometry values from wheel encoders, the IMU sensor value for odometry, and Gazebo's state values.

We will use the clone of the TurtleBot package in which the robot model and simulation parameters are different. We can perform this cloning for most of the mobile robot that has a differential steering system. We will create the packages for our robot by cloning the TurtleBot code. We will name our custom robot as `chefbot` instead of `turtlebot`, and all our packages will be named according to this.

Creating the Gazebo model from TurtleBot packages

In TurtleBot packages, the simulation and kinematic models are implemented using two packages, that is, `turtlebot_gazebo` and `turtlebot_description`. The `turtlebot_gazebo` package has files to launch simulation in Gazebo. The `turtlebot_description` package contains the Gazebo and the kinematic model of the robot.

We customized and reused the turtlebot packages and recreated the same packages for our robot. We named our robot as `chefbot`; we can create `chefbot_gazebo`, which contains the simulation launch files. The launch files in ROS are a kind of an XML file in which we can launch multiple nodes and set multiple parameters by running a single file. To run the launch file, we have to use the `roslaunch` command.

 We can check out the implemented ROS packages of ChefBot at `http://wiki.ros.org/roslaunch` for reference.

The following command clones the complete ROS packages of the ChefBot:

```
$git clone https://github.com/qboticslabs/Chefbot_ROS_pkg.git
```

The `chefbot_description` package contains the kinematic model and the Gazebo model of the robot. The following figure shows the various files in these two packages:

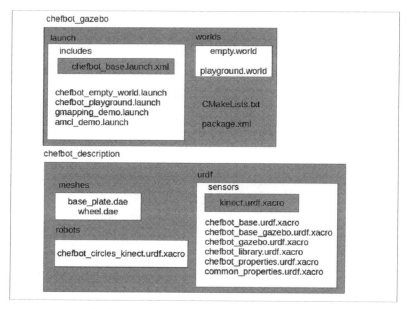

The Chefbot_description and the Chefbot_Gazebo package

Switch to `catkin_ws`, which we created to develop ROS packages. In the `src` folder, first create a folder called `chefbot`. Then, we can create all the packages of ChefBot in it, using the following commands:

```
$ cd ~/catkin_ws/src
$ mkdir chefbot
$ cd chefbot
```

The `chefbot_gazebo` can be created using the following command with the required dependencies:

```
$ catkin_create_pkg chefbot_gazebo depthimage_to_laserscan
  diagnostic_aggregator gazebo_ros kobuki_gazebo_plugins
  robot_pose_ekf robot_state_publisher xacro yocs_cmd_vel_mux
  create_gazebo_plugins create_description create_driver create_node
```

After creating the package, you can copy the two folders in `chefbot_gazebo` from the source code of the chapter that can be downloaded from the Packt Publishing website. This code is adapted from the `turtlebot_gazebo` package; you can also refer to its code for further reference.

Here is the explanation of each file usage. First, we discussed the `chefbot_gazebo` package. In the `launch` folder, there are launch files for each functionality:

- **chefbot_empty_world.launch**: This file will launch the ChefBot model in Gazebo with an empty world, where the **world** is a Gazebo file containing information about the robot environment.

- **chefbot_playground.launch**: This file will launch the Chefbot model in Gazebo. The simulated Gazebo environment contains some random objects like cylinders and boxes.

- **gmapping_demo.launch**: This file will start **Simultaneous Localization And Mapping (SLAM)**. Using SLAM, we can map the environment and store it for future use. In our case, we can map a hotel environment using this package. We will discuss more on gmapping in the upcoming chapter. For more information on SLAM, refer to http://wiki.ros.org/gmapping.

- **amcl_demo.launch**: AMCL stands for **Adaptive Monte Carlo Localization** (`http://wiki.ros.org/amcl`). After mapping the environment, the robot can autonomously navigate by localizing itself on the map and also by giving the feedback from wheels. The feedback from the robot is called odometry. The localization algorithm AMCL and the navigation algorithm, such as path planning is performed in this launch file.

- **chefbot_base.launch.xml**: This XML file will parse an xacro file called `chefbot_circles_kinect.urdf.xacro` to URDF present in the `chefbot_description` folder. After converting the xacro file to URDF, it will generate the robot model equivalent to ROS. We will learn more about URDF and xacro after this section.

After generating the robot model in URDF, this file will generate the Gazebo-compatible model from the URDF robot description. Also, it will start a velocity muxer node that will prioritize the command velocity of the robot. An example of command velocity is the teleoperation by keyboard or joystick. According to the priority assigned, the command velocity will reach the robot. Let's discuss more on URDF and xacro to get a clear picture of the description of the robot.

What is a robot model, URDF, xacro, and robot state publisher?

Robot model in ROS contains packages to model the various aspects of the robot, which is specified in the XML Robot Description Format (URDF). The core package of this stack is URDF, which parses URDF files and constructs an object model of the robot.

Unified Robot Description Format (URDF) is an XML specification to describe the model of a robot. We can represent the following features of the robot using URDF:

- The kinematic and dynamic description of the robot
- The visual representation of the robot
- The collision model of the robot

The description of the robot consists of a set of **link** (part), elements, and a set of **joint** elements, which connect these links together. A typical robot description is shown in the following code:

```
<robot name="chefbot">
   <link> ... </link>
   <link> ... </link>
   <link> ... </link>

   <joint>  .... </joint>
   <joint>  .... </joint>
   <joint>  .... </joint>
</robot>
```

It will be good if you refer to the following links for more information on URDF:

http://wiki.ros.org/urdf

http://wiki.ros.org/urdf/Tutorials

Xacro (XML Macros) is an XML macro language. With xacro, we can create shorter and readable XML files. We can use xacro along with URDF to simplify the URDF file. If we add xacro to urdf, we have to call the additional parser node to convert xacro to urdf.

 The following link can give you more idea about xacro:

http://wiki.ros.org/xacro

robot_state_publisher allows you to publish the state of the robot to **tf** (http://wiki.ros.org/tf). Once the state gets published, it's available to all the components in the system that also use tf. The package takes the joint angles of the robot as input and publishes the 3D poses of the robot links using the kinematic tree model of the robot. The package can be used as a library and as an ROS node. This package has been well tested and the code is stable. No major changes are planned in the near future.

- **World files**: These represent the environment of Gazebo, which have to be loaded along with the robot. The empty.world and playground.world world files are included in the launch files, so it will load when Gazebo starts.

- **CMakeList.txt and package.xml**: These files are created during the creation of package. CmakeList.txt file helps to build the nodes or libraries within a package and the package.xml file holds the list of all the dependencies of this package.

Creating a ChefBot description ROS package

The chefbot_description package contains the urdf model of our robot. Before creating this package by your own, you can go through the downloaded packages of ChefBot. It can help you to speed up the process.

Let's check how to create the `chefbot_description` package. Following procedure will guide you in creating this package:

1. First, we need to switch to the `chefbot` folder in the `src` folder:

   ```
   $ cd ~/catkin_ws/src/chefbot
   ```

2. The following command will create the robot description package along with dependencies, such as urdf, xacro, and the description package of Kobuki, and create mobile robots:

   ```
   $ catkin_create_pkg chefbot_description urdf xacro
     kobuki_description create_description
   ```

3. Copy the `meshes`, `urdf`, and `robots` folders from the downloaded source to the `package` folder. The `mesh` folder holds the 3D parts of the robot and the `urdf` folder contains the urdf description and the sensors of the robot. The entire robot model is divided into a set of xacro files for easier debugging and better readability.

Let's see the functionality of each files inside this package. You can refer the downloaded source code for checking these files, and you can also copy these files from the downloaded files to the newly created folder. The functionality of each urdf folder is as follows:

- **chefbot_base.urdf.xacro**: This xacro represents the kinematic model of the entire robot. It models the entire joints of the robot using the URDF tags. The joint includes two wheels, two caster wheels, gyro sensors, and so on. The 3D kinect sensor is not modeled in this file. It will also attach meshes to each links. This file is reused from the Kobuki mobile-based package.

- **chefbot_base_gazebo.urdf.xacro**: This is the Gazebo model representation of each link of the robot. It includes the actuator definition, sensor definitions, the parameter setting of the differential robot, and so on. Gazebo uses this value to perform the simulation. The robot parameters can change by changing the values in this file.

- **chefbot_gazebo.urdf.xacro**: The previous Gazebo urdf does not have the definitions of the 3D sensor kinect. This file starts the `kinect_openni` Gazebo plugin to simulate the kinect sensor on the robot.

- **chefbot_library.urdf.xacro**: This file includes all the xacro files and sensors of the robot. This single file can launch all the descriptions of the robot.

- **chefbot_properties.urdf.xacro**: This file includes the 3D kinect sensor position on the robot model.

- **common_properties.urdf.xacro**: This file contains properties of meshes such as color.
- **kinect.urdf.xacro**: This file contains the Gazebo parameter of kinect and is present inside the `sensors` folder. This file is included in the `chefbot_gazebo.urdf.xacro` and `chefbot_properties.urdf.xacro` files to set the kinect parameters.
- **chefbot_circles_kinect_urdf.xacro**: This file is inside the `robot` folder. It includes the `chefbot_library.urdf.xacro` file, which will load all the robot description files needed to start the simulation.

In the `meshes` folder, we mainly have the wheel and the body of the robot, the 3D model parts of ChefBot.

Similar to TurtleBot, we can launch the ChefBot simulation using the following command:

```
$ roslaunch chefbot_gazebo chefbot_empty_world.launch
```

When we execute this command, launch files will execute in the order, as shown in the following screenshot:

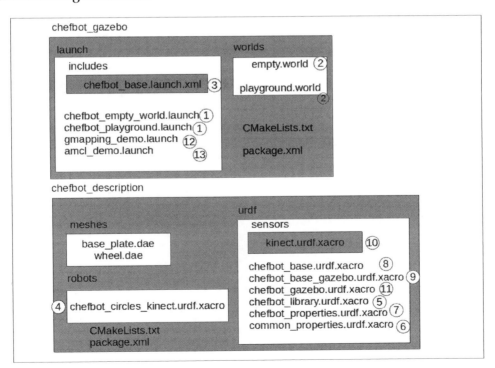

We have already seen the functionality of each file. The important files we need to discuss are:

- `chefbot_gazebo.urdf.xacro`
- `kinect.urdf.xacro`
- `chefbot_base.urdf.xacro`

chefbot_base_gazebo.urdf.xacro

Let's take a look at `chefbot_base_gazebo.urdf.xacro`. The actual file definition is pretty long, so we will only discuss the important parts.

Before discussing Gazebo definitions, we can refer to the Gazebo tags parameters mentioned in URDF. The various tags that can be used in the URDF can be found at `http://osrf-distributions.s3.amazonaws.com/sdformat/api/1.5.html`.

The Gazebo definition for each link is mentioned in URDF as `<gazebo> </gazebo>`. The following URDF definitions for individual joints of the robot are modeled using the Gazebo parameters. The joints include wheel joints and caster wheel joints. The `mu1` and `mu2` parameters are coefficients of friction. `Kp` and `kd` indicate the dynamical stiffness and damping of a joint. `MinDepth` is the minimum allowable depth before the contact correction impulse is applied. `MaxVel` is the maximum contact correction velocity truncation term:

```xml
<?xml version="1.0"?>
<robot name="kobuki_sim" xmlns:xacro="http://ros.org/wiki/xacro">
  <xacro:macro name="kobuki_sim">
    <gazebo reference="wheel_left_link">
      <mu1>1.0</mu1>
      <mu2>1.0</mu2>
      <kp>1000000.0</kp>
      <kd>100.0</kd>
      <minDepth>0.001</minDepth>
      <maxVel>1.0</maxVel>
    </gazebo>

    <gazebo reference="wheel_right_link">
      <mu1>1.0</mu1>
      <mu2>1.0</mu2>
      <kp>1000000.0</kp>
      <kd>100.0</kd>
      <minDepth>0.001</minDepth>
```

```
      <maxVel>1.0</maxVel>
  </gazebo>

  <gazebo reference="caster_front_link">
    <mu1>0.0</mu1>
    <mu2>0.0</mu2>
    <kp>1000000.0</kp>
    <kd>100.0</kd>
    <minDepth>0.001</minDepth>
    <maxVel>1.0</maxVel>
  </gazebo>

  <gazebo reference="caster_back_link">
    <mu1>0.0</mu1>
    <mu2>0.0</mu2>
    <kp>1000000.0</kp>
    <kd>100.0</kd>
    <minDepth>0.001</minDepth>
    <maxVel>1.0</maxVel>
  </gazebo>
```

The following section is used for the **Inertial Measurement Unit (IMU)** sensor in the robot (http://en.wikipedia.org/wiki/Inertial_measurement_unit) modeled in Gazebo. The main use of IMU in the robot is to generate a good odometry value:

```
  <gazebo reference="gyro_link">
    <sensor type="imu" name="imu">
      <always_on>true</always_on>
      <update_rate>50</update_rate>
      <visualize>false</visualize>
      <imu>
        <noise>
          <type>gaussian</type>
          <rate>
            <mean>0.0</mean>
            <stddev>${0.0014*0.0014}</stddev> <!-- 0.25 x 0.25
              (deg/s) -->
            <bias_mean>0.0</bias_mean>
            <bias_stddev>0.0</bias_stddev>
          </rate>
          <accel> <!-- not used in the plugin and real robot,
            hence using tutorial values -->
            <mean>0.0</mean>
            <stddev>1.7e-2</stddev>
```

```
                <bias_mean>0.1</bias_mean>
                <bias_stddev>0.001</bias_stddev>
            </accel>
          </noise>
        </imu>
      </sensor>
    </gazebo>
```

The differential-drive controller plugin for Gazebo is given in the following code. We will reuse the Kobuki differential-drive plugin for the drive system. We will also mention the main measurements of the robot, such as the wheel separation, wheel diameter, torque of the motor, and so on, in this section. This section will also include the cliff sensor, which will not be used in our model. We may ignore this section if we don't want to use it:

```
    <gazebo>
      <plugin name="kobuki_controller"
        filename="libgazebo_ros_kobuki.so">
        <publish_tf>1</publish_tf>
        <left_wheel_joint_name>wheel_left_joint
        </left_wheel_joint_name>
        <right_wheel_joint_name>wheel_right_joint
        </right_wheel_joint_name>
          <wheel_separation>.30</wheel_separation>
          <wheel_diameter>0.09</wheel_diameter>
          <torque>18.0</torque>
          <velocity_command_timeout>0.6</velocity_command_timeout>
        <cliff_sensor_left_name>cliff_sensor_left
          </cliff_sensor_left_name>
        <cliff_sensor_center_name>cliff_sensor_front
          </cliff_sensor_center_name>
        <cliff_sensor_right_name>cliff_sensor_right
          </cliff_sensor_right_name>
        <cliff_detection_threshold>0.04
          </cliff_detection_threshold>
        <bumper_name>bumpers</bumper_name>
          <imu_name>imu</imu_name>
      </plugin>
    </gazebo>
```

kinect.urdf.xacro

This file mainly has the definitions of joints and links of the kinect sensor. This file also includes two launch files:

```
<xacro:include filename="$(find
  chefbot_description)/urdf/chefbot_gazebo.urdf.xacro"/>
<xacro:include filename="$(find
  chefbot_description)/urdf/chefbot_properties.urdf.xacro"/>
```

The `chefbot_gazebo.urdf.xacro` file consists of the kinect plugin for Gazebo. We will reuse this plugin from TurtleBot. The kinect plugin is actually the `libgazebo_ros_openni_kinect.so` file; we can also define the parameters of Kinect, as shown in the following code:

```
<plugin name="kinect_camera_controller"
  filename="libgazebo_ros_openni_kinect.so">
  <cameraName>camera</cameraName>
  <alwaysOn>true</alwaysOn>
  <updateRate>10</updateRate>
  <imageTopicName>rgb/image_raw</imageTopicName>
  <depthImageTopicName>depth/image_raw
    </depthImageTopicName>
  <pointCloudTopicName>depth/points</pointCloudTopicName>
  <cameraInfoTopicName>rgb/camera_info
    </cameraInfoTopicName>
  <depthImageCameraInfoTopicName>depth/camera_info
    </depthImageCameraInfoTopicName>
  <frameName>camera_depth_optical_frame</frameName>
  <baseline>0.1</baseline>
  <distortion_k1>0.0</distortion_k1>
  <distortion_k2>0.0</distortion_k2>
  <distortion_k3>0.0</distortion_k3>
  <distortion_t1>0.0</distortion_t1>
  <distortion_t2>0.0</distortion_t2>
  <pointCloudCutoff>0.4</pointCloudCutoff>
</plugin>
```

chefbot_base.urdf.xacro

This file defines the links and joints of the robot and also includes the `chefbot_gazebo.urdf.xacro` file. The joints of the robot are wheels, caster wheels, and so on. Here is the XML definition of the body of the robot, the wheel of the robot, and the caster wheel of the robot.

The base link of the robot includes the robot body, excluding the wheels. We can export the robot body mesh from the blender and export it to the .DAE extension using MeshLab (http://en.wikipedia.org/wiki/COLLADA). The base joint is a fixed type. There is no movement on the base plate. We can define the collision profile and inertia for each link of the robot. These files are reused from TurtleBot, as shown in the following code:

```
<xacro:macro name="kobuki">
  <link name="base_footprint"/>
  <!--
      Base link is set at the bottom of the base mould.
      This is done to be compatible with the way base link
      was configured for turtlebot 1. Refer to

      https://github.com/turtlebot/turtlebot/issues/40

      To put the base link at the more oft used wheel
      axis, set the z-distance from the base_footprint
      to 0.352.
      -->
  <joint name="base_joint" type="fixed">
    <origin xyz="0 0 0.0102" rpy="0 0 0" />
    <parent link="base_footprint"/>
    <child link="base_link" />
  </joint>
  <link name="base_link">
    <visual>
      <geometry>
        <!-- new mesh -->
        <mesh filename="package://chefbot_description/
          meshes/base_plate.dae" />
      </geometry>
<!--      <origin xyz="0.001 0 0.05199" rpy="0 0 ${M_PI/2}"/> -->
  <origin xyz="0.001 0 -0.034" rpy="0 0 ${M_PI/2}"/>
    </visual>
    <collision>
      <geometry>
        <cylinder length="0.10938" radius="0.178"/>
      </geometry>
      <origin xyz="0.0 0 0.05949" rpy="0 0 0"/>
    </collision>
    <inertial>
```

```
<!-- COM experimentally determined -->
<origin xyz="0.01 0 0"/>
<mass value="2.4"/> <!-- 2.4/2.6 kg for small/big battery
  pack -->
<!-- Kobuki's inertia tensor is approximated by a
  cylinder with homogeneous mass distribution
      More details: http://en.wikipedia.org/wiki/
        List_of_moment_of_inertia_tensors
      m = 2.4 kg; h = 0.09 m; r = 0.175 m
      ixx = 1/12 * m * (3 * r^2 + h^2)
      iyy = 1/12 * m * (3 * r^2 + h^2)
      izz = 1/2 * m * r^2
  -->
<inertia ixx="0.019995" ixy="0.0" ixz="0.0"
         iyy="0.019995" iyz="0.0"
         izz="0.03675" />
</inertial>
</link>


<!--One of the wheel joint is given below. The kind of joint
  used here is a continuous joint. -->

  <joint name="wheel_left_joint" type="continuous">
    <parent link="base_link"/>
    <child link="wheel_left_link"/>
    <origin xyz="0 ${0.28/2} 0.026" rpy="${-M_PI/2} 0 0"/>
    <axis xyz="0 0 1"/>
  </joint>
  <link name="wheel_left_link">
    <visual>
      <geometry>
        <mesh filename="package://
          chefbot_description/meshes/wheel.dae"/>
      </geometry>
      <origin xyz="0 0 0" rpy="0 0 0"/>
    </visual>
    <collision>
      <geometry>
        <cylinder length="0.0206" radius="0.0352"/>
      </geometry>
      <origin rpy="0 0 0" xyz="0 0 0"/>
    </collision>
```

```
<inertial>
  <mass value="0.01" />
  <origin xyz="0 0 0" />
  <inertia ixx="0.001" ixy="0.0" ixz="0.0"
           iyy="0.001" iyz="0.0"
           izz="0.001" />
</inertial>
</link>
```

Simulating ChefBot and TurtleBot in a hotel environment

After discussing each file, we can try the simulation of two robots in a hotel environment. The procedures and screenshots of the simulation are as follows.

Similar to TurtleBot, we can start ChefBot using the following commands:

```
$ roslaunch chefbot_gazebo chefbot_empty_world.launch
```

It will show the robot in Gazebo, as shown in the following screenshot:

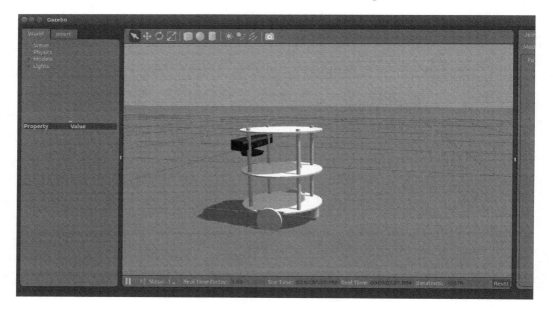

We can exit Gazebo and start building the hotel environment for the robot.

The first procedure is to create a world file and save it with the `.world` file extension. A typical hotel environment with nine block-like tables is shown in the following screenshot. You can take an empty Gazebo world using the following command and make an environment using the basic shapes available in Gazebo:

1. Start `roscore` using the following command:

    ```
    $ roscore
    ```

2. Start Gazebo with an empty world using the following command:

    ```
    $ rosrun gazebo_ros gazebo
    ```

3. Now we have created an environment, as shown in the following screenshot, and saved it as `empty.world`.

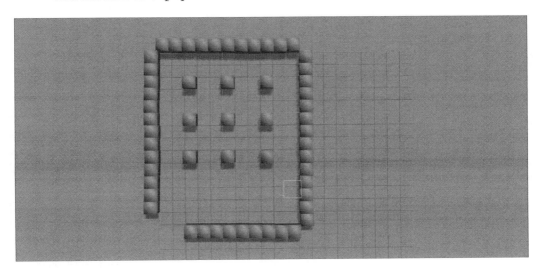

4. Copy `empty.world` to the world folder in the `chefbot_decription` package. Start the robot with this environment using the following command:

    ```
    $ roslaunch chefbot_gazebo chefbot_empty_world.launch
    ```

This will bring the same environment that we created before along with ChefBot. The procedure remains the same for TurtleBot.

Instead of `chefbot_description`, we have to copy the `turtlebot_description` folder for TurtleBot users:

1. Start the gmapping launch file to start mapping this area. We can use the following command to launch the gmapping process:

    ```
    $ roslaunch chefbot_gazebo gmapping_demo.launch
    ```

2. In TurtleBot, use the following command:

    ```
    $ roslaunch turtlebot_gazebo gmapping_demo.launch
    ```

3. It will start the gmapping process and if we want to view the mapping process, start **rviz**, a tool in ROS to visualize sensor data (http://wiki.ros.org/rviz). The command is the same as it was for TurtleBot:

    ```
    $ roslaunch turtlebot_rviz_launchers view_navigation.launch
    ```

    The screenshot of rviz is as follows:

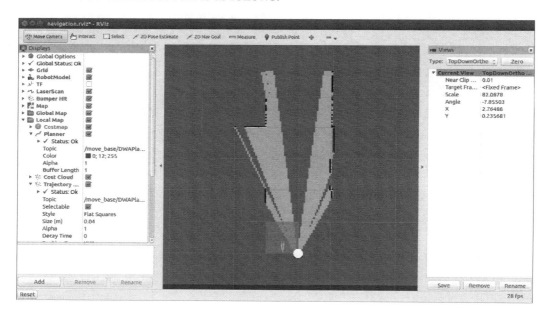

To create a map of the room, we have to start the keyboard teleoperation:

1. Using the keyboard teleoperation function, we can move the robot using the keyboard so that it can map the entire area:

    ```
    $ roslaunch turtlebot_teleop keyboard_teleop.launch
    ```

2. The command is same for TurtleBot. A complete map of the surrounding is shown in the following screenshot:

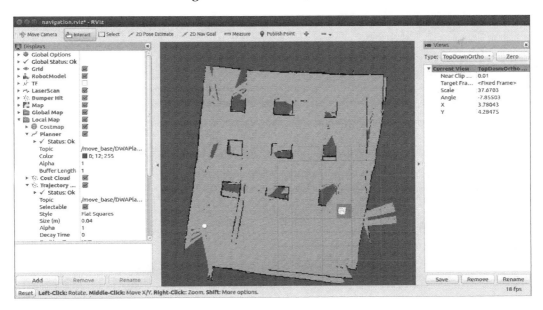

3. After building the map, we can save the name **hotel_world** using the following command:

```
$ rosrun map_server map_saver -f ~/hotel_world
```

The command is same for TurtleBot

4. After saving the map, exit all the other applications that are currently in use.

5. After the map is generated, the next step is autonomous navigation and the localization of the robot using the built map.

6. Start Gazebo using the following command:

```
$ roslaunch chefbot_gazebo chefbot_empty_world.launch
```

7. In TurtleBot, use the following command:

```
$ roslaunch turtlebotbot_gazebo chefbot_empty_world.launch
```

8. Start the amcl demo in ChefBot. Note the path because it may vary for each user.

9. For ChefBot, use the following commands:

```
$ roslaunch chefbot_gazebo amcl_demo.launch
  map_file:=/home/lentin/hotel_world.yaml
```

10. For TurtleBot, use the following commands:

```
$ roslaunch turtlebot_gazebo amcl_demo.launch
  map_file:=/home/lentin/hotel_world.yaml
```

11. Start `rviz` using the following command. This is the same for both robots:

```
$ roslaunch turtlebot_rviz_launchers view_navigation.launch
```

Now we can command the robot to navigate to a position on the map using the **2D Nav Goal** button. Click on this button and select a position that is near a table. After clicking on this position, it will plan the path to that point and navigate to that position, as shown in the following screenshot:

The robot can avoid obstacles and also plan the shortest path to the goal position. After several runs, we found that the robot works perfectly if the map we build was accurate. The map building procedure can be fine-tuned using the instructions at (http://wiki.ros.org/costmap_2d). For an application such as serving food, it requires pretty good accuracy in the map, so that the robot can deliver food to the correct position.

Questions

1. What is robot simulation and what are the popular robot simulators?
2. What is ROS and Gazebo?
3. What is the robot model in ROS?
4. What is gmapping and AMCL?

Summary

In this chapter, you learned how to simulate a custom robot called ChefBot. We discussed the design of the the robot in the previous chapter. After the robot design, we moved on to simulate the robot in a virtual environment to test the design of the robot, and checked whether it met our specifications. In this chapter, you learned about simulation and various simulator applications used in industry, research, and education in detail. After that, we discussed how the ROS framework and Gazebo simulator was used to perform the simulator work. We also created a sample hello_world package using ROS. We installed the TurtleBot stack and created ROS packages from the TurtleBot stack. Finally, we simulated the robot and performed gmapping and autonomous navigation in a hotel environment. We got to know that the accuracy of the simulation depends on the map, and that the robot will work better in simulation if the generated map is perfect.

Designing ChefBot Hardware

4

In this chapter, we will discuss the design and working of ChefBot hardware and selection of its hardware components. In the previous chapter, we designed and simulated the basic robot framework in a hotel environment using Gazebo and ROS, and tested various measurements like robot body mass, motor torque, wheel diameter, and so on. Also, we tested the autonomous navigation capability of ChefBot in a hotel environment.

To achieve this goal in hardware, we need to select all hardware components and find how to interconnect all these components. We know that the main functionality of this robot is navigation; this robot will have the ability to navigate from the start position to the end position without any collision with its surroundings. We will discuss the different sensors and hardware components required to achieve this goal. We will see a block diagram representation and its explanation, and also discuss the main working of the robot. Finally, we need to select the components required to build the robot. We can also see the online stores where we can purchase these components.

If you have a TurtleBot, you may skip this chapter because it is only for those who need to create the robot hardware. Let's see what specifications we have to meet in the hardware design. The robot hardware mainly includes robot chassis, sensors, actuators, controller boards, and PC.

Specifications of the ChefBot hardware

In this section, we will discussing some of the important specifications that we mentioned in *Chapter 2, Mechanical Design of a Service Robot*. The final robot prototype will meet the following specifications:

- **Simple and cost effective robot chassis design**: The robot chassis design should be simple and cost effective.

- **Autonomous navigation functionality**: The robot should autonomously navigate and it should contain necessary sensors for doing this.

- **Long Battery life**: The robot should have a long battery life in order to work continuously. The working time should be greater than 1 hour.

- **Obstacle avoidance**: The robot should be able to avoid static and dynamic objects in the surroundings.

The robot hardware design should meet these specifications. Let's look at one of the possible ways of interconnecting the components in this robot. The next section shows the block diagram of a robot and explains it.

Block diagram of the robot

The robot's movement is controlled by two **Direct Current** (**DC**) gear motors with an encoder. The two motors are driven using a motor driver. The motor driver is interfaced into an embedded controller board, which will send commands to the motor driver to control the motor movements. The encoder of the motor is interfaced into the controller board for counting the number of rotations of the motor shaft. This data is the odometry data from the robot. There are ultrasonic sensors, which are interfaced into the controller board for sensing the obstacles and measuring the distance from the obstacles. There is an IMU sensor to improve odometry calculation. The embedded controller board is interfaced into a PC, which does all the high-end processing in the robot. Vision and sound sensors are interfaced into the PC and Wi-Fi is attached for remote operations.

Each block of the robot is explained in the following diagram:

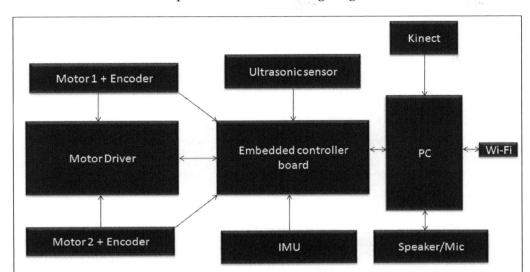

Robot Hardware block Diagram

Motor and encoder

The robot that we are going to design is a differential drive robot with two wheels, so we require two motors for its locomotion. Each motor consists of quadrature encoders (`http://letsmakerobots.com/node/24031`) to get the motor rotation feedback.

The quadrature encoder will give a feedback of the rotation of the motor as square pulses; we can decode the pulse to get the number of ticks of the encoder, which can be used for feedback. If we know the wheel diameter and the number of ticks of the motor, we can compute the displacement and the angle of the robot that traversed. This computation is very useful for navigation of the robot.

Selecting motors, encoders, and wheels for the robot

From the simulation, we got an idea about the robot parameters. On the simulation parameters, we mentioned that the motor torque needed to drive the robot is 18 kg-cm, but the calculated torque is less than this; we are selecting a high torque motor for better performance. One of the economical motors that we might consider using is from Pololu. We can select a high torque DC gear motor with an encoder working at 12 V DC and having speed of 80 RPM according to our design. We are choosing the following motor for the drive system in this robot:

http://www.pololu.com/product/1447

The following figure shows the image of the selected motor for this robot. The motor comes with an integrated quadrature encoder with a resolution of 64 counts per revolution of the motor shaft, which corresponds to 8400 counts per revolution of the gearbox's output shaft.

DC Gear motor with encoder and wheel

This motor has 6 pins with different colors. The pin description of this motor is given in the following table:

Color	Function
Red	Motor power (connects to one motor terminal)
Black	Motor power(connects to the other motor terminal)
Green	Encoder GND
Blue	Encoder Vcc (3.5 V - 20 V)
Yellow	Encoder A output
White	Encoder B output

According to our design, we chose a wheel diameter of 90 mm. Pololu provides a 90 mm wheel, which is available at http://www.pololu.com/product/1439. The preceding figure showed the motor assembled with this wheel.

The other connectors needed to connect the motors and wheels together are available as follows:

- The mounting hub required to mount the wheel to the motor shaft is available at http://www.pololu.com/product/1083
- The L- bracket for the motor to mount on robot chassis is available at http://www.pololu.com/product/1084

Motor driver

A motor driver or motor controller is a circuit that can control the speed of the motor. Controlling motors means that we can control the voltage across the motor and can also control the direction and speed of the motor. Motors can rotate clockwise or counter clockwise, if we change the polarity of motor terminal.

H-bridge circuits are commonly used in motor controllers. **H-bridge** is an electronic circuit that can apply voltage in either direction of load. It has high current handling properties and can change the direction of current flow.

The following screenshot shows a basic H-bridge circuit using switches:

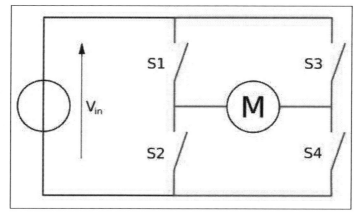

H Bridge circuit

The direction of the motor, depending on the four switches, is given as follows:

S1	S2	S3	S4	Result
1	0	0	1	Motor moves right
0	1	1	0	Motor moves left
0	0	0	0	Motor free runs
0	1	0	1	Motor brakes
1	0	1	0	Motor brakes
1	1	0	0	Motor shoots through
0	0	1	1	Motor shoots through
1	1	1	1	Motor shoots through

We have seen the basics of an H-bridge circuit on the motor driver circuit. Now, we can select one of the motor drivers for our application and discuss how it works.

Selecting a motor driver/controller

There are some motor drivers available with Pololu, which are compatible with the selected motor. The following figure shows one of the motor drivers that we will use in our robot:

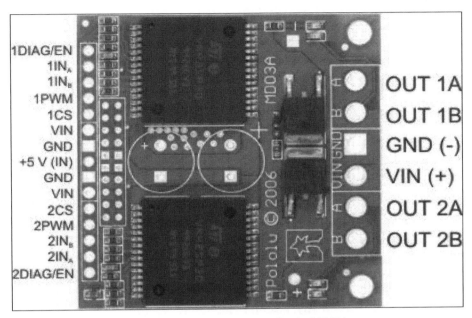

Dual VNH2SP30 Motor Driver Carrier MD03A

This motor driver is available at http://www.pololu.com/product/708.

This driver can drive two motors with a combined maximum current rating of 30 A, and contains two integrated IC for driving each of the motors. The pin description of this driver is given in the upcoming sections.

Input pins

The following pins are the input pins of the motor driver, by which we can control mainly the motor speed and direction:

Pin Name	Function
1DIAG/EN, 2DIAG/EN	This monitors the fault condition of motor driver 1 and 2. In normal operation, it will remain disconnected.
1INa, 1INb, 2INa, 2INb	These pins will control the direction of motor 1 and 2 in the following manner: <ul><li>If INA = INB = 0, motor will break</li><li>If INA = 1, INB = 0, motor will rotate clockwise</li><li>If INA = 0, INB = 1, motor rotate counter clockwise</li><li>If INA = INB = 1, motor will break</li></ul>
1PWM, 2PWM	This will control the speed of motor 1 and 2 by rapidly turning them on and off.
1CS, 2CS	This is the current sensing pin for each motor.

Output pins

The output pins of the motor driver will drive the two motors. The following are the output pins:

Pin Name	Function
OUT 1A, OUT 1B	These pins connect to motor 1 power terminals
OUT 2A, OUT 2B	These pins connect to motor 2 power terminals

Power supply pins

The following are the power supply pins:

Pin name	Function
VIN (+), GND (-)	These are the supply pins of the two motors. The voltage ranges from 5.5 V to 16 V.
+5 VIN, GND (-)	This is the supply of motor driver. The voltage should be 5 V.

Embedded controller board

Controller boards are typically I/O boards, which can send control signals in the form of digital pulses to the H-Bridge/motor driver board and can receive inputs from sensors such as ultrasonic and IR sensors. We can also interface motor encoders to the control board for the motor feedback.

The main functionalities of Launchpad in this robot are:

- Interfacing the motor driver and encoder
- Interfacing the ultrasonic sound sensor
- Sending and receiving sensor values to PC and from PC

We will deal with I/O boards and interfacing with different components in the upcoming chapters. Some of the popular I/O boards are Arduino (`arduino.cc`) and Tiva C LaunchPad (`http://www.ti.com/tool/EK-TM4C123GXL`) by Texas Instruments. We are selecting Tiva C LaunchPad over Arduino because of following factors:

- Tiva C LaunchPad has a microcontroller based on 32-bit ARM Cortex-M4 with 256 KB Flash memory, 32 KB SRAM, and 80 MHz operation; however, most of the Arduino boards run below this specification.
- Outstanding processing performance, combined with fast interrupt handling.
- 12 Timers.
- 16 PWM Outputs.
- Two quadrature encoder inputs.
- Eight **Universal Asynchronous Receiver/Transmitter (UART)**.
- 5 V tolerant **General-Purpose Input/Output (GPIO)**.
- Low cost and size compared to Arduino boards.
- Easy programmable interface IDE called Energia (`http://energia.nu/`). The code written in Energia is Arduino board compatible.

The following image shows the Texas Instrument's Tiva C LaunchPad:

Tiva C Launchpad

The pinout of Texas Instrument Launchpad series is given at http://energia.nu/ pin-maps/guide_stellarislaunchpad/. This pinout is compatible with all the Launchpad series. This is also used while programming in Energia IDE.

Ultrasonic sensors

Ultrasonic sensors are also called ping sensors, and are mainly used to measure the robot's distance from an object. The main application of ping sensors is to avoid obstacles. The ultrasonic sensor sends high frequency sound waves and evaluates the echoes that are received from the object. The sensor will calculate the delay between sending and receiving the echo, and from that, determine its distance from an object.

In our robot, collision-free navigation is an important aspect, otherwise there will be damage to the robot. You will see a figure showing an ultrasonic sensor in the next section. This sensor can be employed on the sides of a robot to detect collision on the sides and back of the robot. The kinect is also mainly used for obstacle detection and collision avoidance. The accuracy of kinect can only be expected from 0.8 m, so that distance in between 0.8 m can be detected using ultrasonic sensor. It is actually an add-on to our robot for increasing collision avoidance and detection.

Selecting the ultrasonic sensor

One of the popular and cheap ultrasonic sensors available is **HC-SR04**. We are selecting this sensor for our robot because of the following factors:

- Range of detection is from 2 cm to 4 m
- Working voltage is 5 V
- Working current is very low typically 15 mA

We can use this sensor for accurate detection of obstacles; it also works with 5 V. Here is the image of HC-SR04 and its pinout:

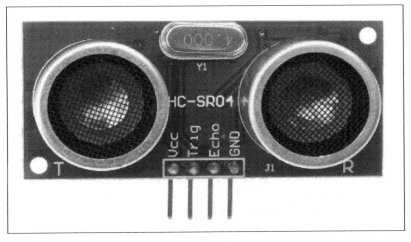

Ultrasonic sound sensor

The pins and description are given as follows:

Pins	Function
Vcc, GND	These are the supply pins of ultrasonic sensor. Normally, we need to apply 5 V for a normal operation.
Trig	This is the input pin of the sensor. We need to apply a pulse with a particular duration to this pin to send the ultrasonic sound waves.
Echo	This is the output pin of the sensor. It will generate a pulse on this pin with a time duration, according to the delay in receiving the triggered pulse.

Inertial Measurement Unit

We will use **Inertial Measurement Unit (IMU)** in this robot to get a good estimate of the odometry value and the robot pose. The odometry values computed from the encoder alone may not be sufficient for efficient navigation, it could contain errors. To compensate for errors during the robot's movement, we will use IMU in this robot. We are selecting MPU 6050 for IMU because of following reasons:

- In MPU 6050, the accelerometer and gyroscope are integrated on a single chip
- It provides high accuracy and sensitivity
- There is provision to interface magnetometer for better IMU performance
- The breakout board of MPU 6050 is very cheap
- The MPU 6050 can directly interface to Launchpad, both are 3.3 V compatible and software libraries are also available for easier interfacing

The following figure shows the breakout board of MPU 6050:

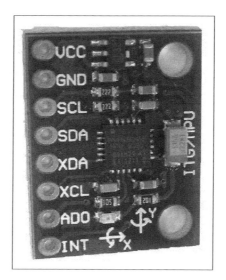

The pins and their descriptions are given as follows:

Pins	Functions
VDD, GND	Supply voltage 2.3 V - 3.4 V
INT	This pin will generate an interrupt when data comes to the device buffer
SCL, SDA	**Serial Data Line (SDA)** and **Serial Clock Line** (SCL) are used for I2C communication
ASCL, ASDA	Auxiliary I2C for communication with Magnetometer

We can purchase the breakout board from `https://www.sparkfun.com/products/11028`.

Kinect

Kinect is a 3D vision sensor, mainly used in 3D vision application and motion gaming. We are using kinect for 3D vision. Using kinect, the robot will get the 3D image of its surroundings. The 3D images are converted to finer points called point cloud. The point cloud data will have all 3D parameters of the surrounding.

The main use of kinect on the robot is to mock the functionality of a laser scanner. The laser scanner data is essential for an algorithm called SLAM, used for building a map of the environment. The laser scanner is a very costly device, so instead of buying an expensive laser scanner, we can convert a kinect into a virtual laser scanner. Another alternative to kinect is Asus Xtion PRO (`http://www.asus.com/Multimedia/Xtion_PRO/`). This will support the same software written for kinect. The point cloud to laser data conversion is done on the software, so no need to change the hardware parts. After generating a map of the environment, the robot can navigate its surroundings.

The following image shows the various parts of a kinect sensor:

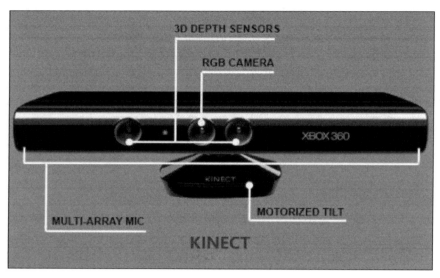

Kinect

The kinect mainly has an IR camera and IR projector and also has an RGB camera. The IR camera and projector generates the 3D point cloud of the surroundings. It also has a mic array and motorized tilt for moving the kinect up and down.

We can purchase kinect from `http://www.amazon.co.uk/Xbox-360-Kinect-Sensor-Adventures/dp/B0036DDW2G`.

Central Processing Unit

The robot is mainly controlled by its navigational algorithm that is running on its PC. We can choose a laptop or mini PC or netbook for the processing. Recently, Intel launched a minicomputer called Intel **Next Unit of Computing** (**NUC**). It has an ultra small form factor (small size), is lightweight, and has a good computing processor with Intel Celeron, Core i3, or Core i5. It can support upto 16 GB of RAM and has integrated Wi-Fi/Bluetooth. We are choosing Intel NUC because of its performance, ultra small form factor, and lightweight. We are not going for a popular board, such as Raspberry Pi (`http://www.raspberrypi.org/`) or BeagleBone (`http://beagleboard.org/`) because we require high computing power in this case, which cannot be provided by these boards.

The NUC we are using is **Intel DN2820FYKH**. Here are the specifications of this computer:

- Intel Celeron Dual Core processor with 2.39 GHz
- 4 GB RAM
- 500 GB hard disk
- Intel integrated graphics
- Headphone/microphone jack
- 12 V supply

The following image shows the Intel NUC minicomputer:

Intel NUC DN2820FYKH

We can purchase NUC from `http://goo.gl/Quzi7a`.

Speakers/ mic

The main function of the robot is autonomous navigation. We are adding an additional feature in which the robot can interact with users through speech. The robot can be given commands using voice and can speak to the user using a **text to speech** (TTS) engine, which can convert text to speech format. A microphone and speakers are essential for this application. There is no particular selection for this hardware. If the speaker and mic are USB compatible, then it will be great. Another alternative is a Bluetooth headset.

Power supply/battery

One of the important hardware component is the power supply. We saw in the specification that the robot has to work for more than 1 hour; it will be good if the supply voltage of the battery is common to the components. Also, if the size and weight of the battery is less, it will not affect the robot's payload. Another concern is that the maximum current needed for the entire circuit should not exceed the battery's maximum current, which it can source. The maximum voltage and current distribution of each part of the circuit is as follows:

Components	Maximum current (Ampere)
Intel NUC PC	12 V, 3 A
Kinect	12 V, 1 A
Motors	12 V,0.7 A
Motor driver, Ultrasonic sensor, IMU, Speakers	5 V, < 0.5 A

To meet these specifications, we are selecting a 12V, 9 AH Li-Polymer battery for our operation. This battery can also source maximum current up to 5 Ampere.

The following image shows our selected battery for this robot:

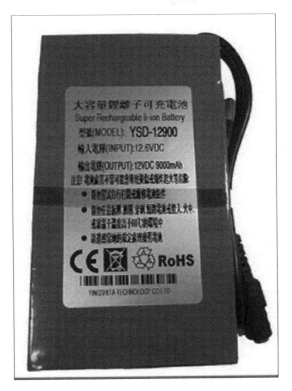

We can buy the following battery from http://goo.gl/Clzk6I.

Working of the ChefBot hardware

We can explain the working of the ChefBot hardware using the following block diagram. This improved version of our first block diagram mentions the voltage of each component and its interconnection:

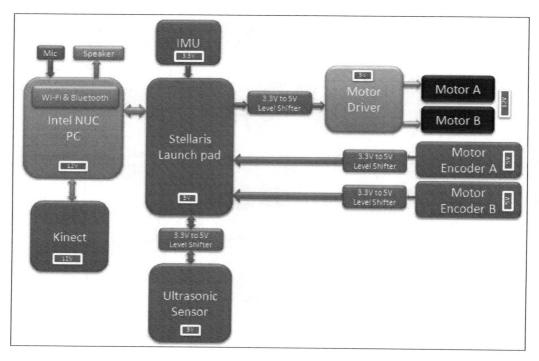

The main aim of this chapter was to design the hardware for ChefBot, which included finding the appropriate hardware components and finding the interconnection between each part. The main functionality of this robot is to perform autonomous navigation. The hardware design of robot is optimized for autonomous navigation.

The robot drive is based on differential drive system, which consists of two motors and two wheels. There are caster wheels for supporting the main wheels. These two motors can move the robot in any pose in a 2D plane by adjusting their velocities and direction.

For controlling the velocity and direction of the wheels, we have to interface a motor controller, which can do these functions. The motor driver we chose should able to control two motors at a time and change the direction and speed.

The motor driver pins are interfaced to a microcontroller board called Tiva C LaunchPad, which can send the commands to change the direction and speed of the motor. The motor driver is interfaced into Launchpad with the help of a level shifter. The **level shifter** is a circuit, which can shift voltage levels from 3.3 V to 5 V and vice versa. We are using a level shifter because the motor driver is operating at 5 V level, but the Launchpad is operating at 3.3 V.

Each motor has a rotation feedback sensor called the encoder, which can be used to estimate the robot's position. The encoders are interfaced into the Launchpad along with the level shifter.

Other sensors interfaced into Launchpad include ultrasonic sound sensor and IMU. Ultrasonic sound sensor can detect objects that are close by, but cannot be detected by the kinect sensor. IMU is used along with the encoders, to get a good robot pose estimation.

All sensor values are received on the Launchpad and sent to PC via USB. The Launchpad runs a firmware code that can receive all sensor values and send to the PC.

The PC is interfaced to kinect, Launchpad, Speaker, and Mic. The PC has ROS running on it and it will receive kinect data and converted to data equivalent to laser scanner. This data can be used to build the map of the environment using SLAM. The speaker/mic is used for communication between the user and robot. The speed commands generated in ROS nodes are sent to Launchpad. Launchpad will then process the speed commands and send appropriate PWM values to the motor driver circuit.

After designing and discussing the working of the robot hardware, we will discuss the detailed interfacing of each component and the firmware coding necessary for the interfacing.

Questions

1. What is robot hardware designing all about?
2. What is H-bridge and what are its functions?
3. Which are the components essential for the robot navigation algorithm?
4. What is the criteria that has to be kept in mind while selecting robotic components?
5. What are the main applications of Kinect on this robot?

Summary

In this chapter, we have seen the features of the robot that we are going to design. The main feature of this robot is autonomous navigation. The robot can navigate in its surrounding by analyzing sensor readings. We went through the robot block diagram in which we discussed the role of each block, and we then selected appropriate components that satisfy these requirements. This chapter also suggested some economical components to build this robot. In the next chapter, we will find out more about actuators and their interfacing that we using on this robot.

5
Working with Robotic Actuators and Wheel Encoders

In this chapter, we will cover:

- Interfacing a DC Geared motor with Tiva C LaunchPad
- Interfacing a quadrature encoder with Tiva C LaunchPad
- Explanation of interfacing code
- Interfacing Dynamixel actuators

In the previous chapter, we have discussed the selection of hardware components needed to build our robot. One of the important components in robot hardware is the actuator. Actuators provide mobility to the robot. In this chapter, we are concentrating on the different types of actuators that we are going to use in this robot and how they can be interfaced with Tiva C LaunchPad, which is a 32-bit ARM micro controller board from Texas Instrument that works at 80 MHz. The first actuator that we are going to discuss is a DC geared motor with an encoder. A DC geared motor works using direct current, and has gear reduction to reduce the shaft speed and increase the torque of the final shaft. These kind of motors are very economic and we can use this kind of motor in our robot prototype.

In the first section of this chapter, we will deal with the design of our robot drive system. The **Drive system** of our robot consists of two DC geared motors with encoders and a motor driver. The motor driver is controlled by Tiva C LaunchPad. We will see interfacing of motor driver and quadrature encoder with Tiva C Launchpad.

In the last section, we will explore some of the latest actuators which can replace the existing DC geared motor with encoder. If the desired robot needs more payload and accuracy, we have switch to these kind of actuators.

Interfacing DC geared motor with Tiva C LaunchPad

In the previous chapter, we selected a DC geared motor with an encoder from Pololu and the embedded board from Texas Instruments called Tiva C LaunchPad. We need the following components to interface the motor with Launchpad:

- Two Pololu metal gear motors 37Dx57L mm with 64 count per revolution encoder
- Pololu wheel 90x10 mm and a matching hub
- Pololu dual VNH2SP30 motor driver carrier MD03A
- A sealed lead acid/Lithium Ion battery of 12 V
- A logic level convertor of 3.3 V to 5 V https://www.sparkfun.com/products/11978.
- A Tiva C LaunchPad and its compatible interfacing wires

The following figure shows the interfacing circuit of two motors using Pololu H-Bridge:

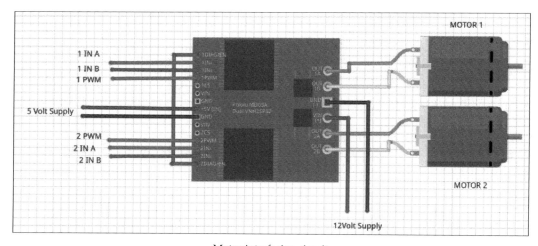

Motor interfacing circuit

To interface with Launchpad, we have to connect a level shifter board in between these two. The motor driver works in 5 V but the Launchpad works in 3.3 V, so we have to connect a level shifter, as shown in the following figure:

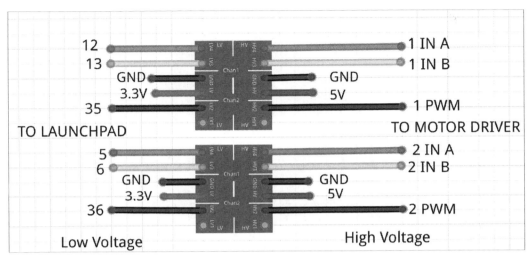

Level shifter circuit

The two geared DC motors are connected to **OUT1A, OUT1B**, and **OUT2A, OUT2B** of the motor driver. **VIN(+)** and **GND(-)** are the supply voltages of the motor. These DC motors can work with 12 Volt supply, so we give 12 Volt as the input voltage. The motor driver will support an input voltage range of 5.5 V to 16 V.

The control signals/input pins of motor drivers are on the left-hand side of the driver. The first pin is **1DIAG/EN**, in most cases we leave this pin disconnected. These pins are externally pulled high in the driver board itself. The main use of this pin is to enable or disable the H-bridge chip. It is also used to monitor the faulty condition of the H-bridge IC. Pins **1INA** and **1INB** control the direction of rotation of the motor. The **1PWM** pin will switch the motor to ON and OFF state. We achieve speed control using **PWM** pins. The **CS** pin will sense the output current. It will output 0.13 Volts per Ampere of the output current. The **VIN** and **GND** pins give the same input voltage that we supplied to the motor. We are not using these pins here. The **+5V(IN)** and **GND** pins are the supply for the motor driver IC. The supply to the motor driver and motors is different.

The following table shows the truth table of the input and output combinations:

INA	INB	DIAGA/ ENA	DIAGB/ENB	OUTA	OUTB	CS	Operating mode
1	1	1	1	H	H	High Imp	Brake to Vcc
1	0	1	1	H	L	Isense = Iout / K	Clockwise (CW)
0	1	1	1	L	H	Isense = Iout / K	Counterclockwise (CCW)
0	0	1	1	L	L	High Imp	Braker to GND

The value **DIAG/EN** pins are always high because this pin is externally pulled high in the driver board itself. Using these signal combinations, we can move the robot in any direction and by adjusting the PWM Signal, we can adjust the speed of the motor too. This is the basic logic behind controlling a DC motor using an H-bridge circuit.

While interfacing motor to Launchpad, we may require a level shifter. This is because the output pins of Launchpad can only supply 3.3 Volt but the motor driver needs 5 V to trigger; so, we have to connect 3.3 V to a 5 V logic level convertor to start working.

The two motors work in a differential drive mechanism. The following section discusses differential drive and its operation.

Differential wheeled robot

The robot we have designed is a differential wheeled robot. In a differential wheeled robot, the movement is based on two separately driven wheels placed on either side of the robot's body. It can change its direction by changing the relative rate of rotation of its wheels, and hence, doesn't require additional steering motion. To balance the robot, a free turning wheel or caster wheels may be added.

The following figure shows a typical representation of differential drive:

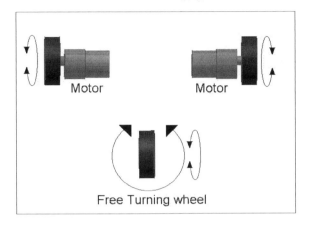

If the two motors are moving in the same direction, the robot will move forward or backward. If one motor has more speed than the other, then the robot turns to the slower motor side; so to turn left, stop the left motor and move the right motor. The following figure shows how we connect the two motors in our robot. The two motors are mounted on the opposite sides of the base plate and we put two casters in front and back of the robot in order to balance it:

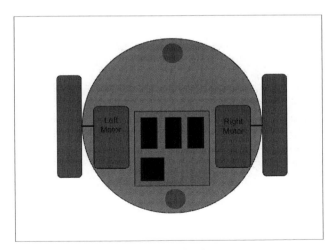

Top view of robot base

Next, we can program the motor controller using Launchpad according to the truth table data. Programming is done using an IDE called **Energia** (http://energia.nu/). We are programming Launchpad using a language called **Wiring** (http://wiring.org.co/).

Installing the Energia IDE

We can download the latest version of Energia from the following link:

`http://energia.nu/download/`

We will discuss the installation procedure mainly on Ubuntu 14.04.2, 64-bit. The Energia version that we will use is 0101E0013:

1. Download Energia for Linux 64-bit from the above link.

2. Extract the Energia compressed file into the Home folder of the user.

3. Add rules to set read and write permission to Tiva C LaunchPad. This is essential for writing firmware to Launchpad. The following command will add permission for USB device:

   ```
   $ echo 'ATTRS{idVendor}=="1cbe", ATTRS{idProduct}=="00fd",
   GROUP="users", MODE="0660"' | \
   sudo tee /etc/udev/rules.d/99-tiva-launchpad.rules
   ```

4. After entering the command, plug Launchpad to PC.

5. Start Energia using the following command inside the folder:

   ```
   $ ./energia
   ```

   The following screenshot shows the Energia IDE:

6. Now, select the board by navigating to **Tools | Boards | Launchpad (Tiva C) w/tm4c123 (80MHz)** as shown in the following screenshot:

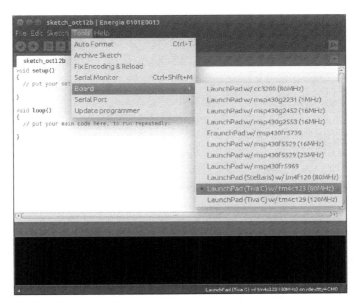

7. Then, select the **Serial Port** by navigating to **Tools | Serial Port | /dev/ ttyACM0** as shown in the following screenshot:

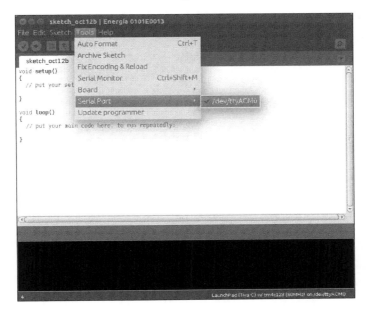

8. Compile the code using the compile button. The screenshot of a successful compilation is given here:

9. After successful compilation, upload the code into the board by clicking on the **Upload** button. The uploaded code was an empty code which performs no operations.

   If the uploading is successful, the following message will be shown:

Use the following tutorial to install Energia on Mac OS X and Windows:

- Refer to `http://energia.nu/Guide_MacOSX.html` for Mac OS X
- Refer to `http://energia.nu/Guide_Windows.html` for Windows

Interfacing code

The following code can be used to test the two motors in differential drive configuration. This code can move the robot forward for 5 seconds and backward for 5 seconds. Then, it moves the robot to the left for 5 seconds and right for 5 seconds. After each movement, the robot will stop for 1 second.

At the beginning of the code, we define pins for INA, INB, and PWM of the two motors as follows:

```
///Left Motor  Pins
#define INA_1 12
#define INB_1 13
#define PWM_1 PC_6

///Right Motor Pins
#define INA_2 5
#define INB_2 6
#define PWM_2 PC_5
```

The pinout for Launchpad is given at:

`http://energia.nu/pin-maps/guide_tm4c123launchpad/`

The following code shows the five functions to move the robot forward, backward, left and right. The fifth function is to stop the robot. We will use the `digitalWrite()` function to write a digital value to a pin. The first argument of `digitalWrite()` is the pin number and second argument is the value to be written to the pin. The value can be `HIGH` or `LOW`. We will use the `analogWrite()` function to write a PWM value to a pin. The first argument of this function is the pin number and second is the PWM value. The range of this value is from 0-255. At high PWM, the motor driver will switch fast and have more speed. At low PWM, switching inside the motor driver will be slow, so the motor will also be slow. Currently, we are running at full speed.

```
voidmove_forward()
{
  //Setting CW rotation to and Left Motor  and CCW to Right Motor
  //Left Motor
```

```
digitalWrite(INA_1,HIGH);
digitalWrite(INB_1,LOW);
analogWrite(PWM_1,255);
  //Right Motor
digitalWrite(INA_2,LOW);
digitalWrite(INB_2,HIGH);
analogWrite(PWM_2,255);
}

/////////////////////////////////////////////////////

voidmove_left()
{
    //Left Motor
digitalWrite(INA_1,HIGH);
digitalWrite(INB_1,HIGH);
analogWrite(PWM_1,0);
  //Right Motor
digitalWrite(INA_2,LOW);
digitalWrite(INB_2,HIGH);
analogWrite(PWM_2,255);
}

/////////////////////////////////////////////////////

voidmove_right()
{
      //Left Motor
digitalWrite(INA_1,HIGH);
digitalWrite(INB_1,LOW);
analogWrite(PWM_1,255);
  //Right Motor
digitalWrite(INA_2,HIGH);
digitalWrite(INB_2,HIGH);
analogWrite(PWM_2,0);
}

/////////////////////////////////////////////////////

void stop()
{
  //Left Motor
```

```
digitalWrite(INA_1,HIGH);
digitalWrite(INB_1,HIGH);
analogWrite(PWM_1,0);
  //Right Motor
digitalWrite(INA_2,HIGH);
digitalWrite(INB_2,HIGH);
analogWrite(PWM_2,0);
}


/////////////////////////////////////////////////

voidmove_backward()

{
    //Left Motor
digitalWrite(INA_1,LOW);
digitalWrite(INB_1,HIGH);
analogWrite(PWM_1,255);
  //Right Motor
digitalWrite(INA_2,HIGH);
digitalWrite(INB_2,LOW);
analogWrite(PWM_2,255);
}
```

We first set the INA, INB pins of the two motor to the OUTPUT mode, so that we can write HIGH or LOW values to these pins. The function pinMode() is used to set the mode of the I/O pin. The first argument of pinMode() is the pin number and second argument is the mode. We can set a pin as input or output. To set a pin as output, give OUTPUT argument as the second argument; to set it as input, give INPUT as the second argument as shown in following code. There is no need to set the PWM pin as the output because analogWrite() writes the PWM signal without setting pinMode():

```
void setup()
{
    //Setting Left Motor pin as OUTPUT
pinMode(INA_1,OUTPUT);
pinMode(INB_1,OUTPUT);
pinMode(PWM_1,OUTPUT);

    //Setting Right Motor pin as OUTPUT
pinMode(INA_2,OUTPUT);
pinMode(INB_2,OUTPUT);
pinMode(PWM_2,OUTPUT);
}
```

The following snippet is the main loop of the code. It will call each function, move forward(), move_backward(), move_left(), and move_right() for 5 seconds. After calling each function, the robot stops for 1 second.

```
void loop()
{
  //Move forward for 5 sec
move_forward();
delay(5000);
  //Stop for 1 sec
stop();
delay(1000);

  //Move backward for 5 sec
move_backward();
delay(5000);
  //Stop for 1 sec
stop();
delay(1000);

  //Move left for 5 sec
move_left();
delay(5000);
  //Stop for 1 sec
stop();
delay(1000);

  //Move right for 5 sec
move_right();
delay(5000);
  //Stop for 1 sec
stop();
delay(1000);
}
```

Interfacing quadrature encoder with Tiva C Launchpad

The wheel encoder is a sensor attached to the motor to sense the number of rotations of the wheel. If we know the number of rotations, we can compute the displacement, velocity, acceleration, and angle of the wheel.

For this robot, we have chosen a motor with an in-built encoder. This encoder is a quadrature type, which can sense both the direction and speed of the motor. Encoders use different types of sensors, such as optical and hall sensors, to detect these parameters. This encoder uses Hall effect to sense the rotation. The quadrature encoder has two channels, namely Channel A and Channel B. Each channel will generate digital signals with ninety degree phase shift. The following figure shows the wave form of a typical quadrature encoder:

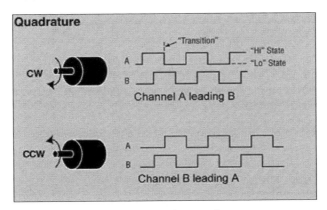

Quadrature encoder waveforms

If the motor rotates clockwise, **Channel A** will lead **Channel B,** and if the motor rotates counterclockwise, **Channel B** will lead **Channel A**. This reading will be useful to sense the direction of rotation of the motor. The following section discusses how we can translate the encoder output to useful measurements like displacement and velocity.

Processing encoder data

Encoder data is a two channel pulse out with 90 degree out of phase. Using this data, we can find the direction of rotation and how many times the motor has rotated, and thereby find the displacement and velocity.

Some of the terms that specify encoder resolution are **pulses per revolution (PPR)** or **lines per revolution (LPR)** and **counts per revolution (CPR)**. PPR specifies how many electrical pulses (0 to 1 transitions) there will be during one revolution of a motor's final shaft. Some manufacturers use the name CPR instead of PPR. Because each pulse will contain two edges (rising and falling) and there are two pulse channels (A and B) with a 90 degree phase shift, the total number of edges will be four times the number of PPR. Most quadrature receivers use the so called 4X decoding to count all the edges from an encoder's A and B channels yielding 4X resolution compared to the raw PPR value.

In our motor, Pololu specifies that the CPR is 64 for the motor shaft, which corresponds to 8400 CPR of the gearbox's output shaft. In effect, we get 8400 counts from the gearbox output shaft when the motor's final shaft completes one revolution. The following figure shows how we can compute the count from the encoder pulses:

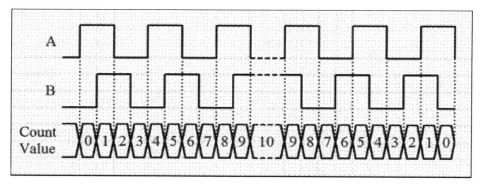

Encoder waveform with count waveform

In this encoder specification, they give the count per revolution; it is calculated by the encoder channel edge transitions. One pulse of an encoder channel corresponds to four counts. So to get 8400 counts in our motor, the PPR will be *8400 / 4 = 2100*. From the preceding figure, we will be able to calculate the number of counts in one revolution, but we also need to sense the direction of the movement. This is because irrespective of whether the robot moves forward or backward, the counts that we get will be same; so sensing the direction is important in order to decode the signal. The following figure shows how we can decode the encoder pulses:

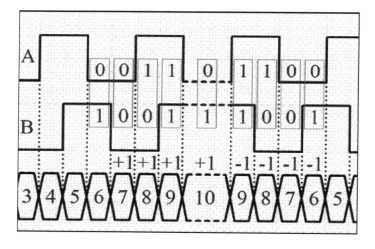

If we observe the code pattern, we can understand that it follows the 2-bit Gray code. A Gray code is encoding of numbers, such that adjacent numbers have a single digit differing by 1. Gray codes (http://en.wikipedia.org/wiki/Gray_code) are commonly used in rotary encoders for efficient coding.

We can predict the direction of rotation of a motor by state transitions. The state transition table is given in the following figure:

State	Clockwise transition	Counterclockwise transition
0,0	0,1 to 0,0	1,0 to 0,0
1,0	0,0 to 1,0	1,1 to 1,0
1,1	1,0 to 1,1	0,1 to 1,1
0,1	1,1 to 0,1	0,0 to 0,1

It will be more convenient if we represent it in a state transition diagram:

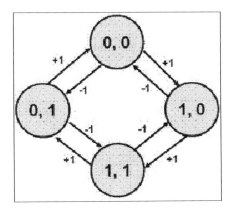

After getting this Gray code, we can process the pulses using a microcontroller. The channel pins of the motor have to be connected to the interrupt pins of the microcontroller. So when the channel has edge transitions, it will generate an interrupt or trigger in the pins, and if any interrupts arrives in that pin, an interrupt service routine or simply a function will be executed inside the microcontroller program. It can read the current state of the two pins. According to the current state of pins and previous values, we can determine the direction of rotation and can decide whether we have to increment or decrement the count. This is the basic logic of encoder handling.

After getting the count, we can calculate the angle of rotation (in degrees) using *Angle = (Count Value / CPR) * 360*. Here, if we substitute CPR with 8400, the equation becomes *Angle = 0.04285 * Count Value*, that is, for turning one degree, 24 counts have to be received or 6 encoded channel pulses have to come.

The following figure shows the interfacing circuit of one motor encoder with Tiva C LaunchPad:

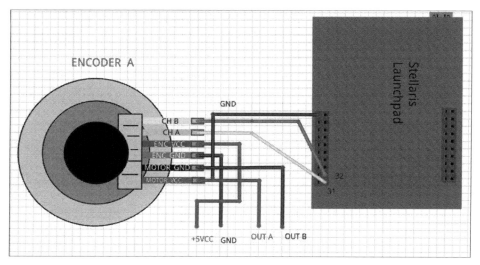

Interfacing Motor encoder with Tiva C Launchpad

The maximum level of output pulse is between 0 V to 5 V from the encoder. In this case, we can directly interface the encoder with Launchpad because it can receive input of up to 5 V, or we can use a 3.3 V to 5 V level shifter like we used for motor driver interfacing earlier.

In the next section, we will write a code in Energia to test the quadrature encoder signal. We need to check whether we get a proper count from encoder.

Quadrature encoder interfacing code

This code will print the count of the left and right motor encoder via a serial port. The two encoders are in 2X decoding scheme, so we will get 4200 CPR. In the first section of the code, we are defining pins for two channel outputs of two encoders and we are declaring the count variable for two encoders. The encoder variable uses a volatile keyword before the variable data type.

The main use of `volatile` is that the variable with `volatile` keyword will be stored in the RAM, whereas normal variables are in CPU registers. Encoder values will change very quickly, so using an ordinary variable will not be accurate. In order to get accuracy, we will use `volatile` for encoder variables, as follows:

```
//Encoder pins definition

// Left encoder

#define Left_Encoder_PinA 31
#define Left_Encoder_PinB 32

volatile long Left_Encoder_Ticks = 0;

//Variable to read current state of left encoder pin
volatile bool LeftEncoderBSet;

//Right Encoder

#define Right_Encoder_PinA 33
#define Right_Encoder_PinB 34
volatile long Right_Encoder_Ticks = 0;
//Variable to read current state of right encoder pin
volatile bool RightEncoderBSet;
```

The following code snippet is the definition of the `setup()` function. In wiring language, `setup()` is a built-in function used for initialization and for one-time execution of variables and functions. Inside `setup()`, we initialize the serial data communication with a baud rate of `115200` and call a user-defined function `SetupEncoders()` to initialize pins of the encoders. The serial data communication is mainly done to check the encoder count via the serial terminal.

```
void setup()
{
    //Init Serial port with 115200 buad rate
    Serial.begin(115200);
  SetupEncoders();
}
```

The definition of SetupEncoders() is given in the code that follows. To receive the encoder pulse, we need two pins in Launchpad as the input. Configure the encoder pins to Launchpad as the input and activate its pull-up resistor. The attachInterrupt () function will configure one of the encoder pins as an interrupt. The attachInterrupt () function has three arguments. First argument is the pin number, second argument is the **Interrupt Service Routine (ISR)**, and the third argument is the interrupt condition, that is, the condition in which the interrupt has to fire ISR. In this code, we are configuring PinA of the left and right encoder pins as the interrupt; it calls the ISR when there is a rise in the pulse.

```
void SetupEncoders()
{
  // Quadrature encoders
  // Left encoder
  pinMode(Left_Encoder_PinA, INPUT_PULLUP);
  // sets pin A as input
  pinMode(Left_Encoder_PinB, INPUT_PULLUP);
  // sets pin B as input
  attachInterrupt(Left_Encoder_PinA, do_Left_Encoder, RISING);

  // Right encoder
  pinMode(Right_Encoder_PinA, INPUT_PULLUP);
  // sets pin A as input
  pinMode(Right_Encoder_PinB, INPUT_PULLUP);
  // sets pin B as input

  attachInterrupt(Right_Encoder_PinA, do_Right_Encoder, RISING);
}
```

The following code is the built-in loop() function in wiring language. The loop() function is an infinite loop where we put our main code. In this code, we call the Update_Encoders() function to print the encoder value continuously through serial terminal.

```
void loop()
{
  Update_Encoders();
}
```

The following code is the function definition of the `Update_Encoders()` function. It prints two encoder values in a line with a starting character "e", and the values are separated by tab spaces. The `Serial.print()` function is a built-in function that will print the character/string given as the argument.

```
void Update_Encoders()
{
  Serial.print("e");
  Serial.print("\t");
  Serial.print(Left_Encoder_Ticks);
  Serial.print("\t");
  Serial.print(Right_Encoder_Ticks);
  Serial.print("\n");
}
```

The following code is the ISR definition of the left and right encoders. When a rising edge is detected on each of the pins, one of the ISRs will be called. The current interrupt pins are `PinA` of each of the encoders. After getting the interrupt, we can assume that the rising `PinA` has a higher value state, so there is no need to read that pin. Read `PinB` of both the encoders and store the pin state to `LeftEncoderBSet` or `RightEncoderBSet`. The current state is compared to the previous state of `PinB` and can detect the direction and decide whether the count has to be incremented or decremented according to the state transition table.

```
void do_Left_Encoder()
{
  LeftEncoderBSet = digitalRead(Left_Encoder_PinB);
  // read the input pin
  Left_Encoder_Ticks -= LeftEncoderBSet ? -1 : +1;
}

void do_Right_Encoder()
{
  RightEncoderBSet = digitalRead(Right_Encoder_PinB);
  // read the input pin
  Right_Encoder_Ticks += RightEncoderBSet ? -1 : +1;
}
```

Upload the sketch and view the output using the serial monitor in Energia. Navigate to **Tools | Serial monitor**. Move the two motors manually and you can see the count changing. Set the baud rate in the serial monitor, which is the same as initialized in the code; in this case, it is **115200**.

The output will look like this:

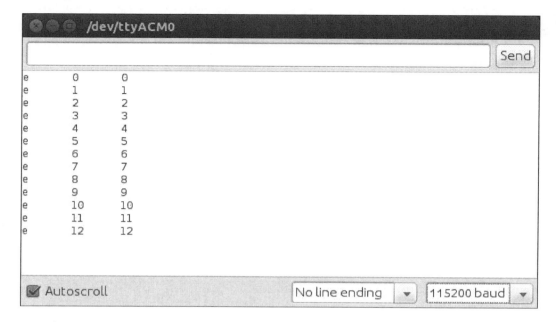

If we want to upgrade the robot to high accuracy and payload, we have to think about high quality actuators such as Dynamixel. Dynamixels are intelligent actuators, which have in-built PID control and monitoring of the servo and encoder parameters, such as torque, position, and so on.

Working with Dynamixel actuators

Dynamixel is a kind of networked actuator for robots developed by Korean manufacture ROBOTIS. It is widely used by companies, universities, and hobbyists due to its versatile expansion capability, power feedback function, position, speed, internal temperature, input voltage, and so on.

The Dynamixel servos can be connected in a daisy chain; it is a method of connecting device in a serial fashion, that is, connecting one device to another through the connected devices, and can control all the connected servos from one controller. Dynamixel servos communicate via RS485 or TTL. The list of available Dynamixel servos is given at http://www.robotis.com/xe/dynamixel_en.

The interfacing of Dynamixel is very easy. Dynamixel comes with a controller called USB2Dyanmixel, which will convert USB to Dynamixel compatible TTL/RS485 levels. The following figure shows the interfacing diagram of Dynamixel:

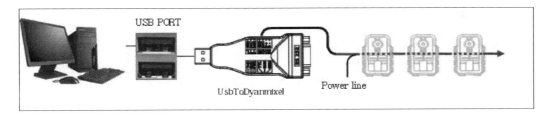

ROBOTIS provides Dynamixel SDK for accessing motor registers; we can read and write values to Dynamixel registers and retrieve data such as position, temperature, voltage, and so on.

 The instructions to set USB2Dynamixel and Dynamixel SDK are given at support.robotis.com/en/.

Dynamixel can be programed using Python libraries. One of the Python libraries for handling Dynamixel servos is **pydynamixel**. This package is available for Windows and Linux. Pydynamixel will support RX, MX, and EX series servos.

We can download the pydynamixel Python package from https://pypi.python.org/pypi/dynamixel/.

Download the package and extract it to the home folder. Open a terminal/DOS prompt and execute the following command:

```
sudo python setup.py install
```

After installing the package, we can try the following Python example, which will detect the servo attached to the USB2Dynamixel and write some random position to the servo. This example will work with RX and MX servos.

```
#!/usr/bin/env python
```

The following code will import the necessary Python modules required for this example. This includes Dynamixel Python modules too:

```
import os
import dynamixel
import time
import random
```

The following code defines the main parameters needed for Dynamixel communication parameters.The nServos variable denoted number of Dynamixel servos connected to the bus. The portName variable indicates the serial port of USB2Dynamixel to which Dynamixel servos are connected. The baudRate variable is the communication speed of USB2Dynamixel and Dynamixel.

```
# The number of Dynamixels on our bus.
nServos = 1

# Set your serial port accordingly.
if os.name == "posix":
    portName = "/dev/ttyUSB0"
else:
    portName = "COM6"

# Default baud rate of the USB2Dynamixel device.
baudRate = 1000000
```

The following code is the Dynamixel Python function to connect to Dynamixel servos. If it is connected, the program will print it and scan the communication bus to find the number of servos starting from ID 1 to 255. The Servo ID is the identification of each servo. We are given nServos as 1, so it will stop scanning after getting one servo on the bus:

```
# Connect to the serial port
print "Connecting to serial port", portName, '...',
serial = dynamixel.serial_stream.SerialStream( port=portName,
baudrate=baudRate, timeout=1)
print "Connected!"
net = dynamixel.dynamixel_network.DynamixelNetwork( serial )
net.scan( 1, nServos )
```

The following code will append the Dynamixel ID and the servo object to the myActuators list. We can write servo values to each servo using servo id and servo object. We can use the myActuators list for further processing:

```
# A list to hold the dynamixels
myActuators = list()
print myActuators
```

```
This will create a list for storing  dynamixel actuators details.
```

```
print "Scanning for Dynamixels...",
for dyn in net.get_dynamixels():
    print dyn.id,
    myActuators.append(net[dyn.id])
print "...Done"
```

The following code will write random positions from 450 to 600 to each Dynamixel actuator that is available on the bus. The range of positions in Dynamixel is 0 to 1023. This will set the servo parameters such as speed, torque, torque_limt, max_torque, and so on:

```
# Set the default speed and torque
for actuator in myActuators:
    actuator.moving_speed = 50
    actuator.synchronized = True
    actuator.torque_enable = True
    actuator.torque_limit = 800
    actuator.max_torque = 800
```

The following code will print the current position of the current actuator:

```
# Move the servos randomly and print out their current positions
while True:
    for actuator in myActuators:
        actuator.goal_position = random.randrange(450, 600)
    net.synchronize()
```

The following code will read all data from actuators:

```
    for actuator in myActuators:
        actuator.read_all()
        time.sleep(0.01)


    for actuator in myActuators:
        print actuator.cache[dynamixel.defs.REGISTER['Id']], actuator.
cache[dynamixel.defs.REGISTER['CurrentPosition']]


    time.sleep(2)
```

Questions

1. What is the H-Bridge circuit?
2. What is a quadrature encoder?
3. What is the 4X encoding scheme?
4. How do we calculate displacement from encoder data?
5. What are the features of the Dynamixel actuator?

Summary

In this chapter we have discussed the interfacing of motor that we are using in our robot. We have seen motor and encoder interfacing with a controller board called Tiva C LaunchPad. We have discussed the controller code for interfacing motor and encoder. In the future, if the robot requires high accuracy and torque, we have seen Dynamixel servos that can substitute current DC motors. In the next chapter, we will see different kinds of sensors that can be used in robots and its interfacing.

6
Working with Robotic Sensors

In the previous chapter, we have seen the interfacing of some actuators for our service robot. The next important section that we need to cover is about the robotic sensors used in this robot.

We are using sensors in this robot to find the distance from an obstacle, to get the robot odometry data, and for robotic vision and acoustics.

The sensors are ultrasonic distance sensors, or IR proximity sensors are used to detect the obstacles and to avoid collisions. The vision sensors such as Kinect to acquire 3D data of the environment, for visual odometry; object detection, for collision avoidance; and audio devices such as speakers and mics, for speech recognition and synthesis.

In this chapter, we are not including vision and audio sensors interfacing because in the upcoming chapter we will discuss them and their interfacing in detail.

Working with ultrasonic distance sensors

One of the most important features of a mobile robot is navigation. An ideal navigation means a robot can plan its path from its current position to the destination and can move without any obstacles. We use ultrasonic distance sensors in this robot for detecting objects in close proximity that can't be detected using the Kinect sensor. A combination of Kinect and ultrasonic sound sensors provides ideal collision avoidance for this robot.

Ultrasonic distance sensors work in the following manner. The transmitter will send an ultrasonic sound which is not audible to human ears. After sending an ultrasonic wave, it will wait for an echo of the transmitted wave. If there is no echo, it means there are no obstacles in front of the robot. If the receiving sensor receives an echo, a pulse will be generated on the receiver, and it can calculate the total time the wave will take to travel to the object and return to the receiver sensors. If we get this time, we can compute the distance to the obstacle using the following formula:

*Speed of Sound * Time Passed /2 = Distance from Object.*

Here, the speed of sound can be taken as 340 m/s.

Most of the ultrasonic range sensors have a distance range from 2 cm to 400 cm. In this robot, we use a sensor module called HC-SR04. We can see how to interface HC-SR04 with Tiva C LaunchPad to get the distance from the obstacles.

Interfacing HC-SR04 to Tiva C LaunchPad

The following figure is the interfacing circuit of the HC-SR04 ultrasonic sound sensor with Tiva C LaunchPad:

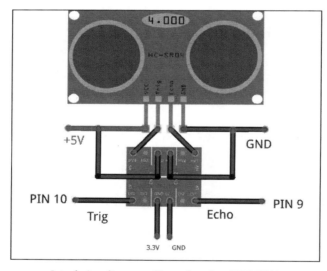

Interfacing diagram of Launchpad and HC-SR04

The working voltage of the ultrasonic sensor is 5 V and the input/output of this sensor is also 5 Volt, so we need a level shifter on the **Trig** and **Echo** pins for the interfacing into the **3.3 V** level Launchpad. In the level shifter, we need to apply high voltage, that is, 5 Volt, and low voltage, that is, 3.3 Volt, as shown in the figure, to switch from one level to another level. **Trig** and **Echo** pins are connected on the high voltage side of the level shifter and the low voltage side pins are connected to Launchpad. The **Trig** pin and **Echo** pin are connected to the 10th and 9th pins of Launchpad. After interfacing the sensor, we can see how to program the two I/O pins.

Working of HC-SR04

The timing diagram of waveform on each pin is shown in the following diagram. We need to apply a short 10 μs pulse to the trigger input to start the ranging and then the module will send out an eight cycle burst of ultrasound at 40 KHz and raise its echo. The echo is a distance object that is pulse width and the range in proportion. You can calculate the range through the time interval between sending trigger signals and receiving echo signals using the following formula:

*Range = high level time of echo pin output * velocity (340 M/S) / 2.*

It will be better to use a delay of 60 ms before each trigger, to avoid overlapping between the trigger and echo:

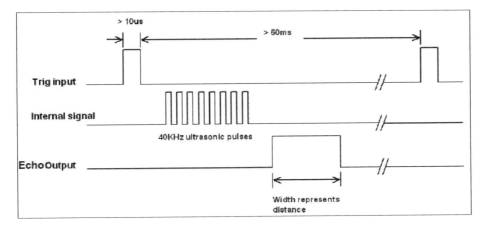

Interfacing code of Tiva C LaunchPad

The following Energia code for Launchpad reads values from the ultrasound sensor and monitors the values through a serial port.

The following code defines the pins in Launchpad to handle ultrasonic echo and trigger pins and also defines variables for the duration of the pulse and the distance in centimeters:

```
const int echo = 9, Trig = 10;
long duration, cm;
```

The following code snippet is the setup() function. The setup() function is called when a sketch/code starts. Use this to initialize variables, pin modes, start using libraries, and so on. The setup function will only run once, after each power up or reset of the Launchpad board. Inside setup(), we initialize serial communication with a baud rate of 115200 and setup the mode of ultrasonic handling pins by calling a function SetupUltrasonic();

```
void setup()
{

  //Init Serial port with 115200 buad rate
  Serial.begin(115200);
  SetupUltrasonic();
}
```

The following is the setup function for the ultrasonic sensor; it will configure the Trigger pin as OUTPUT and the Echo pin as INPUT. The pinMode() function is used to set the pin as INPUT or OUTPUT.

```
void SetupUltrasonic()
{
 pinMode(Trig, OUTPUT);
 pinMode(echo, INPUT);

}
```

After creating a setup() function, which initializes and sets the initial values, the loop() function does precisely what its name suggests, and loops consecutively, allowing your program to change and respond. Use it to actively control the Launchpad board.

The main loop of this is in the following code. This function is an infinite loop and calls the `Update_Ultra_Sonic()` function to update and print the ultrasonic readings through a serial port:

```
void loop()
{
    Update_Ultra_Sonic();
    delay(200);
}
```

The following code is the definition of the `Update_Ultra_Sonic()` function. This function will do the following operations. First, it will take the trigger pin to the LOW state for 2 microseconds and HIGH for 10 microseconds. After 10 microseconds, it will again return the pin to the LOW state. This is according to the timing diagram. We already saw that 10 µs is the trigger pulse width.

After triggering with 10 µs, we have to read the time duration from the Echo pin. The time duration is the time taken for the sound to travel from the sensor to the object and from the object to the sensor receiver. We can read the pulse duration by using the `pulseIn()` function. After getting the time duration, we can convert the time into centimeters by using the `microsecondsToCentimeters()` function, as shown in the following code:

```
void Update_Ultra_Sonic()
{
    digitalWrite(Trig, LOW);
    delayMicroseconds(2);
    digitalWrite(Trig, HIGH);
    delayMicroseconds(10);
    digitalWrite(Trig, LOW);

    duration = pulseIn(echo, HIGH);
    // convert the time into a distance
    cm = microsecondsToCentimeters(duration);

    //Sending through serial port
    Serial.print("distance=");
    Serial.print("\t");
    Serial.print(cm);
    Serial.print("\n");

}
```

The following code is the conversion function from microseconds to distance in centimeters. The speed of sound is 340 m/s, that is, 29 microseconds per centimeter. So we get the total distance by dividing the total microseconds by 29/2:

```
long microsecondsToCentimeters(long microseconds)
{
return microseconds / 29 / 2;
}
```

After uploading the code, open the serial monitor from the Energia menu under **Tools | Serial Monitor** and change the baud rate into **115200**. You can see the values from the ultrasonic sensor, like this:

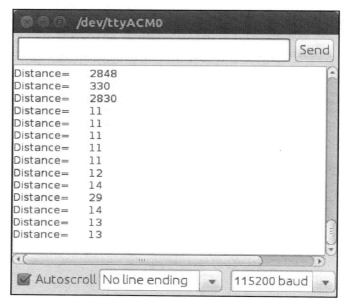

Output of the energia serial monitor

Interfacing Tiva C LaunchPad with Python

In this section, we can see how to connect Tiva C LaunchPad with Python to receive data from Launchpad.

The **PySerial** module can be used for interfacing Launchpad to Python. The detailed documentation of PySerial and its installation procedure for Window, Linux, and OS X is on the following link:

http://pyserial.sourceforge.net/pyserial.html

PySerial is available in the Ubuntu package manager and it can be easily installed in Ubuntu using the following command in terminal:

```
$ sudo apt-get install python-serial
```

After installing the `python-serial` package, we can write a python code to interface Launchpad. The interfacing code is given in following section.

The following code imports the python `serial` module and the `sys` module. The `serial` module handles the serial ports of Launchpad and performs operations such as reading, writing, and so on. The `sys` module provides access to some variables used or maintained by the interpreter and to functions that interact strongly with the interpreter. It is always available:

```
#!/usr/bin/env python
import serial
import sys
```

When we plug Launchpad to the computer, the device registers on the OS as a virtual serial port. In Ubuntu, the device name looks like /dev/ttyACMx. Where **x** can be a number, if there is only one device, it will probably be 0. To interact with the Launchpad, we need to handle this device file only.

The following code will try to open the serial port /dev/ttyACM0 of Launchpad with a baud rate of 115200. If it fails, it will print Unable to open serial port.

```
try:
    ser = serial.Serial('/dev/ttyACM0',115200)
except:
    print "Unable to open serial port"
```

The following code will read the serial data until the serial character becomes a new line (`'\n'`) and prints it on the terminal. If we press *Ctrl* + *C* on the keyboard, to quit the program, it will exit by calling `sys.exit(0)`.

```
while True:
    try:
        line = ser.readline()
        print line
    except:
        print "Unable to read from device"
        sys.exit(0)
```

After saving the file, change the permission of the file to executable using the following command:

```
$ sudo chmod +X script_name
$ ./script_name
```

The output of the script will look like this:

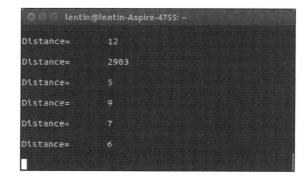

Working with the IR proximity sensor

Infrared sensors are another method to find obstacles and the distance from the robot. The principle of infrared distance sensors is based on the infrared light that is reflected from a surface when hitting an obstacle. An IR receiver will capture the reflected light and the voltage is measured based on the amount of light received.

One of the popular IR range sensors is Sharp GP2D12, the product link is as follows:

http://www.robotshop.com/en/sharp-gp2y0a21yk0f-ir-range-sensor.html

The following figure shows the Sharp GP2D12 sensor:

The sensor sends out a beam of IR light and uses triangulation to measure the distance. The detection range of the GP2D12 is between 10 cm and 80 cm. The beam is 6 cm wide at a distance of 80 cm. The transmission and reflection of the IR light sensor is illustrated in the following figure:

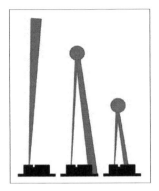

On the left of the sensor is an IR transmitter, which continuously sends IR radiation, after hitting into some objects, the IR light will reflect and it will be received by the IR receiver. The interfacing circuit of the IR sensor is shown here:

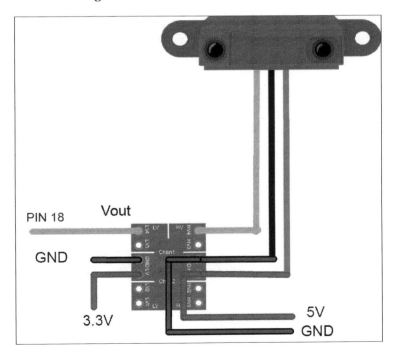

The analog out pin **Vo** can be connected to the ADC pin of Launchpad. The interfacing code of the Sharp distance sensor with the Tiva C Launchpad is given further in this section. In this code, we select the 18th pin of Launchpad and set it to the ADC mode and read the voltage levels from the Sharp distance sensor. The range equation of the GP2D12 IR sensor is given as follows:

Range = (6787 / (Volt - 3)) – 4

Here, Volt is the analog voltage value from ADC of the Vout pin.

In this first section of the code, we set the 18th pin of Tiva C LaunchPad as the input pin and start a serial communication at a baud rate of 115200:

```
int IR_SENSOR = 18; // Sensor is connected to the analog A3
int intSensorResult = 0; //Sensor result
float fltSensorCalc = 0; //Calculated value

void setup()
{
Serial.begin(115200); // Setup communication with computer
  to present results serial monitor
}
```

In the following section of code, the controller continuously reads the analog pin and converts it to the distance value in centimeters:

```
void loop()
{

// read the value from the ir sensor
intSensorResult = analogRead(IR_SENSOR); //Get sensor value

//Calculate distance in cm according to the range equation
fltSensorCalc = (6787.0 / (intSensorResult - 3.0)) - 4.0;

Serial.print(fltSensorCalc); //Send distance to computer
Serial.println(" cm"); //Add cm to result
delay(200); //Wait
}
```

This is the basic code to interface a Sharp distance sensor. There are some drawbacks with the IR sensors. Some of them are as follows:

- We can't use them in direct or indirect sunlight, so it's difficult to use them in an outdoor robot
- They may not work if an object is reflective
- The range equation only works within the range

In the next section, we can discuss IMU and its interfacing with Tiva C LaunchPad. IMU can give the odometry data and it can be used as the input to navigation algorithms.

Working with Inertial Measurement Unit

An **Inertial Measurement Unit (IMU)** is an electronic device that measures velocity, orientation, and gravitational forces using a combination of accelerometers, gyroscopes, and magnetometers. An IMU has a lot of applications in robotics; some of the applications are in balancing of **Unmanned Aerial Vehicles (UAVs)** and robot navigation.

In this section, we discuss the role of IMU in mobile robot navigation and some of the latest IMUs on the market and its interfacing with Launchpad.

Inertial Navigation

An IMU provides acceleration and orientation relative to inertial space, if you know the initial position, velocity, and orientation, you can calculate the velocity by integrating the sensed acceleration and the second integration gives the position. To get the correct direction of the robot, the orientation of the robot is required; this can be obtained by integrating sensed angular velocity from gyroscope.

The following figure illustrates an inertial navigation system, which will convert IMU values to odometric data:

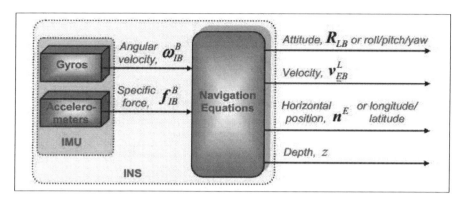

The values we get from the IMU are converted into navigational information using navigation equations and feeding into estimation filters such as the Kalman filter. The **Kalman** filter is an algorithm that estimates the state of a system from the measured data (http://en.wikipedia.org/wiki/Kalman_filter). The data from **Inertial Navigation System (INS)** will have some drift because of the error from the accelerometer and gyroscope. To limit the drift, an INS is usually aided by other sensors that provide direct measurements of the integrated quantities. Based on the measurements and sensor error models, the Kalman filter estimates errors in the navigation equations and all the colored sensors' errors. The following figure shows a diagram of an aided inertial navigation system using the Kalman filter:

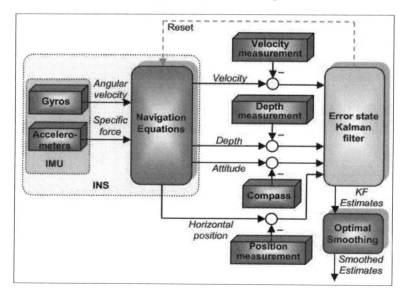

Along with the motor encoders, the value from the IMU can be taken as the odometer value and it can be used for **dead reckoning**, the process of finding the current position of a moving object by using a previously determined position.

In the next section, we are going to see one of the most popular IMUs from InvenSense called **MPU 6050**.

Interfacing MPU 6050 with Tiva C LaunchPad

The MPU-6000/MPU-6050 family of parts are the world's first and only 6-axis motion tracking devices designed for the low power, low cost, and high performance requirements of smart phones, tablets, wearable sensors, and robotics.

The MPU-6000/6050 devices combine a 3-axis gyroscope and 3-axis accelerometer on the silicon die together with an onboard digital motion processor capable of processing complex 9-axis motion fusion algorithms. The following figure shows the system diagram of MPU 6050 and breakout of MPU 6050:

The breakout board of MPU 6050 is shown in the following figure and it can be purchased from the following link:

https://www.sparkfun.com/products/110286

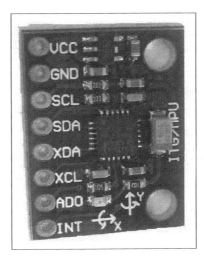

The connection from Launchpad to MPU 6050 is given in the following table. The remaining pins can be left disconnected:

Launchpad pins	MPU6050 pins
+3.3V	VCC/VDD
GND	GND
PD0	SCL
PD1	SDA

The following figure shows the interfacing diagram of MPU 6050 and Tiva C Launchpad:

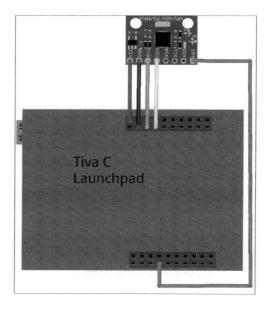

The MPU 6050 and Launchpad communicate using the I2C protocol, the supply voltage is 3.3 Volt and it is taken from Launchpad.

Setting up the MPU 6050 library in Energia

The interfacing code of Energia is discussed in this section. The interfacing code uses the `https://github.com/jrowberg/i2cdevlib/zipball/master` library for interfacing MPU 6050.

Download the ZIP file from the preceding link and navigate to **Preference** from **File | Preference** in Energia, as shown in the following screenshot:

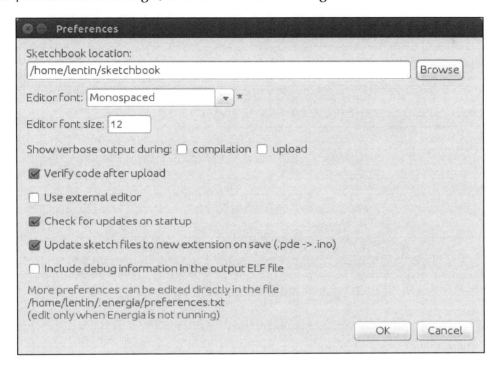

Go to **Sketchbook location** under **Preferences**, as seen in the preceding screenshot, and create a folder called libraries. Extract the files inside the **Arduino** folder inside the ZIP file to the sketchbook/libraries location. The Arduino packages in this repository are also compatible with Launchpad. The extracted files contain the I2Cdev, Wire, and MPU6050 packages that are required for the interfacing of the MPU 6050 sensor. There are other sensors packages that are present in the libraries folder but we are not using them now.

The preceding procedure is done in Ubuntu, but it is the same for Windows and Mac OS X.

Interfacing code of Energia

This code is used to read the raw value from MPU 6050 to Launchpad, it uses a MPU 6050 third-party library that is compatible with Energia IDE. The following are the explanations of each block of the code.

In this first section of code, we include the necessary headers for interfacing MPU 6050 to Launchpad such as I2C, Wire and the MPU6050 library and create an object of MPU6050 with the name accelgyro. The MPU6050.h library contains a class named MPU6050 to send and receive data to and from the sensor:

```
#include "Wire.h"

#include "I2Cdev.h"
#include "MPU6050.h"

MPU6050 accelgyro;
```

In the following section, we start the I2C and serial communication to communicate with MPU 6050 and print sensor values through the serial port. The serial communication baud rate is 115200 and Setup_MPU6050() is the custom function to initialize the MPU 6050 communication:

```
void setup()
{

  //Init Serial port with 115200 buad rate
  Serial.begin(115200);
  Setup_MPU6050();
}
```

The following section is the definition of the Setup_MPU6050() function. The Wire library allows you to communicate with the I2C devices. MPU 6050 can communicate using I2C. The Wire.begin() function will start the I2C communication between MPU 6050 and Launchpad; also, it will initialize the MPU 6050 device using the initialize() method defined in the MPU6050 class. If everything is successful, it will print **connection successful**, otherwise it will print **connection failed**:

```
void Setup_MPU6050()
{
   Wire.begin();

      // initialize device
```

```
      Serial.println("Initializing I2C devices...");
      accelgyro.initialize();

      // verify connection
      Serial.println("Testing device connections...");
      Serial.println(accelgyro.testConnection() ? "MPU6050 connection
  successful" : "MPU6050 connection failed");
}
```

The following code is the `loop()` function, which continuously reads the sensor value and prints its values through the serial port: The `Update_MPU6050()` custom function is responsible for printing the updated value from MPU 6050:

```
void loop()
{

    //Update MPU 6050
    Update_MPU6050();


}
```

The definition of `Update_MPU6050()` is given as follows. It declares six variables to handle the accelerometer and gyroscope value in 3-axis. The `getMotion6()` function in the MPU 6050 class is responsible for reading the new values from the sensor. After reading, it will print via the serial port:

```
void Update_MPU6050()
{

    int16_t ax, ay, az;
    int16_t gx, gy, gz;

      // read raw accel/gyro measurements from device
    accelgyro.getMotion6(&ax, &ay, &az, &gx, &gy, &gz);

    // display tab-separated accel/gyro x/y/z values
    Serial.print("i");Serial.print("\t");
    Serial.print(ax); Serial.print("\t");
    Serial.print(ay); Serial.print("\t");
    Serial.print(az); Serial.print("\t");
    Serial.print(gx); Serial.print("\t");
    Serial.print(gy); Serial.print("\t");
    Serial.println(gz);
    Serial.print("\n");
}
```

The output from the serial monitor is shown here:

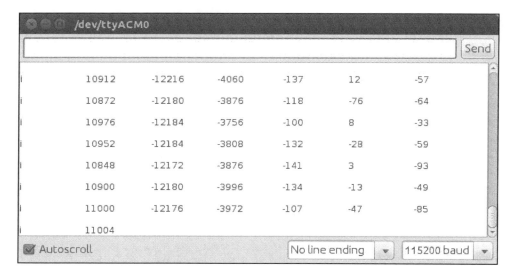

We can read these values using the python code that we used for ultrasonic. The following is the screenshot of the terminal when we run the python script:

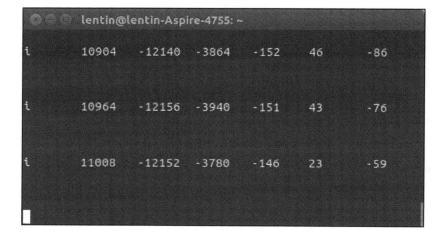

Interfacing MPU 6050 to Launchpad with the DMP support using Energia

In this section, we will see the interfacing code of MPU 6050 by activating DMP, which can give us direct orientation values in quaternion or yaw, pitch, and roll. This value can be directly applied to our robotic application too.

The following section of code imports all the necessary header files to interface and create an MPU6050 object like the previous code:

```
#include "Wire.h"
#include "I2Cdev.h"
#include "MPU6050_6Axis_MotionApps20.h"

//Creating MPU6050 Object
MPU6050 accelgyro(0x68);
```

The following code initializes and declares variables to handle DMP:

```
//DMP options
//Set true if DMP initialization was successful
bool dmpReady = false;

//Holds actual interrupt status byte from MPU
uint8_t mpuIntStatus;

//return status after each device operation
uint8_t devStatus;

//Expected DMP packet size
uint16_t packetSize;

//count of all bytes currently in FIFO
uint16_t fifoCount;

//FIFO storate buffer
uint8_t fifoBuffer[64];

//Output format will be in quaternion
#define OUTPUT_READABLE_QUATERNION
```

The following code declares various variables to handle orientation variables:

```
//quaternion variable
Quaternion q;
```

The following function is an interrupt service routine, which is called when MPU 6050 **INT** pin generates an interrupt:

```
//Interrupt detection routine for DMP handling
volatile bool mpuInterrupt = false;
// indicates whether MPU interrupt pin has gone high
void dmpDataReady() {
    mpuInterrupt = true;
}
```

The following code is the definition of the setup() function. It initializes the serial port with a baud rate of 115200 and calls the Setup_MPU6050() function:

```
void setup()
{
  //Init Serial port with 115200 buad rate
  Serial.begin(115200);
  Setup_MPU6050();
}
```

The following code is the definition of the Setup_MPU6050() function. It will initialize MPU 6050 and checks whether it's initialized or not. If it's initialized, it will initialize DMP by calling the Setup_MPU6050_DMP() function:

```
void Setup_MPU6050()
{
    Wire.begin();
   // initialize device
    Serial.println("Initializing I2C devices...");
    accelgyro.initialize();

    // verify connection
    Serial.println("Testing device connections...");
    Serial.println(accelgyro.testConnection() ?
      "MPU6050 connection successful" : "MPU6050
      connection failed");

    //Initialize DMP in MPU 6050
    Setup_MPU6050_DMP();
}
```

The following code is the definition of the Setup_MPU6050_DMP() function. It initializes DMP and sets offset in three axis. If DMP is initialized, it will start functioning and configure the PF_0/PUSH2 pin as an interrupt. When the data is ready on the MPU 6050 buffer, an interrupt will be generated, which will read values from the bus:

```
//Setup MPU 6050 DMP
void Setup_MPU6050_DMP()
{

    //DMP Initialization
   devStatus = accelgyro.dmpInitialize();
   accelgyro.setXGyroOffset(220);
   accelgyro.setXGyroOffset(76);
   accelgyro.setXGyroOffset(-85);
   accelgyro.setXGyroOffset(1788);
   if(devStatus == 0){

        accelgyro.setDMPEnabled(true);
        pinMode(PUSH2,INPUT_PULLUP);
        attachInterrupt(PUSH2, dmpDataReady, RISING);
        mpuIntStatus = accelgyro.getIntStatus();
        dmpReady = true;
        packetSize = accelgyro.dmpGetFIFOPacketSize();

}

else{

//Do nothing
;
    }
}
```

The following code is the definition the of the loop() function. It will call Update_MPU6050(), which will read buffer values and print it on the serial terminal:

```
void loop()
{
    //Update MPU 6050
    Update_MPU6050();
}
```

This is the definition of `Update_MPU6050()`, which will call the `Update_MPU6050_DMP()` function:

```
void Update_MPU6050()
{
    Update_MPU6050_DMP();
}
```

The following function reads from the FIFO register of MPU 6050 and the quaternion value gets printed on the serial terminal:

```
//Update MPU6050 DMP functions
void Update_MPU6050_DMP()
{

    //DMP Processing
    if (!dmpReady) return;
    while (!mpuInterrupt && fifoCount < packetSize)
    {
        ;
    }

    mpuInterrupt = false;
    mpuIntStatus = accelgyro.getIntStatus();

    //get current FIFO count
    fifoCount = accelgyro.getFIFOCount();

    if ((mpuIntStatus & 0x10) || fifoCount > 512) {
        // reset so we can continue cleanly
        accelgyro.resetFIFO();
    }

else if (mpuIntStatus & 0x02) {
        // wait for correct available data length,
          should be a VERY short wait

        while (fifoCount < packetSize) fifoCount =
          accelgyro.getFIFOCount();

        // read a packet from FIFO
        accelgyro.getFIFOBytes(fifoBuffer, packetSize);
```

```
        // track FIFO count here in case there is > 1
           packet available
        // (this lets us immediately read more without
           waiting for an interrupt)
        fifoCount -= packetSize;

        #ifdef OUTPUT_READABLE_QUATERNION

        // display quaternion values in easy matrix form: w x y z
        accelgyro.dmpGetQuaternion(&q, fifoBuffer);

        Serial.print("i");Serial.print("\t");
        Serial.print(q.x); Serial.print("\t");
        Serial.print(q.y); Serial.print("\t");
        Serial.print(q.z); Serial.print("\t");
        Serial.print(q.w);
        Serial.print("\n");
        #endif
    }
}
```

The output from the serial monitor is shown in the following screenshot. The serial monitor shows the quaternion values of x, y, z, and w starting with an "i" character:

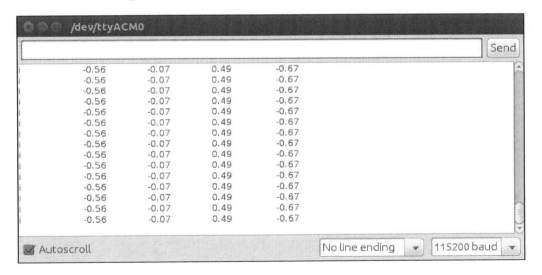

We can also use the Python script to view these values. The output of the Python script is shown in the following screenshot:

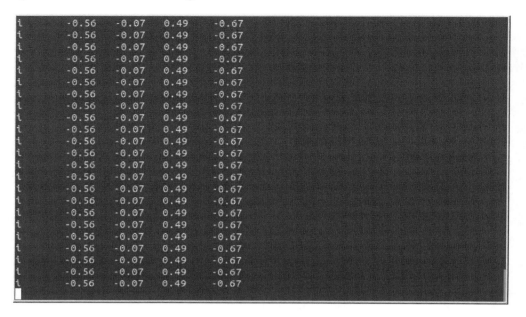

In the next chapters, we will see some of the vision and audio sensors that can be used on this robot and its interfacing with Python.

Questions

1. What are ultrasonic sensors and how do they work?
2. How do you calculate distance from the ultrasonic sensor?
3. What is the IR proximity sensor and how does it work?
4. How do you calculate distance from the IR sensor?
5. What is IMU and how do you get the odometric data?
6. What is the Aided Inertial Navigation system?
7. What are the main features of MPU 6050?

Summary

In this chapter, we have seen some robotic sensors, which can be used in our robot. The sensors we discussed are ultrasonic distance sensors, IR proximity sensors, and IMUs. These three sensors help in the navigation of the robot. We also discussed the basic code to interface these sensors to Tiva C LaunchPad. We will see more on vision and audio sensors interfacing using Python in the next chapter.

7
Programming Vision Sensors Using Python and ROS

In the previous chapter, we have seen some of the robotic sensors used in our robot and its interfacing with the Launchpad board. In this chapter, we will mainly discuss vision sensors and its interface used in our robot.

The robot we are designing will have a 3D sensor and we can interface it with vision libraries such as OpenCV, OpenNI, and **Point Cloud Library (PCL)**. Some of the applications of the 3D vision sensor in our robot are autonomous navigation, obstacle avoidance, object detection, people tracking, and so on.

We will also discuss the interfacing of vision sensors and image processing libraries with ROS. In the last section of the chapter, we will see a navigational algorithm for our robot called **SLAM (Simultaneous Localization and Mapping)** and its implementation using a 3D sensor, ROS, and image processing libraries.

In the first section, we will see some 2D and 3D vision sensors available on the market that we will use in our robot.

List of robotic vision sensors and image processing libraries

A 2D vision sensor or an ordinary camera delivers 2D image frames of the surroundings, whereas a 3D vision sensor delivers 2D image frames and an additional parameter called depth of each image point. We can find the x, y, and z distance of each point from the 3D sensor with respect to the sensor axis.

There are quite a few vision sensors available on the market. Some of the 2D and 3D vision sensors that can be used in our robot are mentioned in this chapter.

The following figure shows the latest 2D vision sensor called Pixy/CMU cam 5 (http://www.cmucam.org/), which is able to detect color objects with high speed and accuracy and can be interfaced to an Arduino board. Pixy can be used for fast object detection and the user can teach which object it needs to track. Pixy module has a CMOS sensor and NXP (http://www.nxp.com/) processor for image processing:

Pixy/CMU Cam 5

The commonly available 2D vision sensors are webcams. They contain a CMOS sensor and USB interface, but there is no inbuilt processing for the object detection. The following image shows a popular webcam from Logitech that can capture pictures of up to 5 megapixel resolution and HD videos:

Logitech HD Cam

We can take a look at some of the 3D vision sensors available on the market. Some of the popular sensors are Kinect, Asus Xtion Pro, and Carmine.

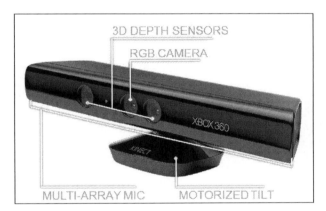

Kinect

Kinect is a 3D vision sensor used along with the Microsoft Xbox 360 game console. It mainly contains an RGB camera, an infrared projector, a depth sensor, a microphone array, and a motor for tilt. The RGB and depth camera capture images at a resolution of 640 x 480 at 30 Hz. The RGB camera captures 2D color images, whereas the depth camera captures monochrome depth images. Kinect has a depth sensing range from 0.8 m to 4 m.

Some of the applications of Kinect are 3D motion capture, skeleton tracking, face recognition, and voice recognition.

Kinect can be interfaced to PC using the USB 2.0 interface and programmed using Kinect SDK, OpenNI, and OpenCV. Kinect SDK is only available for Windows platforms and is developed and supplied by Microsoft. The other two libraries are open source and available for all platforms. The Kinect we are using here is the first version; the latest versions of Kinect only support Kinect SDK running on Windows.

Asus Xtion Pro

Asus Xtion Pro is a 3D sensor designed for PC-based motion sensing applications. Xtion Pro is only for 3D sensing and it doesn't have any sound sensing facilities. It has an infrared projector and a monochrome CMOS sensor to capture the infrared data. Xtion Pro communicates to the PC via the USB 2.0 interface. Xtion can be powered from the USB itself and can calculate a sense depth from 0.8 m to 3.5 m from the sensor.

The applications of Kinect and Xtion Pro are the same except for voice recognition. It will work in Windows, Linux, and Mac. We can develop applications in Xtion Pro using OpenNI and OpenCV.

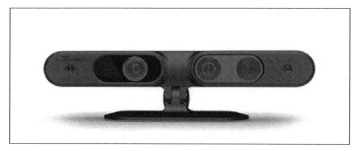

PrimeSense Carmine

The Prime Sense team developed the Microsoft Kinect 3D vision system. Later, they developed their own 3D vision sensor called Carmine. The technology behind Carmine is similar to Kinect. It works with an IR projector and a depth image CMOS sensor. The following figure shows the block diagram of Carmine:

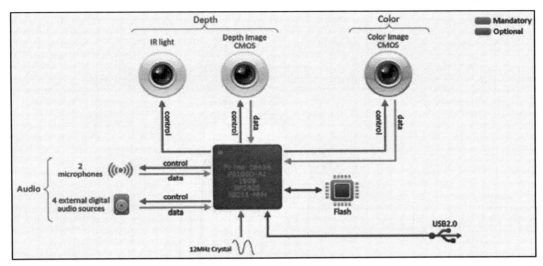

Carmine block diagram

Similar to Kinect, Carmine has an RGB CMOS sensor, a depth image CMOS, and an IR light source. It also has an array of microphones for voice recognition. All sensors are interfaced in **System On Chip (SOC)**. Interfacing and powering is performed through USB.

Carmine can capture RGB and depth frames in 640 x 480 resolution and can sense depth from 0.35 m to 3.5 m. Compared to Kinect, the advantages are small power consumption, small form factor, and good depth sensing range.

Carmine can be interfaced to a PC and it will support Windows, Linux, Mac, and Android platforms. Carmine is supported by OpenNI; developers can program the device using OpenNI and its wrapper libraries.

Apple Inc bought Prime Sense in November 2013. You can buy Carmine at the following link:

```
http://www.amazon.com/dp/B00KO908MM?psc=1
```

Introduction to OpenCV, OpenNI, and PCL

Let's discuss about the software frameworks and libraries that we are using in our robots. First, we can discuss OpenCV. This is one of the libraries that we are going to use in this robot for object detection and other image processing functionalities.

What is OpenCV?

OpenCV is an open source BSD-licensed computer vision based library that includes hundreds of computer vision algorithms. The library, mainly aimed for real-time computer vision, was developed by Intel Russia research, and is now actively supported by Itseez (http://itseez.com/).

OpenCV logo

OpenCV is written mainly in C and C++ and its primary interface is in C++. It also has good interfaces in Python, Java, Matlab/Octave and wrappers in other languages such as C# and Ruby.

In the new version of OpenCV, there is support for CUDA and OpenCL to get GPU acceleration (http://www.nvidia.com/object/cuda_home_new.html).

OpenCV will run on most of the OS platforms (such as Windows, Linux, Mac OS X, Android, FreeBSD, OpenBSD, iOS, and Blackberry).

In Ubuntu, OpenCV, and Python, wrappers are already installed when we install the ros-indigo-desktop-full package. If this package is not installed, then we can install the OpenCV library, ROS interface, and Python interface of OpenCV using the following command:

```
$ sudo apt-get install ros-indigo-vision-opencv
```

If you want to install only the OpenCV Python wrapper, then use the following command:

```
$ sudo apt-get install python-opencv
```

If you want to try OpenCV in Windows, you can try the following link:

http://docs.opencv.org/doc/tutorials/introduction/windows_install/
windows_install.html

The following link will guide you through the installation process of OpenCV on Mac OS X:

http://jjyap.wordpress.com/2014/05/24/installing-opencv-2-4-9-on-mac-
osx-with-python-support/

The main applications of OpenCV are in the field of:

- Object detection
- Gesture recognition
- Human-computer interaction
- Mobile robotics
- Motion tracking
- Facial recognition

Now we can see how to install OpenCV in Ubuntu 14.04.2 from source code.

Installation of OpenCV from source code in Ubuntu 14.04.2

We can install OpenCV from source code in Linux based on the following documentation of OpenCV:

http://docs.opencv.org/doc/tutorials/introduction/linux_install/
linux_install.html

After the installation of OpenCV, we can try some examples using the Python wrappers of OpenCV.

Reading and displaying an image using the Python-OpenCV interface

The first example will load an image in grayscale and display it on screen.

In the following section of code, we will import the `numpy` module for image array manipulation and the `cv2` module is the OpenCV wrapper for Python in which we can access OpenCV Python APIs. NumPy is an extension to the Python programming language, adding support for large multidimensional arrays and matrices along with a large library of high-level mathematical functions to operate on these arrays (`https://pypi.python.org/pypi/numpy`):

```python
#!/usr/bin/env python
import numpy as np
import cv2
```

The following function will read the `robot.jpg` image and load this image in grayscale. The first argument of the `cv2.imread()` function is the name of the image and the next argument is a flag that specifies the color type of the loaded image. If the flag is > 0, the image returns a three channel RGB color image, if the flag = 0, the loaded image will be a grayscale image, and if the flag is < 0, it will return the same image as loaded:

```python
img = cv2.imread('robot.jpg',0)
```

The following section of code will show the read image using the `imshow()` function. The `cv2.waitKey(0)` function is a keyboard binding function. Its argument is time in milliseconds. If it's 0, it will wait indefinitely for a key stroke:

```python
cv2.imshow('image',img)
cv2.waitKey(0)
```

The `cv2.destroyAllWindows()` function simply destroys all the windows we created:

```python
cv2.destroyAllWindows()
```

Save the preceding code with a name called `image_read.py` and copy a JPG file with `robot.jpg` as its name. Execute the code using the following command:

```
$python image_read.py
```

The output will load an image in grayscale because we used 0 as the value in the imread() function:

The following example will try to open webcam. The program will quit when the user presses any button.

Capturing from web camera

The following code will capture the webcam having device name /dev/video0 or /dev/video1.

We need to import the following modules if we are using OpenCV API's:

```
#!/usr/bin/env python
import numpy as np
import cv2
```

The following function will create a VideoCapture object. The VideoCapture class is used to capture videos from video files or cameras. The initialization arguments of the VideoCapture class is the index of a camera or a name of a video file. Device index is just a number to specify the camera. The first camera index is 0 having device name /dev/video0; that's why we use 0 here:

```
cap = cv2.VideoCapture(0)
```

The following section of code is looped to read image frames from the `VideoCapture` object and shows each frame. It will quit when any key is pressed:

```
while(True):
    # Capture frame-by-frame
    ret, frame = cap.read()
    # Display the resulting frame
    cv2.imshow('frame',frame)
    if cv2.waitKey(10):
        break
```

The following is a screenshot of the program output:

You can explore more OpenCV-Python tutorials from the following link:

```
http://opencv-python-tutroals.readthedocs.org/en/latest/py_tutorials/
py_tutorials.html
```

In the next section, we will look at OpenNI library and its application.

What is OpenNI

OpenNI is a Multilanguage, cross-platform framework that defines API's to write applications using **Natural interaction (NI)**. Natural interaction is defined in terms of experience. It means, people naturally communicate through gestures, expressions, movements, and discover the world by looking around and manipulating physical stuff.

OpenNI API's are composed of a set of interfaces to write NI applications. The following figure shows a three-layered view of the OpenNI library:

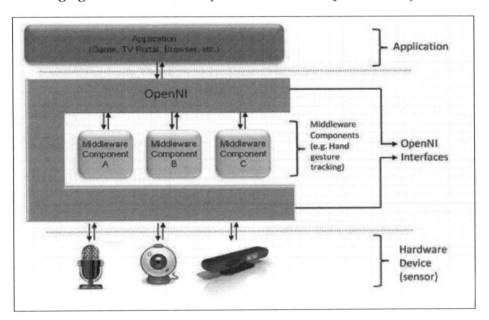

The top layer represents the application layer that implements natural interaction-based application. The middle layer is the OpenNI layer and it will provide communication interfaces that interact with sensors and middleware components that analyze the data from the sensor. Middleware can be used for full body analysis, hand point analysis, gesture detection, and so on. One of the examples of middle layer is NITE, which can detect gesture and skeleton.

The bottom layer shows the hardware devices that capture visuals and audio elements of the scene. It includes 3D sensors, RGB cameras, an IR camera, and a microphone.

OpenNI is cross-platform and has been successfully compiled and deployed on Linux, Mac OS X, and Windows.

In the next section, we will see how we to install OpenNI in Ubuntu 14.04.2.

Installing OpenNI in Ubuntu 14.04.2

We can install the OpenNI library along with ROS packages. ROS is already interfaced with OpenNI, but the complete installation of `ros-indigo-desktop-full` may not install OpenNI packages; we need to install it from the package manager.

The following is the installation command:

```
$ sudo apt-get install ros-indigo-openni-launch
```

The source code and latest build of OpenNI for Windows, Linux, and MacOS X is available at the following link:

```
http://structure.io/openni
```

In the next section, we will see how to install PCL.

What is PCL?

PCL is a large scale, open project for 2D/3D image, and Point Cloud processing. The PCL framework contains numerous algorithms included to perform filtering, feature estimation, surface reconstruction, registration, model fitting, and segmentation. Using these methods, we can process Point Cloud and extract key descriptors to recognize objects in the world based on their geometric appearance and create surfaces from the Point Clouds and visualize them.

PCL logo

PCL is released under the BSD license. It's open source, and free for commercial, or research use. PCL is cross-platform and has been successfully compiled and deployed on Linux, Mac OS X, Windows, and Android/iOS.

You can download PCL at the following link:

```
http://pointclouds.org/downloads/
```

PCL is already integrated into ROS. The PCL library and its ROS interface will install along with ROS full desktop installation. In the previous chapter, we discussed how to install ROS full desktop installation. PCL is the 3D processing backbone of ROS. Refer to the following link for details on the ROS-PCL package:

```
http://wiki.ros.org/pcl.
```

Programming Kinect with Python using ROS, OpenCV, and OpenNI

Let's look at how we can interface and work with the Kinect sensor in ROS. ROS is bundled with OpenNI driver, which can fetch RGB and the depth image of Kinect. This package can be used for Microsoft Kinect, PrimeSense Carmine, Asus Xtion Pro, and Pro Live.

This driver mainly publishes raw depth, RGB, and IR image streams. The openni_launch package will install packages such as openni_camera and openni_launch. The openni_camera package is the Kinect driver that publishes raw data and sensor information, whereas the openni_launch package contains ROS launch files. It's basically an XML file that launches multiple nodes at a time and publishes data such as point clouds.

How to launch OpenNI driver

The following command will open the OpenNI device and load all nodelets to convert raw depth/RGB/IR streams to depth images, disparity images, and point clouds. The ROS nodelet package is designed to provide a way to run multiple algorithms in the same process with zero copy transport between algorithms.

```
$ roslaunch openni_launch openni.launch
```

You can view the RGB image using a ROS tool called image_view

```
$ rosrun image_view image_view image:=/camera/rgb/image_color
```

In the next section, we will see how to interface these images to OpenCV for image processing.

The ROS interface of OpenCV

ROS is integrated into many libraries. OpenCV is also integrated into ROS mainly for image processing. The `vision_opencv` ROS stack includes the complete OpenCV library and interface to ROS.

The `vision_opencv` provides several packages:

- `cv_bridge`: This contains the `CvBridge` class; this class converts from ROS image messages to OpenCV image data type and vice versa
- `image_geometry`: This contains a collection of methods to handle image and pixel geometry

The following diagram shows how OpenCV is interfaced to ROS:

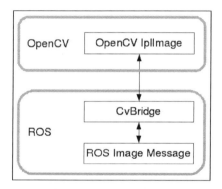

OpenCV-ROS interfacing

The image data type of OpenCV are IplImage and Mat. If we want to work with OpenCV in ROS, we have to convert IplImage or Mat to ROS Image messages. The ROS package `vision_opencv` has the `CvBridge` class; this class can convert IplImage to ROS image and vice versa.

The following section shows how to create a ROS package; this package contains node to subscribe RGB, depth image, process the RGB image to detect edges, and display all images after converting to an image type equivalent to OpenCV.

Creating ROS package with OpenCV support

We can create a package called `sample_opencv_pkg` with the following dependencies, that is, `sensor_msgs`, `cv_bridge`, `rospy`, and `std_msgs`. The `sensor_msgs` dependency defines messages for commonly used sensors, including cameras and scanning laser rangefinders; `cv_bridge` is the OpenCV interface of ROS.

The following command will create the ROS package with the preceding dependencies:

```
$ catkin-create-pkg sample_opencv_pkg sensor_msgs cv_bridge
rospy std_msgs
```

After creating the package, create a `scripts` folder inside the package and save the code in the mentioned in the next section.

Displaying Kinect images using Python, ROS, and cv_bridge

The first section of the Python code is given below. It mainly includes importing of `rospy`, `sys`, `cv2`, `sensor_msgs`, `cv_bridge`, and the `numpy` module. The `sensor_msgs` dependency imports the ROS data type of `Image` and `CameraInfo`. The `cv_bridge` module imports the `CvBridge` class for converting ROS image data type to the OpenCV data type and vice versa:

```python
import rospy
import sys
import cv2
import cv2.cv as cv
from sensor_msgs.msg import Image, CameraInfo
from cv_bridge import CvBridge, CvBridgeError
import numpy as np
```

The following section of code is a class definition in Python to demonstrate `CvBridge` functions. The class is named as `cvBridgeDemo`:

```python
class cvBridgeDemo():
    def __init__(self):
        self.node_name = "cv_bridge_demo"
        #Initialize the ros node
        rospy.init_node(self.node_name)

        # What we do during shutdown
        rospy.on_shutdown(self.cleanup)

        # Create the OpenCV display window for the RGB image

        self.cv_window_name = self.node_name
        cv.NamedWindow(self.cv_window_name, cv.CV_WINDOW_NORMAL)
        cv.MoveWindow(self.cv_window_name, 25, 75)

        # And one for the depth image
```

```
cv.NamedWindow("Depth Image", cv.CV_WINDOW_NORMAL)
cv.MoveWindow("Depth Image", 25, 350)

# Create the cv_bridge object
self.bridge = CvBridge()

# Subscribe to the camera image and depth topics and set
# the appropriate callbacks
self.image_sub =
rospy.Subscriber("/camera/rgb/image_color", Image,
self.image_callback)
        self.depth_sub =
rospy.Subscriber("/camera/depth/image_raw", Image,
self.depth_callback)

rospy.loginfo("Waiting for image topics...")
```

The following code gives a callback function of the color image from Kinect. When a color image comes on the /camera/rgb/image_color topic, it will call this function. This function will process the color frame for edge detection and show the edge detected and raw color image:

```
def image_callback(self, ros_image):
    # Use cv_bridge() to convert the ROS image to OpenCV format
    try:
        frame = self.bridge.imgmsg_to_cv(ros_image, "bgr8")
    except CvBridgeError, e:
        print e

    # Convert the image to a Numpy array since most cv2
functions

    # require Numpy arrays.
    frame = np.array(frame, dtype=np.uint8)

    # Process the frame using the process_image() function
    display_image = self.process_image(frame)

    # Display the image.
    cv2.imshow(self.node_name, display_image)

    # Process any keyboard commands
    self.keystroke = cv.WaitKey(5)
    if 32 <= self.keystroke and self.keystroke < 128:
        cc = chr(self.keystroke).lower()
```

```
if cc == 'q':
    # The user has press the q key, so exit
    rospy.signal_shutdown("User hit q key to quit.")
```

The following code gives a callback function of the depth image from Kinect. When a depth image comes on the /camera/depth/raw_image topic, it will call this function. This function will show the raw depth image:

```
def depth_callback(self, ros_image):
    # Use cv_bridge() to convert the ROS image to OpenCV
format
    try:
        # The depth image is a single-channel float32 image
        depth_image = self.bridge.imgmsg_to_cv(ros_image,
"32FC1")
    except CvBridgeError, e:
        print e

    # Convert the depth image to a Numpy array since most cv2
functions
    # require Numpy arrays.
    depth_array = np.array(depth_image, dtype=np.float32)

    # Normalize the depth image to fall between 0 (black) and
1 (white)
    cv2.normalize(depth_array,
depth_array, 0, 1, cv2.NORM_MINMAX)

    # Process the depth image
    depth_display_image =
self.process_depth_image(depth_array)

    # Display the result
    cv2.imshow("Depth Image", depth_display_image)
```

The following function is called process_image(), which will convert the color image to grayscale, then blur the image, and find the edges using the canny edge filter:

```
def process_image(self, frame):
    # Convert to grayscale
    grey = cv2.cvtColor(frame, cv.CV_BGR2GRAY)

    # Blur the image
    grey = cv2.blur(grey, (7, 7))
```

```
# Compute edges using the Canny edge filter
edges = cv2.Canny(grey, 15.0, 30.0)

return edges
```

The following function is called `process_depth_image()`. It simply returns the depth frame:

```
def process_depth_image(self, frame):
    # Just return the raw image for this demo
    return frame
```

This function will close the image window when the node shuts down:

```
def cleanup(self):
    print "Shutting down vision node."
    cv2.destroyAllWindows()
```

The following code is the `main()` function. It will initialize the `cvBridgeDemo()` class and call the ros `spin()` function:

```
def main(args):
    try:
        cvBridgeDemo()
        rospy.spin()
    except KeyboardInterrupt:
        print "Shutting down vision node."
        cv.DestroyAllWindows()

if __name__ == '__main__':
    main(sys.argv)
```

Save the preceding code to `cv_bridge_demo.py` and change the permission of the node using the following command. The node is only visible to the `rosrun` command if we give it executable permission.

```
$ chmod +X cv_bridge_demo.py
```

The following are the commands to start the driver and node. Start the Kinect driver using the following command:

```
$ roslaunch openni_launch openni.launch
```

Run the node using the following command:

```
$ rosrun sample_opencv_pkg cv_bridge_demo.py
```

The following is the screenshot of the output:

RGB, depth, and edge images

Working with Point Clouds using Kinect, ROS, OpenNI, and PCL

A Point Cloud is a data structure used to represent a collection of multidimensional points and is commonly used to represent 3D data. In a 3D Point Cloud, the points usually represent the x, y, and z geometric coordinates of an underlying sampled surface. When the color information is present, the Point Cloud becomes 4D.

Point Clouds can be acquired from hardware sensors (such as stereo cameras, 3D scanners, or time-of-flight cameras). It can be generated from a computer program synthetically. PCL supports the OpenNI 3D interfaces natively; thus it can acquire and process data from devices (such as Prime Sensor's 3D cameras, Microsoft Kinect, or Asus XTion PRO).

PCL will be installed along with the ROS indigo full desktop installation. Let's see how we can generate and visualize Point Cloud in RViz, a data visualization tool in ROS.

Opening device and Point Cloud generation

Open a new terminal and launch the ROS OpenNI driver along with the Point Cloud generator nodes using the following command:

```
roslaunch openni_launch openni.launch
```

This command will activate the Kinect driver and process the raw data into convenient outputs like Point Cloud.

We will use RViz 3D visualization tool to view Point Clouds.

The following command will start the RViz tool:

```
$ rosrun rviz rviz
```

Set the RViz options for **Fixed Frame** (at the top of the **Displays** panel under **Global Options**) to **camera_link**.

On the left-hand side of the **RViz** panel, click on the **Add** button and choose the **PointCloud2** display option. Set its topic to **/camera/depth/points**.

Change **Color Transformer** of **PointCloud2** to **AxisColor**.

The following figure shows a screenshot of RViz Point Cloud data. In this screenshot, the near object is marked in red and the far object is marked in violet and blue. The object in front of Kinect is represented as cylinder and cube:

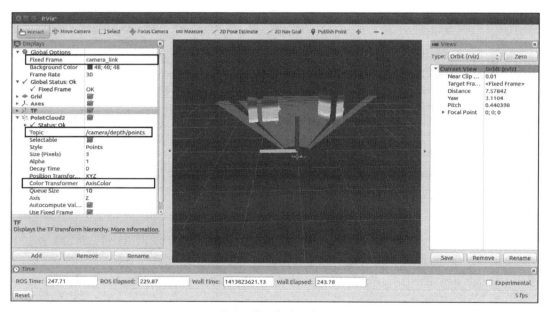

Point Cloud of a robot

Conversion of Point Cloud to laser scan data

We are using Kinect in this robot for replicating the function of expensive laser range scanner. Kinect can deliver Point Cloud data which contains the depth of each point of surrounding. The Point Cloud data is processed and converted to data equivalent to a laser scanner using the ROS `depthimage_to_laserscan` package. The main function of this package is to slice a section of the Point Cloud data and convert it to a laser scan equivalent data type. The `Pointcloud2` data type is `sensor_msgs/PointCloud2` and for the laser scanner, the data type is `sensor_msgs/LaserScan`. This package will perform this processing and fake the laser scanner. The laser scanner output can be viewed using RViz. In order to run the conversion, we have to start the convertor nodelets that will perform this operation. We have to specify this in our launch file to start the conversion. The following is the required code in the launch file to start the `depthimage_to_laserscan` conversion:

```
<!-- Fake laser -->
<node pkg="nodelet" type="nodelet"
name="laserscan_nodelet_manager" args="manager"/>
<node pkg="nodelet" type="nodelet"
name="depthimage_to_laserscan"
      args="load depthimage_to_laserscan/
DepthImageToLaserScanNodelet
laserscan_nodelet_manager">
   <param name="scan_height" value="10"/>
   <param name="output_frame_id" value="/camera_depth_frame"/>
   <param name="range_min" value="0.45"/>
   <remap from="image" to="/camera/depth/image_raw"/>
   <remap from="scan" to="/scan"/>
</node>
```

Along with starting the nodelet, we need to set certain parameters of the nodelet for better conversion. Refer to `http://wiki.ros.org/depthimage_to_laserscan` for a detailed explanation of each parameter.

The laser scan of the preceding view is shown in the following screenshot. To view the laser scan, add the **LaserScan** option. This is similar to how we add the **PointCloud2** option and change the **Topic** value of **LaserScan** to **/scan**:

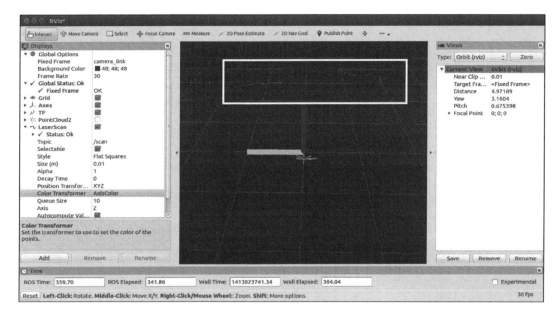

Working with SLAM using ROS and Kinect

The main aim of deploying vision sensors in our robot is to detect objects and perform robot navigation in an environment. SLAM is a technique used in mobile robots and vehicles to build up a map of an unknown environment or update a map within a known environment by tracking the current location of a robot.

Maps are used to plan the robot trajectory and to navigate through this path. Using maps, the robot will get an idea about the environment. The main two challenges in mobile robot navigation are mapping and localization.

Mapping involves generating a profile of obstacles around the robot. Through mapping, the robot will understand how the world looks. Localization is the process of estimating a pose of the robot relative to the map we build.

SLAM fetches data from different sensors and uses it to build maps. The 2D/3D vision sensor can be used as an input to SLAM. The 2D vision sensors such as laser range finders and 3D sensors such as Kinect are mainly used as an input for a SLAM algorithm.

ROS is integrated into a SLAM library using OpenSlam (`http://openslam.org/gmapping.html`). The `gmapping` package provides laser-based SLAM as a node called `slam_gmapping`. This can create a 2D map from the laser and pose data collected by a mobile robot.

The `gmapping` package is available at `http://wiki.ros.org/gmapping`.

To use `slam_gmapping`, you will need a mobile robot that provides odometry data and is equipped with a horizontally mounted, fixed, laser range finder. The `slam_gmapping` node will attempt to transform each incoming scan into the odom (odometry) tf frame.

The `slam_gmapping` node takes in `sensor_msgs/LaserScan` messages and builds a map (`nav_msgs/OccupancyGrid`). The map can be retrieved via a ROS topic or service.

The following code can be used to make a map from a robot with a laser publishing scans on the `base_scan` topic:

```
$ rosrun gmapping slam_gmapping scan:=base_scan
```

Questions

1. What are 3D sensors and how are they different from ordinary cams?
2. What are the main features of a robotic operating system?
3. What are the applications of OpenCV, OpenNI, and PCL?
4. What is SLAM?
5. What is RGB-D SLAM and how does it work?

Summary

In this chapter, we saw vision sensors to be used in our robot. We used Kinect in our robot and discussed OpenCV, OpenNI, PCL and their application. We also discussed the role of vision sensors in robot navigation and a popular SLAM technique and its application using ROS. In the next chapter, we will discuss speech processing and synthesis to be used in this robot.

8

Working with Speech Recognition and Synthesis Using Python and ROS

In this chapter, we will mainly discuss the following topics:

- Introducing speech recognition, synthesis, and various speech processing frameworks
- Working with speech recognition and synthesis using Python in Ubuntu/Linux, Windows and Mac OS X
- Working with speech recognition and synthesis packages in ROS using Python

If the robots are able to recognize and respond the way human beings communicate, then the robot-human interaction will be much more easier and effective than any other method. However, extracting speech parameters such as meaning, pitch, duration, and intensity from human speech is a very tough task. Researchers found numerous ways to solve this problem. Now, there are some algorithms that are doing a good job in speech processing.

In this chapter, we will discuss the applications of speech recognition and synthesis in our robot and also look at some of the libraries to perform speech recognition and synthesis.

The main objective of speech synthesis and recognition system in this robot is to make the robot-human interaction easier. If a robot has these abilities, it can communicate with the surrounding people and they can ask various questions about the food and the cost of each item. The speech recognition and synthesis functionality can be added using the framework that we will discuss in this chapter.

In the first section of this chapter, you will learn about the steps involved in speech recognition and synthesis.

Understanding speech recognition

Speech recognition basically means talking to a computer and making it recognize what we are saying in real time. It converts natural spoken language to digital format that can be understood by a computer. We are mainly discussing the conversion of speech-to-text process here. Using the speech recognition system, the robot will record the sentence or word commanded by the user. The text will be passed to another program and the program will decide which action it has to execute. We can take a look at the block diagram of the speech recognition system that explains how it works.

Block diagram of a speech recognition system

The following is a block diagram of a typical speech recognition system. We can see each block and understand how a speech signal is converted to text:

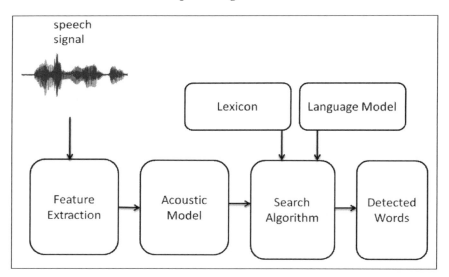

Speech recognition system block diagram

The speech signal is received through a microphone and will be converted to a digital format such as **PCM (Pulse Code Modulation)** by the sound card inside the PC. This digital format can be processed by the software inside the PC. In a speech recognition process, the first phase is to extract the speech features from the digital sound format.

In the speech recognition system, the following are the common components:

- **Feature extraction**: In this process, the raw digital sound is converted to sound feature vectors, which carry information of sounds and suppress the irrelevant sources of sound. The sound feature vectors can be mathematically represented as a vector with respect to time. After getting the sound feature vectors, they will be decoded to text from a list of possible strings and selected according to its probability.

- **Acoustic model**: The first stage of decoding is acoustic models. Acoustic models are trained statistical models and are capable of predicting the elementary units of speech called phonemes after getting the sound feature vectors. Popular acoustic modeling in speech recognition is **HMM (Hidden Markov Models)** and another hybrid approach is to use artificial neural networks.

- **Lexicon**: A lexicon (also known as dictionary) contains the phonetic script of words that we use in training the acoustic model.

- **Language model**: This provides a structure to the stream of words that is detected according to the individual word probability. The language model is trained using large amounts of training text (which includes the text used to train the acoustic model). It helps to estimate the probabilities and find the appropriate word detected.

- **Search algorithm**: This is used to find the most probable sequence of words in the sound vectors with the help of the language model and lexicon.

- **Recognized words**: The output of the search algorithm is a list of words that has the highest probability for given sound vectors.

Speech recognition libraries

The following are some good and popular implementations of speech recognition algorithms in the form of libraries.

CMU Sphinx/Pocket Sphinx

Sphinx is a group of speech recognition tools developed by Carnegie Mellon University. The entire library is open source and it comes with acoustic models and sample applications. The acoustic model trainer improves the accuracy of detection. It allows you to compile its language model and provides a lexicon called **cmudict**. The current Sphinx version is 4. The Sphinx version customized for an embedded system is called Pocket Sphinx. It's a lightweight speech recognition engine that will work on desktop as well as on mobile devices. Sphinx libraries are available for Windows, Linux, and Mac OS X.

There are Python modules available to handle Pocket Sphinx APIs from Python. The following is the official website of CMU Sphinx:

```
http://cmusphinx.sourceforge.net/
```

Julius

This is a high performance and continuous speech recognition library based on HMM and can detect continuous stream of words or N-grams. It's an open source library that is able to work in real time. There are Python modules to handle Julius functions from Python. Julius is available in Windows, Linux, and Mac OS X. The official website of Julius is:

```
http://julius.sourceforge.jp/en_index.php
```

Windows Speech SDK

Microsoft provides a SDK to handle speech recognition and synthesis operation. SDK contains APIs to handle speech-related processing that can be embedded inside the Microsoft application. The SDK only works on Windows and it has some ports for Python like the PySpeech module. These speech APIs are comparatively accurate than other open source tools.

Speech synthesis

Speech synthesis is the process of converting text data to speech. The following block diagram shows the process involved in converting text to speech:

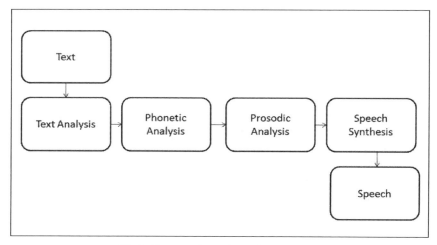

Block diagram of speech synthesis process

For more details, refer to page 6 of *Spoken Language Processing, X. Huang, A. Acero, H.-W. Hon, Prentice Hall PTR*, published in 2001.

Let us take a look at the speech synthesis stages:

- **Text analysis**: In text analysis, the text to be converted to speech will check for the structure of text, linguistic analysis, and text normalization to convert numbers and abbreviations to words

- **Phonetic analysis**: In phonetic analysis, each individual text data called grapheme is converted to an individual indivisible sequence of sound called phoneme

- **Prosodic analysis**: In prosodic analysis, the prosody of speech (such as rhythm, stress, and intonations of speech) added to the basic sound makes it more realistic

- **Speech synthesis**: This unit finally binds the short units of speech and produces the final speech signal

Speech synthesis libraries

Let's now discuss a bit about the various speech synthesis libraries.

eSpeak

eSpeak is an open source lightweight speech synthesizer mainly for English language and it will also support several other languages. Using eSpeak, we can change the voices and its characteristics. eSpeak has the module to access its APIs from Python. eSpeak works mainly in Windows and Linux and it's also compatible with Mac OS X. The official website of eSpeak is as follows:

```
http://espeak.sourceforge.net/
```

Festival

Festival is an open source and free speech synthesizer developed by **Centre of Speech Technology Research (CSTR)** and is written completely in C++. It provide access to the APIs from Shell in the form of commands and also in C++, Java, and Python. It has multi language support (such as English and Spanish). Festival mainly supports Linux-based platform. The code can also be built in Windows and Mac OS X. The following is the official website of the Festival speech synthesis system:

```
http://www.cstr.ed.ac.uk/projects/festival/
```

Working with speech recognition and synthesis in Ubuntu 14.04.2 using Python

In this section, we will discuss Python interfacing with Pocket Sphinx, Julius, and Microsoft Speech SDK and speech synthesis frameworks such as eSpeak and Festival. Let's start with speech recognition libraries and their installation procedures.

Setting up Pocket Sphinx and its Python binding in Ubuntu 14.04.2

The following packages are required to install Pocket Sphinx and its Python bindings:

- `python-pocketsphinx`
- `pocketsphinx-hmm-wsj1`
- `pocketsphinx-lm-wsj`

The packages can be installed using the `apt-get` command. The following commands are used to install Pocket Sphinx and its Python interface.

Installing Pocket Sphinx in Ubuntu can be done either through source code or by package managers. Here, we will install Pocket Sphinx using the package manager:

- The following command will install HMM of Pocket Sphinx:

  ```
  $ sudo apt-get install pocketsphinx-hmm-wsj1
  ```

- The following command will install LM of Pocket Sphinx:

  ```
  $ sudo apt-get install pocketsphinx-lm-wsj
  ```

- The following command will install the Python extension of Pocket Sphinx:

  ```
  $ sudo apt-get install python-pocketsphinx
  ```

Once we are done with the installation, we can work with Python scripting for speech recognition.

Working with Pocket Sphinx Python binding in Ubuntu 14.04.2

The following is the code to perform speech recognition using Pocket Sphinx and Python. The following code demonstrates how we can decode the speech recognition from a wave file:

```python
#!/usr/bin/env python
import sys

#In Ubuntu 14.04.2, the pocketsphinx module shows error in first
import and will work for the second import. The following code is
a temporary fix to handle that issue
try:
   import pocketsphinx

except:
   import pocketsphinx
```

The preceding code will import the `pocketsphinx` Python module and Python `sys` module. The `sys` module contain functions that can be called during program runtime. In this code, we will use the `sys` module to get the wave filename from the command-line argument:

```python
if __name__ == "__main__":
    hmdir = "/usr/share/pocketsphinx/model/hmm/en_US/hub4wsj_sc_8k"
    lmdir = "/usr/share/pocketsphinx/model/lm/en_US/hub4.5000.DMP"
    dictd = "/usr/share/pocketsphinx/model/lm/en_US/cmu07a.dic"
```

The `hmdir`, `lmdirn`, and `dictd` variables hold the path of HMM, **LM (Language Model)**, and dictionary of Pocket Sphinx:

```python
#Receiving wave file name from command line argument
wavfile = sys.argv[1]
```

The following code will pass HMM, LM, and the dictionary path of Pocket Sphinx to Pocket Sphinx's `Decoder` class. Read and decode the wave file. In the end, it will print the detected text:

```python
speechRec = pocketsphinx.Decoder(hmm = hmdir, lm = lmdir,
dict = dictd)
    wavFile = file(wavfile,'rb')
    speechRec.decode_raw(wavFile)
    result = speechRec.get_hyp()

    print "\n\n\nDetected text:>",result
    print "\n\n\n"
```

Output

The preceding code can be run using the following command:

```
$ python <code_name.py> <wave_file_name.wav>
```

The following is a screenshot of the output. The detected text was not the content on the wave file. The detection accuracy with the default acoustic model and LM is low; we have to train a new model or adapt an existing model to improve accuracy:

```
INFO: ngram_search.c(1214): </s> not found in last frame, using <sil>.1326 inste
ad
INFO: ngram_search.c(1266): lattice start node <s>.0 end node <sil>.1296
INFO: ngram_search.c(1294): Eliminated 0 nodes before end node
INFO: ngram_search.c(1399): Lattice has 425 nodes, 1725 links
INFO: ps_lattice.c(1365): Normalizer P(O) = alpha(<sil>:1296:1326) = -7472594
INFO: ps_lattice.c(1403): Joint P(O,S) = -7490696 P(S|O) = -18102
INFO: ngram_search.c(888): bestpath 0.01 CPU 0.001 xRT
INFO: ngram_search.c(891): bestpath 0.01 wall 0.001 xRT


Detected text:> ("to news and i'm", '000000000', -143373)



INFO: ngram_search_fwdtree.c(430): TOTAL fwdtree 3.02 CPU 0.228 xRT
INFO: ngram_search_fwdtree.c(433): TOTAL fwdtree 3.10 wall 0.234 xRT
INFO: ngram_search_fwdflat.c(174): TOTAL fwdflat 0.11 CPU 0.009 xRT
INFO: ngram_search_fwdflat.c(177): TOTAL fwdflat 0.11 wall 0.009 xRT
INFO: ngram_search.c(317): TOTAL bestpath 0.01 CPU 0.001 xRT
INFO: ngram_search.c(320): TOTAL bestpath 0.01 wall 0.001 xRT
lentin@lentin-Aspire-4755:~/Desktop/Chapter-8/codes$
```

The previous method we discussed was an offline recognition; in the next section, we will see how to perform real-time speech recognition using Pocket Sphinx, GStreamer, and Python. In this approach, real-time speech data comes through the GStreamer framework and is decoded using Pocket Sphinx. To work with the GStreamer Pocket Sphinx interface, install the following packages:

The following command will install the GStreamer plugin for Pocket Sphinx:

```
$ sudo apt-get install gstreamer0.10-pocketsphinx
```

The following package will install the GStreamer Python binding. It will enable you to use GStreamer APIs from Python:

```
$ sudo apt-get install python-gst0.10
```

The following package will install the GStreamer plugin to get information from GConf:

```
$ sudo apt-get install gstreamer0.10-gconf
```

Real-time speech recognition using Pocket Sphinx, GStreamer, and Python in Ubuntu 14.04.2

The following is the code for real-time speech recognition using GStreamer:

```python
#!/usr/bin/env python

#The following modules need to import before handling
gstreamer API's

import gobject
import sys
import pygst
pygst.require('0.10')
gobject.threads_init()
import gst

#Module to handle keyboard interrupt signal
import signal

#Keyboard signal handling routine
def signal_handle(signal, frame):
  print "You pressed Ctrl+C"
  sys.exit(0)


#Implementation of Speech recognition class
class Speech_Recog(object):

  #Initializing gstreamer pipeline and pocket sphinx element
  def __init__(self):
    self.init_gst()

  #This function will initialize gstreamer pipeline
  def init_gst(self):
    #The following code create a gstreamer pipeline with
pipeline description. The required descriptors needed
for the code is given as parameters.
        self.pipeline =
gst.parse_launch('gconfaudiosrc !audioconvert ! audioresample '
                    + '! vader name=vad auto-threshold=true '
                    + '! pocketsphinx name=asr ! fakesink')
```

```
#Accessing pocket sphinx element from gstreamer pipeline
        asr = self.pipeline.get_by_name('asr')
#Connecting to asr_result function when a speech to
text conversion is completed
        asr.connect('result', self.asr_result)


    #User can mention lm and dict for accurate detection
    #asr.set_property('lm', '/home/user/mylanguagemodel.lm')
    #asr.set_property('dict','/home/user/mylanguagemodel.dic')


    #This option will set all options are configured well
and can start recognition
        asr.set_property('configured', True)


#Pausing the GStreamer pipeline at first.
        self.pipeline.set_state(gst.STATE_PAUSED)


    #Definition of asr_result
def asr_result(self, asr, text, uttid):
    #Printing the detected text
    print "Detected Text=>      ",text


#This function will start/stop Speech recognition operation
def start_recognition(self):
    #VADER - Voice Activity DEtectoR, which helps when the
speech start and when its ends. Creating VADER object and set the
property silent to False, so no speech will detected until key
press
        vader = self.pipeline.get_by_name('vad')
        vader.set_property('silent', False)


    #Waiting for a key press to start recognition
    raw_input("Press any key to start recognition:>")
    #Start playing the pipeline
    self.pipeline.set_state(gst.STATE_PLAYING)


    #Waiting for stopping the recognition
    raw_input("Press any key to stop recognition:>")
        vader = self.pipeline.get_by_name('vad')
    #Setting silent property of VADER to True
        vader.set_property('silent', True)
    #Pausing GStreamer pipeline
        self.pipeline.set_state(gst.STATE_PAUSED)
```

```
if __name__ == "__main__":

    #Creating an object of Speech_Recog() class
    app_object = Speech_Recog()


    #Assign keyboard interrupt handler
    signal.signal(signal.SIGINT, signal_handle)

    while True:

        #Calling Speech recognition routine
        app_object.start_recognition()
```

The code can be simply executed using the following command:

```
$ python <code_name.py>
```

The following is the screenshot of the output window:

```
INFO: ngram_model_arpa.c(77): No \data\ mark in LM file
INFO: ngram_model_dmp.c(142): Will use memory-mapped I/O for LM file
INFO: ngram_model_dmp.c(196): ngrams 1=5001, 2=436879, 3=418286
INFO: ngram_model_dmp.c(242):    5001 = LM.unigrams(+trailer) read
INFO: ngram_model_dmp.c(288):  436879 = LM.bigrams(+trailer) read
INFO: ngram_model_dmp.c(314):  418286 = LM.trigrams read
INFO: ngram_model_dmp.c(339):   37293 = LM.prob2 entries read
INFO: ngram_model_dmp.c(359):   14370 = LM.bo_wt2 entries read
INFO: ngram_model_dmp.c(379):   36094 = LM.prob3 entries read
INFO: ngram_model_dmp.c(407):     854 = LM.tseg_base entries read
INFO: ngram_model_dmp.c(463):    5001 = ascii word strings read
INFO: ngram_search_fwdtree.c(99): 788 unique initial diphones
INFO: ngram_search_fwdtree.c(147): 0 root, 0 non-root channels, 60 single-phone
words
INFO: ngram_search_fwdtree.c(186): Creating search tree
INFO: ngram_search_fwdtree.c(191): before: 0 root, 0 non-root channels, 60 singl
e-phone words
INFO: ngram_search_fwdtree.c(326): after: max nonroot chan increased to 13428
INFO: ngram_search_fwdtree.c(338): after: 457 root, 13300 non-root channels, 26
single-phone words

(original_code_gst.py:3611): GStreamer-CRITICAL **: gst_clock_get_time: assertio
n 'GST_IS_CLOCK (clock)' failed
Press any key to start recognition:>
```

Press any key to start recognition; after this, we can talk and it will be converted and printed on the terminal window. To stop detection, press any key and it will pause the GStreamer pipeline.

One of the other speech recognition tool is Julius. We will see how to install it and work with it using Python.

Speech recognition using Julius and Python in Ubuntu 14.04.2

In this section, we will see how to install the speech recognition system of Julius and how to connect it to Python. The required packages (such as Julius and audio tools) are available in Ubuntu's package manager, but we also need to download and install the Python wrapper separately. Let's start with the required components for the installation.

Installation of Julius speech recognizer and Python module

The following are the instructions to install Julius and Python binding in Ubuntu 14.04.2:

- The following command will install the speech recognition system of Julius:

  ```
  $ sudo apt-get install julius
  ```

- The following command will install padsp (the pulse audio tool). It may be necessary to run the Julius speech recognizer in Ubuntu 14.04.2:

  ```
  $ sudo apt-get install pulseaudio-utils
  ```

- The following command will install the OSS proxy daemon to emulate the OSS sound device and stream through the ALSA device. It will emulate the **/dev/dsp** device in Ubuntu and stream through ALSA. Julius needs the /dev/dsp device for its functioning:

  ```
  $ sudo apt-get install osspd-alsa
  ```

- Reload the ALSA process to bind osspd to alsa:

  ```
  $ sudo alsa force-reload
  ```

To install pyjulius, the Python extension for Julius, you need to install the setup tools in Python.

1. To install the setup tools, the best option is to download a script from the setup tools website; it's a global script that can be used in any OS. The script can be downloaded from the following link using the wget tool:

   ```
   $ wget https://bootstrap.pypa.io/ez_setup.py
   $ sudo python ez_setup.py
   ```

2. The installation details of setup tools is mentioned at https://pypi.python.org/pypi/setuptools

3. After the installation of setup tools, download pyjulius from
   `https://pypi.python.org/pypi/pyjulius/0.3`

4. Extract the achieve and installation package using the following command:

   ```
   $ sudo python setup.py install
   ```

5. After the installation of pyjulius, install a demo of the Julius tool, which contains HMM, LM, and dictionary of a few words. Download the Julius quick-start files using the following command:

   ```
   $ wget
   http://www.repository.voxforge1.org/downloads/software/julius-
   3.5.2-quickstart-linux.tgz
   ```

6. Extract the files and run the command from the folder.

7. Execute the following command in the extracted folder. It will start the speech recognition in the command line:

   ```
   $ padsp julius -input mic -C julian.jconf
   ```

8. To exit speech recognition, click on *CTRL + C*.

9. To connect to Python, enter the following command:

   ```
   $ padsp julius -module -input mic -C julian.jconf
   ```

This command will start a Julius server. This server listens to clients. If we want to use Julius APIs from Python, we need to connect to a server using a client code as given in the following sections. The Python code is a client that connects to the Julius server and prints the recognized text.

Python-Julius client code

The following code is a Python client of the Julius speech recognition server that we started using the previous command. After connecting to this server, it will trigger speech-to-text conversion and fetch the converted text and print on terminal:

```python
#!/usr/bin/env python
import sys

#Importing pujulius module
import pyjulius

#It an implementation of FIFO(First In First Out) queue suitable for
multi threaded programming.
import Queue
```

```
# Initialize Julius Client object with localhost ip and default port
of 10500 and trying to connect server.
client = pyjulius.Client('localhost', 10500)
try:
    client.connect()
#When the client runs before executing the server it will cause a
connection error.
except pyjulius.ConnectionError:
    print 'Start julius as module first!'
    sys.exit(1)


# Start listening to the server
client.start()
try:
    while 1:
        try:
            #Fetching recognition result from server
             result = client.results.get(False)
        except Queue.Empty:
            continue
        print result
except KeyboardInterrupt:
    print 'Exiting...'
    client.stop()  # send the stop signal
    client.join()  # wait for the thread to die
    client.disconnect()  # disconnect from julius
```

After connecting to Julius server, the Python client will listen to server and print the output from the server.

The acoustic models we used in the preceding programs are already trained, but they may not give accurate results for our speech. To improve the accuracy in the previous speech recognition engines, we need to train new language and acoustic models and create a dictionary or we can adapt the existing language model using our voice. The method to improve accuracy is beyond the scope of this chapter, so some links to train or adapt both Pocket Sphinx and Julius are given.

Improving speech recognition accuracy in Pocket Sphinx and Julius

The following link is used to adapt the existing acoustic model to our voice for Pocket Sphinx:

```
http://cmusphinx.sourceforge.net/wiki/tutorialadapt
```

Julius accuracy can be improved by writing recognition grammar. The following link gives an idea about how to write recognition grammar in Julius:

```
http://julius.sourceforge.jp/en_index.php?q=en_grammar.html
```

In the next section, we will see how to connect Python and speech synthesis libraries. We will work with the eSpeak and Festival libraries here. These are two popular, free, and effective speech synthesizers available in all the OS platforms. There are precompiled binaries available in Ubuntu in the form of packages.

Setting up eSpeak and Festival in Ubuntu 14.04.2

eSpeak and Festival are speech synthesizers available in the Ubuntu/Linux platform. These applications can be installed from the software package repository of Ubuntu. The following are the instructions and commands to install these packages in Ubuntu.

1. The following commands will install the eSpeak application and its wrapper for Python. We can use this wrapper in our program and access eSpeak APIs:

   ```
   $ sudo apt-get install espeak
   $ sudo apt-get install python-espeak
   ```

2. The following command will install the Festival text-to-speech engine. Festival has some package dependencies; all dependencies will be automatically installed using this command:

   ```
   $ sudo apt-get install festival
   ```

3. After the installation of the Festival application, we can download and install Python bindings for Festival.

4. Download Python bindings using the following command. We need the svn tool (Apache Subversion) to download this package. Subversion is a free software versioning and revision control system:

   ```
   $ svn checkout http://pyfestival.googlecode.com/svn/trunk/
   pyfestival-read-only
   ```

5. After the downloading process is complete, switch to the `pyfestival-read-only` folder and you can install this package using the following command:

```
$ sudo python setup.py install
```

Here is the code to work with Python and eSpeak. As you will see, it's very easy to work with Python binding for eSpeak. We need to write only two lines of code to synthesize speech using Python:

```
from espeak import espeak
espeak.synth("Hello World")
```

This code will import the eSpeak-Python wrapper module and call the `synth` function in the wrapper module. The `synth` function will synthesize the text given as argument.

The following code shows how to synthesize speech using Python and Festival:

```
import festival
festival.say("Hello World")
```

The preceding code will import the Festival-Python wrapper module and call the `say` function in the Festival module. It will synthesize the text as speech.

Working with speech recognition and synthesis in Windows using Python

In Windows, there are many tools and frameworks to perform speech recognition and synthesis. The speech recognition libraries, namely, Pocket Sphinx and Julius that we discussed will also be supported in Windows. Microsoft also provides **SAPI (Speech Application Programming Interface)**, a set of APIs that allows you to use speech recognition and synthesis from code. These APIs are either shipped with an operating system or with Microsoft Speech SDK.

In this section, we will demonstrate how to connect Python and Microsoft Speech SDK to perform speech recognition and synthesis. This procedure will work in Windows 8, Windows 7, 32, and 64 bit.

Installation of the Speech SDK

The following is the step-by-step procedure to install Speech SDK and the Python wrapper of Speech SDK:

1. Download Speech SDK from `http://www.microsoft.com/en-in/download/details.aspx?id=27226`

2. Download and install Active State Python 2.7 bit from `http://www.activestate.com/activepython/downloads`

3. Download and install Python wrapper for the Windows Speech SDK from `https://pypi.python.org/pypi/speech/`. Currently, this project is not active, but it will work fine in Windows 7 and 8

4. Install the package using the following command:

   ```
   python setup.py install
   ```

5. The code to do speech recognition using Python is very simple and it's given in the following code:

   ```
   import speech
   result = speech.input("Speak")
   print result
   ```

In this code, we import the speech module. When we import the speech module, the speech recognition panel of Windows will pop up. It will be in *off* state first and we need to turn it *on* to perform the recognition. The recognized text will be printed on the Python command line.

Next, we can look at the speech synthesis using Python. Similar to the speech recognition process, it's very easy to perform the speech module. This can be used to perform speech synthesis. Here is the code:

```
import speech
speech.say("Hello World")
```

In this code, `speech.say()` is the method to convert text to speech.

We have seen some of the speech recognition and synthesis platforms. Now, we can take a look at how we can integrate speech recognition and synthesis in ROS. The following section discusses the integration of speech recognition and synthesis on ROS.

Working with Speech recognition in ROS Indigo and Python

Compared to other speech recognition methods, one of the easiest and effective methods to implement real time speech recognition is Pocket Sphinx and GStreamer pipeline. We discussed Pocket Sphinx, GStreamer and its interfacing with Python previously. Next, we can see a ROS package called `pocketsphinx` that uses the GStreamer `pocketsphinx` interface to perform speech recognition. The `pocketsphinx` ROS package is available in the ROS repository. You will get the package information at the following link

```
http://wiki.ros.org/pocketsphinx
```

Installation of the pocketsphinx package in ROS Indigo

To install the `pocketsphinx` package, first switch to the `catkin` workspace source folder.

1. Download the source code of the `pocketsphinx` package using the following command:

    ```
    $ git clone https://github.com/mikeferguson/pocketsphinx
    ```

2. Execute the `catkin_make` command from the `catkin` workspace folder to build the package

3. Start the speech recognizer demo using the following command. The robotcup demo has some basic commands to drive the robot. We can change the command by adapting acoustic and language models:

    ```
    $ roslaunch pocketsphinx robocup.launch
    ```

4. Subscribe to /recognizer/output using the following command:

    ```
    $ rostopic echo /recognizer/output
    ```

The following is the screenshot of the output:

```
lentin@lentin-desktop:~/ros_ws/pocketsphinx/demo$ rostopic echo /recognizer/output
data: move left
---
data: move right
---
data: full speed
---
data: left
---
data: left
---
data: ''
---
```

This Topic can be subscribed and the command can be processed in some other nodes. In the next section, we will see how to synthesize speech using ROS and Python.

Working with speech synthesis in ROS Indigo and Python

In ROS, there are some ROS packages that perform speech synthesis. Here, we will discuss one ROS package. This package uses Festival as the backend. The package name is sound_play. It has nodes and launch scripts that enable speech synthesis. We need to perform the following steps for speech synthesis:

1. We can install the sound_play package using the following command:

   ```
   $ sudo apt-get install ros-indigo-sound-play
   ```

2. After the installation of package, we have to create a sample ROS package to interact with the sound-play node. The following is the command to create a sample package in ROS with the sound-play package as dependency:

   ```
   $ catkin_create_pkg sample_tts rospy roscpp sound_play std_msgs
   ```

3. We have to create a sound_play python client code for sending text to sound play server node. This client will send the text that needs to be converted to speech to the sound_play server node. The client will send the text to convert to speech in a Topic called /robotsound. The sound play node in the sound play package will subscribe to this Topic and convert the string from Topic to speech.

4. Create a folder inside this `sample_tts` package named `scripts` and create the following code in the `scripts` folder and name it `test.py`. The code snippets of `test.py` is given.

5. The following code will import the `rospy` and `sound_play` modules. This script will act as a `SoundClient`, which will connect to the `sound_play` server and synthesize the speech:

```
#!/usr/bin/env python
import roslib; roslib.load_manifest('sample_tts')
import rospy, os, sys
from sound_play.msg import SoundRequest
from sound_play.libsoundplay import SoundClient
```

6. This code will initialize the `soundplay_test` node and create an object of `SoundClient`:

```
if __name__ == '__main__':
    rospy.init_node('soundplay_test', anonymous = True)
    soundhandle = SoundClient()
    rospy.sleep(1)

    soundhandle.stopAll()
```

7. This code will call a function to synthesize the speech. It can be used to synthesize speech in any package that includes `sound_play` as dependency.

```
    print 'Starting TTS'
    soundhandle.say('Hello world!')
    rospy.sleep(3)

    s = soundhandle.voiceSound("Hello World")
    s.play()
    rospy.sleep(3)
```

8. The following command starts the sound play server:

```
$ roslaunch sound_play soundplay_node.launch
```

9. The following command will start the test script for speech synthesis:

```
$ rosrun sample_tts test.py
```

Questions

1. What are the basic procedures involved in converting speech to text?
2. What is the function of the acoustic model and language model in speech recognition?
3. What are the basic procedures involved in converting text to speech ?
4. What are the procedures involved in phonetic analysis and prosodic analysis?
5. How can we improve the recognition accuracy of Sphinx and Julius?

Summary

The main aim of this chapter was to discuss speech recognition and synthesis and how we can implement it on our robot. By adding speech functionalities in our robot, we can make the robot more interactive than before. We saw what are the processes involved in the speech recognition and synthesis process. We also saw the block diagram of these processes and the functions of each block. After discussing the blocks, we saw some interesting speech recognition frameworks (such as Sphinx/Pocket Sphinx, Julius, and Windows Speech SDK and synthesis libraries such as eSpeak and Festival). After discussing these libraries, we discussed and worked with the Python interfacing of each library. Towards the end of this chapter, we discussed and worked with the ROS packages that perform speech recognition and synthesis functionalities.

9
Applying Artificial Intelligence to ChefBot Using Python

In the previous chapter, we have discussed and implemented speech recognition and speech synthesis using Python and ROS. In this chapter, we will discuss how to apply AI to ChefBot to communicate with people intelligently, like a human. Actually, these features are add-ons in ChefBot, which can increase human-robot interaction and make the robot resemble a human food supplier. In this chapter, we will mainly cover the following topics:

- Block diagram of ChefBot's communication system
- Introduction to AIML and PyAIML
- Interfacing ChefBot's AI module to ROS

AI (Artificial Intelligence) can be defined as the intelligent behavior exhibited by computers or machines. Using AI, we can create a virtual intelligence in machines to perform a specific task like a human. In this chapter, we will use a simple method to apply AI to the robot. This intelligence will work using pattern matching and searching algorithms. The input-output dialog patterns between the user and robot are stored in files called **Artificial Intelligence Markup Language (AIML)** and we will interpret these stored patterns using a Python module called **PyAIML**. The user can store desired patterns in AIML files and the interpreter module will search for appropriate response from the dataset. We can develop our own pattern dataset for our robot simply by writing logical patterns. In one section of this chapter, we will see how to write AIML tags and patterns in a robot. In the first section, we will discuss where we will use AI in ChefBot.

Block diagram of the communication system in ChefBot

The following block diagram shows how ChefBot communicates and interacts with humans using speech:

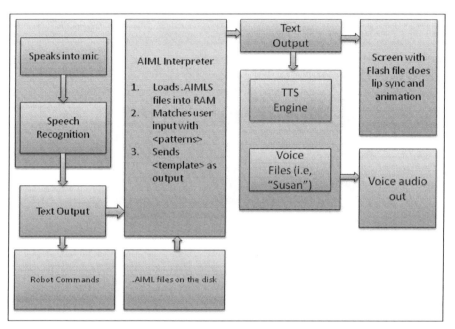

Robot communication block diagram

The robot can convert human speech to text using the speech recognition system and can convert textual data to speech using speech synthesis. We have already discussed these processes in the previous chapter. The AI we will discuss here is contained in between these two blocks. After receiving the text data from a speech to text conversion stage, it is sent to the AIML interpreter. The AIML interpreter retrieves the most meaningful reply from the AIML dataset. The dataset of the robot can be anything, such as food details, casual talks, and so on. The user can write any kind of pattern in AIML files. In the case of ChefBot, the user can ask about food details or can command the robot to do something. The robot command system checks whether the converted text is a command to the robot. If it's a command, it is directly sent to the hardware nodes to execute. The output text from AIML will be converted to speech using a text-to-speech system. Also, we can put an LCD display to show the result of speech in the form of an animated face. All these features enhance the robot's interaction. Before we discuss the Python interpreter for AIML, we will discuss AIML and AIML tags in detail.

Introduction to AIML

AIML files are a subset of **Extensible Mark-up Language (XML)** that can store different text patterns in the form of tags. AIML was developed by the Alicebot free software community (http://www.alicebot.org/). AIML is mainly used to implement Chatbots, a natural language software agent in which a user can ask questions to the robot and it can give an intelligent reply. This same technique is used in ChefBot. Using speech recognition, the robot gets input text from the user and an AIML interpreter; a software program that can interpret AIML files and retrieve an intelligent reply from the AIML dataset. The reply will be converted to speech. AIML files mainly consist of various tags. Here are a set of commonly used AIML tags.

Introduction to AIML tags

AIML files consist of a set of commonly used AIML tags. Let's take a look at them.

The `<aiml>` tag: Each AIML code begins with this tag and is closed using the `</aiml>` tag. This tag also consists of attributes such as the version and encoding scheme of the file. The AIML file can parse even without these attributes, but this will be useful in big projects. The version attribute corresponds to the current version of AIML that we will use. The encoding attribute is the type of character encoding we will use in this file. The following code snippet shows an example usage of AIML tags:

```
<aiml version="1.0.1" encoding="UTF-8">
...
</aiml>
```

The `<category>` tag: The basic knowledge blocks of AIML are called categories. Each category block consists of two sections. One is the user input in the form of a sentence and the other is a corresponding response to user input which comes from robot. The category tag is represented using the opening `<category>` tag and the closing tag is represented using the `</category>` tag. These categories must be inside the `<aiml>` and `</aiml>` tags. The category tags consist of two tags, namely, the `<pattern>` tag and the `<template>` tag. The input given by users is inside the `<pattern>` tag and the answers are in the `<template>` tag. For example, look at this following conversation:

User: How are you?

Robot: I am fine.

In this conversation, the user dialog will be in the `<pattern>` tag and the robot's response will be in the `<template>` tag. The following code shows the representation of the preceding dialogs in the AIML format:

```
<aiml version="1.0.1" encoding="UTF-8">
  <category>
    <pattern> HOW ARE YOU </pattern>
    <template> I AM FINE </template>
  </category>
</aiml>
```

We need to save this file in the `.aiml` or `.xml` format.

The `<pattern>` tag: The pattern tag comprises of possible user inputs. There will be only one `<pattern>` tag in a category block. The `<pattern>` tag will be the first element of the `<category>` tag and, in the `<pattern>` tag, words are separated by single spaces. The sentence in `<pattern>` tag may have words or wild cards such as "*" or "_", which can replace a string in this position. In the preceding example, the `<pattern> HOW ARE YOU </pattern>` code indicates the possible user input in this category.

The `<template>` tag: The `<template>` tag comprises of possible answers for the user input. The `<template>` tag will be within the `<category>` tag and will be placed after the `<pattern>` tag. The `<template>` tag can save a particular answer or it can trigger programs. Also, we can give conditional form of answers too. In the preceding code, the `<template>` tag sentence: "I AM FINE" will be the answer for the "HOW ARE YOU" pattern. We can insert additional tags in the `<template>` tag. The following tags are used in the `<template>` tag:

The `<star index = "n"/>` tag: This tag is used to extract a part of the user text input sentence. The n index indicates which fragment of text has to be extracted and taken from the entire sentence:

- `<star index="1"/>`: This indicates the first fragment of a sentence
- `<star index="2"/>`: This indicates the second fragment of a sentence

The main application of this tag is to extract and store the text from user input. The following is a dialog between the robot and the user. The wildcard can be anything, such as a name or something else. Using this tag, we can extract this wildcard portion and use it in the answering section:

User: My name is *

Robot: Nice to meet you *

So, if the user says, "My name is Lentin", then the robot will reply, "Nice to meet you Lentin". This kind of conversation is only possible using the `<star>` tag and wildcards such as "*". The complete AIML example using the star tag is as follows:

```
<aiml version="1.0.1" encoding="UTF-8">
  <category>
    <pattern> MY NAME IS * </pattern>
    <template>
      NICE TO MEET YOU <star/>
    </template>
  </category>
  <category>
    <pattern> MEET OUR GUEST * AND * </pattern>
    <template>
    NICE TO MEET YOU <star index="1"/> AND <star index="2"/>.
    </template>
  </category>
</aiml>
```

If we load this example to the AIML interpreter, we will get the following reply when we give the following input:

USER: MY NAME IS LENTIN

ROBOT: NICE TO MEET YOU LENTIN

The previous conversation uses one wildcard and the following conversation will use both wildcards:

USER: MEET OUR GUEST TOM AND JOSEPH

ROBOT: NICE TO MEET YOU TOM AND JOSEPH

Here, the name is "TOM", the index number is "1", and "JOSEPH" is indexed as "2".

The `<srai>` tag: Using the `<srai>` tag, we can target multiple patterns from a single `<template>` tag. Using the `<srai>` tag, the AIML interpreter can search recursively for the answer that is replacing the current template text with the template text of another pattern. The following code is an example of the usage of the `<srai>` tag:

```
<aiml version="1.0.1" encoding="UTF-8">
  <category>
    <pattern> WHAT IS A ROBOT? </pattern>
    <template>
    A ROBOT IS A MACHINE MAINLY DESIGNED FOR EXECUTING REPEATED
    TASK WITH SPEED AND PRECISION.
```

```
      </template>
    </category>
    <category>
      <pattern> DO YOU KNOW WHAT A * IS ? </pattern>
      <template>
        <srai> WHAT IS A <star/> </srai>
      </template>
    </category>
  </aiml>
```

When a user asks the robot, "DO YOU KNOW WHAT A ROBOT IS", it will go to the second category template and extract the wildcard section from user input, "ROBOT" and put the complete sentence, "WHAT IS A ROBOT", and put it in the `<srai>` tag. The `<srai>` tag can call the pattern called "WHAT IS A ROBOT" and fill the output of this template to the actual template text.

For more AIML tags, you can refer to `http://www.alicebot.org/documentation/aiml-reference.html`.

After discussing AIML files and tags, we will discuss the Python AIML interpreter to decode AIML files. The AIML interpreter can retrieve the template text from user input. We will use a Python module called PyAIML to interpret AIML files. Let's discuss more about PyAIML.

Introduction to PyAIML

PyAIML is an open source Python AIML interpreter written completely in pure Python without using any third-party dependencies. The module will read all the patterns of AIML from memory and build a directed pattern tree. The backtracking depth-first search algorithm is implemented in this module for pattern matching.

Now, we can check whether we can install PyAIML on our system. The PyAIML module can be installed on Linux, Windows, and Mac OS X. There are prebuilt binaries of PyAIML available on Ubuntu and the source code of this module is also available on GitHub. Currently, we are working with Python version 2.7, or anything less than 2.8, to install PyAIML.

Installing PyAIML on Ubuntu 14.04.2

PyAIML can be installed on Ubuntu using the `apt-get` command. The binaries are available on the Ubuntu package repositories. The Python version we are working with is 2.7.6 and the PyAIML version we are installing is 0.86. The following command will install PyAIML on Ubuntu 14.04.2:

```
$ sudo apt-get install python-aiml
```

You should install Git to get the source code. Also, you should have Python version 2.7 or greater than 2.7 and less than 2.8. We require the latest version of the module if we are performing the installation via source code.

Installing PyAIML from source code

We can retrieve the source code module using the following `git` command:

```
$ git clone git://pyaiml.git.sourceforge.net/gitroot/pyaiml/pyaiml
```

After cloning the code, change the directory to a cloned directory named `pyaiml`:

```
$ cd pyaiml
```

Install the module using the following command:

```
$ sudo python setup.py install
```

Working with AIML and Python

To check whether the module is properly installed on your machine, open a Python IDLE and import the `aiml` module:

```
>>> import aiml
```

If the module is imported correctly, it will not show any error and comes to the next line. Then, we can confirm that the installation is correct.

The most important class we are handling in the `aiml` module is `Kernel()`. We are mainly using this class to learn from AIML files and get a response from the AIML dataset to user input. The following line will create an object of the `aiml.Kernel()` class:

```
>>> mybot = aiml.Kernel()
```

After creating the `Kernel()` object, we can assign the robot name using the following command. We will assign `Chefbot` as the name for this robot:

```
>>> mybot.setBotPredicate("name","Chefbot")
```

The next step is to learn AIML files. We can load either a single AIML file or a group of AIML files. To load a single AIML file, we can use the following command. Note that the `sample.aiml` file must be in the current path:

```
>>> mybot.learn('sample.aiml')
```

The preceding command will load the `sample.aiml` file into memory and the output is as follows:

```
Loading sample.aiml ... done (0.01 seconds)s
```

If you want to learn more than one AIML, it's better to use an AIML/XML file, for example, the `startup.xml` file can load all other AIML files. We will see how `startup.xml` works in the next section. To learn `startup.xml`, use the following command:

```
>>> mybot.learn("startup.xml")
```

After you learn `startup.xml`, let's trigger a pattern in `startup.xml` called "LOAD AIML B". When we call this pattern, it will respond by learning all AIML files and print the response in string after learning each AIML file:

```
>>> mybot.respond("load aiml b")
```

After learning AIML files, we can start inputting text to the kernel object and retrieve the intelligent text using the following code:

```
>>> while True: print k.respond(raw_input("> "))
```

The complete Python code to load one AIML file and get a response from the AIML dataset is given in the code snippet in the following section. We can pass the AIML file as a command-line argument.

Loading a single AIML file from the command-line argument

We can load a single AIML file using the following code:

```
#!/usr/bin/env python
import aiml
import sys
```

```
mybot = aiml.Kernel()
mybot.learn(sys.argv[1])

while True:
    print mybot.respond(raw_input("Enter input >"))
```

The following is the sample AIML file required to load in this code. Save the following code with the name `sample.aiml`:

```
<aiml version="1.0.1" encoding="UTF-8">
  <category>
    <pattern> HOW ARE YOU </pattern>
    <template> I AM FINE </template>
  </category>
</aiml>
```

Save the code as `chatbot.py` and change the permission of the code using the following command:

$ chmod +x chatbot.py

Execute the code using the following command:

$ ./chatbot sample.aiml

It will give you the following result:

```
lentin@lentin-Aspire-4755:~/Desktop/Chapter-9_code$ ./chatbot.py sample.aiml
Loading sample.aiml... done (0.02 seconds)
Enter input >HOW ARE YOU
I AM FINE
Enter input >
```

Press *Ctrl + C* to quit the dialog. We can check whether each AIML example we previously discussed can be tested using this example.

If there is more than one XML file, we can use the following code to load all the AIML files into memory. Let's download some AIML dataset from the **Artificial Linguistic Internet Computer Entity (A.L.I.C.E)** robot and load it using PyAIML.

Working with A.L.I.C.E. AIML files

The AIML files of A.L.I.C.E. chatter are freely available at `https://code.google.com/p/aiml-en-us-foundation-alice/`.

Extract the AIML files to a folder on the desktop or in the `home` directory and copy `startup.xml` to these AIML files. This `startup.xml` file will load all the other AIML files into memory. The following code is an example of a typical `startup.xml` file:

```
<aiml version="1.0">
<category>
  <pattern>LOAD AIML B</pattern>
  <template>
          <!-- Load standard AIML set -->
          <learn>*.aiml</learn>

  </template>
</category>
</aiml>
```

The preceding XML file will learn all the AIML files when we call the LOAD AIML B pattern.

Loading AIML files into memory

The following code will load all the AIML files into memory:

```
#!/usr/bin/env python

import aiml
import sys
import os

#Change the current path to your aiml files path
os.chdir('/home/lentin/Desktop/aiml-files')
mybot = aiml.Kernel()

#Learn startup.xml
mybot.learn('startup.xml')

#Calling load aiml b for loading all AIML files
mybot.respond('load aiml b')

while True:
  print mybot.respond(raw_input("Enter input >"))
```

You will get the following output:

```
PARSE ERROR: Unexpected </category> tag (line 104, column 0)
PARSE ERROR: Unexpected </category> tag (line 144, column 0)
Loading update_mccormick.aiml... done (0.01 seconds)
PARSE ERROR: Unexpected text inside <random> element (line 4311, column 262)
PARSE ERROR: Unexpected text inside <random> element (line 4848, column 172)
PARSE ERROR: Unexpected text inside <random> element (line 8844, column 351)
Loading default.aiml... done (0.72 seconds)
Enter input >How are you
I am fine, thank you.
Enter input >
```

Loading AIML files will take some time. To avoid initial loading time, we can dump the AIML patterns loaded in the memory and save them to brain files. Loading brain files will save initial loading time.

Loading AIML files and saving them in brain files

The following code will load AIML files and save them in brain files:

```python
#!/usr/bin/env python
import aiml
import sys
import os

os.chdir('/home/lentin/Desktop/aiml-files')
mybot = aiml.Kernel()
mybot.learn('startup.xml')
mybot.respond('load aiml b')
#Saving loaded patterns into a brain file
mybot.saveBrain('standard.brn')

while True:
    print mybot.respond(raw_input("Enter input >"))
```

You will get the following output:

```
Loading personality.aiml... done (0.01 seconds)
Loading bot.aiml... done (0.27 seconds)
Loading biography.aiml... done (0.05 seconds)
PARSE ERROR: Unexpected </category> tag (line 104, column 0)
PARSE ERROR: Unexpected </category> tag (line 144, column 0)
Loading update_mccormick.aiml... done (0.01 seconds)
PARSE ERROR: Unexpected text inside <random> element (line 4311, column 262)
PARSE ERROR: Unexpected text inside <random> element (line 4848, column 172)
PARSE ERROR: Unexpected text inside <random> element (line 8844, column 351)
Loading default.aiml... done (0.73 seconds)
Saving brain to standard.brn... done (0.41 seconds)
Enter input >How are you
My logic and cognitive functions are normal.
Enter input >
```

If we want to initialize the robot from the brain file or AIML files, a better way is to use the `bootstrap()` method inside the `Kernel()` class. The `bootstrap()` method takes the brain file or AIML files and some command as argument. The code for loading the brain file if it exists is in the following section; otherwise, load it from AIML and save a new brain file. After this process is complete, respond from the loaded dataset.

Loading AIML and brain files using the Bootstrap method

The following code will load AIML files and brain files using the Bootstrap method:

```python
#!/usr/bin/env python

import aiml
import sys
import os

#Changing current directory to the path of aiml files
#This path will change according to your location of aiml files

os.chdir('/home/lentin/Desktop/aiml-files')
mybot = aiml.Kernel()

#If there is a brain file named standard.brn, Kernel() will initialize
using bootstrap() method
if os.path.isfile("standard.brn"):
  mybot.bootstrap(brainFile = "standard.brn")
```

```
else:
   #If there is not brain file, load all AIML files and save a new
brain
   mybot.bootstrap(learnFiles = "startup.xml", commands =
   "load aiml b")
   mybot.saveBrain("standard.brn")


#This loop ask for response from user and print the output from
Kernel() object
while True:
   print mybot.respond(raw_input("Enter input >"))
```

Integrating PyAIML into ROS

In this section, we are going to develop ROS Python nodes which can handle AIML files. We are using the Python code that we developed in the preceding section. The ROS version we are going to use is Indigo and the Ubuntu version we will use is 14.04.2. We already discussed the interfacing of speech recognition and speech synthesis in ROS and also discussed the Python code to interface AIML files. In this section, we will make a package in ROS to handle AIML files. Currently, there are no active packages in ROS repositories that can handle AIML files. We will build our own package using the code that we develop.

Create a ROS package using the following dependencies. Here the sound_play package is used for speech synthesis:

```
$ catkin_create_pkg ros_aiml rospy std_msgs sound_play
```

Create a scripts folder inside the ros_aiml package and create the following Python files in it. Create a folder called data and copy the ALICE AIML dataset we have already downloaded to this folder.

aiml_server.py

The following code acts as an AIML server in which an AIML client can send user input to the server through the /chatter topic and retrieve the AIML output response through the /response topic:

```
#!/usr/bin/env python
import rospy
import aiml
import os
import sys
from std_msgs.msg import String
```

```
rospy.init_node('aiml_server')
mybot = aiml.Kernel()

#Creating a ROS publisher for the /response topic
response_publisher =
rospy.Publisher('response',String,queue_size=10)

#Function to load AIML files using bootstrap() method
def load_aiml(xml_file):
  #Get the path of aiml data set. We have to mention this path
  on launch file as a rosparameter
  data_path = rospy.get_param("aiml_path")
  os.chdir(data_path)
  if os.path.isfile("standard.brn"):
    mybot.bootstrap(brainFile = "standard.brn")
  else:
    mybot.bootstrap(learnFiles = xml_file, commands = "load
    aiml b")
    mybot.saveBrain("standard.brn")

#Callback function of /chatter topic. It will receive input from user
and feed to respond() method of Kernel() object. and print the results
def callback(data):
  input = data.data
  response = mybot.respond(input)
  rospy.loginfo("I heard:: %s",data.data)
  rospy.loginfo("I spoke:: %s",response)
  response_publisher.publish(response)

#Method to create subscriber in /chatter topic
def listener():
  rospy.loginfo("Starting ROS AIML Server")
  rospy.Subscriber("chatter", String, callback)
  # spin() simply keeps python from exiting until this node is
  stopped
  rospy.spin()

if __name__ == '__main__':
  load_aiml('startup.xml')
  listener()
```

aiml_client.py

This is a simple client code that will send user input taken from the keyboard to the AIML server. The user input is send through the /chatter topic:

```python
#!/usr/bin/env python
import rospy
from std_msgs.msg import String

#Creating a publisher for chatter topic
pub = rospy.Publisher('chatter', String,queue_size=10)
rospy.init_node('aiml_client')
r = rospy.Rate(1) # 10hz

while not rospy.is_shutdown():
  #Receiving text input from user
  input = raw_input("Enter your text :> ")
  #Publishing to chatter topic
  pub.publish(input)
  r.sleep()
```

aiml_tts_client.py

This client will transcribe the response from aiml_server and convert it to speech. This code is adapted from the client code, as we discussed in the previous chapter for speech synthesis, as we discussed in the previous chapter. We will use the sound_play package to perform TTS:

```python
#!/usr/bin/env python
import rospy, os, sys
from sound_play.msg import SoundRequest
from sound_play.libsoundplay import SoundClient
from std_msgs.msg import String

rospy.init_node('aiml_soundplay_client', anonymous = True)
soundhandle = SoundClient()
rospy.sleep(1)
soundhandle.stopAll()
print 'Starting TTS'

#Call back method to receive text from /response topic and convert
to speech
def get_response(data):
  response = data.data
  rospy.loginfo("Response ::%s",response)
```

```
    soundhandle.say(response)

#Method to create a subscriber for /response topic.
def listener():
  rospy.loginfo("Starting listening to response")
  rospy.Subscriber("response",String, get_response,queue_size=10)
  rospy.spin()
if __name__ == '__main__':
  listener()
```

aiml_speech_recog_client.py

This client can send the speech to text data to the AIML server instead of typing on the keyboard. Before running this code, we have to launch the Pocket Sphinx speech recognizer. We can see how to run this code after discussing it:

```
#!/usr/bin/env python
import rospy
from std_msgs.msg import String

rospy.init_node('aiml_speech_recog_client')
pub = rospy.Publisher('chatter', String,queue_size=10)
r = rospy.Rate(1) # 10hz

#The output of pocketsphinx package is sending converted text to
/recognizer/output topic. The following function is the callback
of this topic. The text will receive and send through /chatter
topic, which is received by AIML server
def get_speech(data):
  speech_text=data.data
  rospy.loginfo("I said:: %s",speech_text)
  pub.publish(speech_text)

#Creating a subscriber for pocketsphinx output topic
/recognizer/output
def listener():
  rospy.loginfo("Starting Speech Recognition")
  rospy.Subscriber("/recognizer/output", String, get_speech)
  rospy.spin()

if __name__ == '__main__':
  listener()
```

Let's see how these nodes communicate with the AIML server:

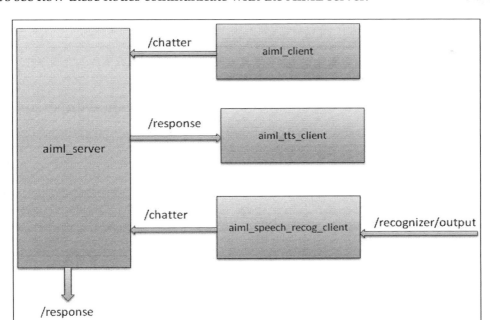

After creating all the scripts in the `scripts` folder, create another folder called `launch` in the `ros_aiml` package to store the launch files. It helps to launch all the nodes in a single run. Create the following launch files in the `launch` folder.

start_chat.launch

This launch file will launch `aiml_server.py` and `aiml_client.py`, in which the user will receive the input as text and the response as text. The `aiml_path` ROS parameter has to mention them in the launch file:

```
<launch>
  <param name="aiml_path" value="/home/lentin/catkin_ws/src/ros_aiml/
data" />
  <node name="aiml_server" pkg="ros_aiml" type="aiml_server.py"
output="screen">
  </node>
  <node name="aiml_client" pkg="ros_aiml" type="aiml_client.py"
output="screen">
  </node>
</launch>
```

start_tts_chat.launch

This launch file will launch the text input and speech synthesis of the AIML response:

```
<launch>
  <param name="aiml_path"
  value="/home/lentin/catkin_ws/src/ros_aiml/data" />
  <node name="aiml_server" pkg="ros_aiml" type="aiml_server.py"
  output="screen">
  </node>

  <include file="$(find
  sound_play)/soundplay_node.launch">
  </include>
  <node name="aiml_tts" pkg="ros_aiml" type="aiml_tts_client.py"
  output="screen">
  </node>

  <node name="aiml_client" pkg="ros_aiml" type="aiml_client.py"
  output="screen">
  </node>
</launch>
```

start_speech_chat.launch

This file will launch the speech recognition client, synthesis client, and AIML server. This will not launch pocket sphinx; we need to launch it separately. This launch file enables you to receive text input from the speech recognizer and convert the response to speech too:

```
<launch>
  <param name="aiml_path"
  value="/home/lentin/catkin_ws/src/ros_aiml/data" />
  <node name="aiml_server" pkg="ros_aiml" type="aiml_server.py"
  output="screen">
  </node>

  <include file="$(find
  sound_play)/soundplay_node.launch"></include>
  <node name="aiml_tts" pkg="ros_aiml" type="aiml_tts_client.py"
  output="screen">
  </node>

  <node name="aiml_speech_recog" pkg="ros_aiml"
  type="aiml_speech_recog_client.py" output="screen">
  </node>
</launch>
```

After creating all the launch files, change the permission of all the launch files using the following command, which we have to execute in the `launch` folder:

```
$ chmod +x *.launch
```

The folder structure of this package is given in the following diagram. After creating this package, verify it with this diagram:

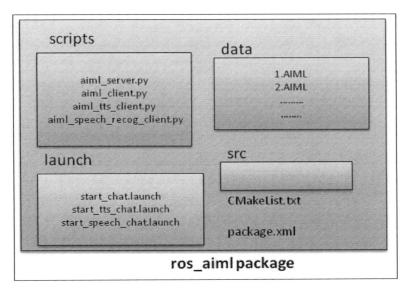

Launch the AIML server and client for text chatting using the following command:

```
$roslaunch ros_aiml start_chat.launch
```

When you launch this file, the user can input the text and the reply will be printed.

Launch the AIML server and client with text chatting and speech synthesis, using the following command:

```
$ roslaunch ros_aiml start_tts_chat.launch
```

When you launch this file, it will start the text chatting interface and the reply text will be synthesized using the speech synthesizer.

Start the `pocketsphinx` demo launch file to start speech recognition. The following launch file is a demo that will detect some words and sentences. If we want more accuracy, we have to train the model:

```
$ roslaunch pocketsphinx robocup.launch
```

Launch the AIML server, speech recognition, and synthesis client using the following command:

```
$ roslaunch ros_aiml start_speech_chat.launch
```

After you run the preceding launch files, the user can interact with the AIML server using speech and the user will get the output as speech as well.

Questions

1. What is Artificial Intelligence?
2. What is the use of an AIML file?
3. Which are the most commonly used AIML tags?
4. What is the use of the PyAIML module?

Summary

In this chapter, we discussed how to add Artificial Intelligence to ChefBot in order to interact with people. This function is an add-on to ChefBot to increase the interactivity of the robot. We used simple AI techniques such as pattern matching and searching in ChefBot. The pattern datasets are stored in a special type of file called AIML. The Python interpreter module is called PyAIML. We used this to decode AIML files. The user can store the pattern data in an AIML format and PyAIML can interpret this pattern. This method is similar to a stimulus-response system. The user has to give a stimulus in the form of text data and from the AIML pattern, the module finds the appropriate reply to the user input. We saw the entire communication system of the robot and how the robot communicates with people. It includes speech recognition and synthesis along with AI. We already discussed speech in the previous chapter. We also saw useful tags used in AIML and the PyAIML installation, how they work, and some examples. Finally, we implemented the entire code in ROS along with the speech recognition and synthesis units. In the next chapter, we will discuss the integration of components in the robot, which we have not discussed until now.

10
Integration of ChefBot Hardware and Interfacing it into ROS, Using Python

In *Chapter 2, Mechanical Design of a Service Robot*, we saw the ChefBot chassis design and now we have got the manufactured parts of this robot. In this chapter, we will see how to assemble this robot using these parts and also the final interfacing of sensors and other electronics components of this robot to Tiva C LaunchPad. We have already discussed interfacing of individual robot components and sensors with Launchpad. In this chapter, we will try to interface the necessary robotic components and sensors of ChefBot and program it in such a way that it will receive the values from all sensors and control the information from the PC. Launchpad will send all sensor values via a serial port to the PC and also receive control information (such as reset command, speed, and so on) from the PC.

After receiving sensor values from the PC, a ROS Python node will receive the serial values and convert it to ROS Topics. There are Python nodes present in the PC that subscribe to the sensor's data and produces odometry. The data from the wheel encoders and IMU values are combined to calculate the odometry of the robot and detect obstacles by subscribing to the ultrasonic sensor and laser scan also, controlling the speed of the wheel motors by using the PID node. This node converts the linear velocity command to differential wheel velocity. After running these nodes, we can run SLAM to map the area and after running SLAM, we can run the AMCL nodes for localization and autonomous navigation.

In the first section of this chapter, *Building ChefBot hardware*, we will see how to assemble the ChefBot hardware using its body parts and electronics components.

Building ChefBot hardware

The first section of the robot that needs to be configured is the base plate. The base plate consists of two motors and its wheels, caster wheels, and base plate supports. The following image shows the top and bottom view of the base plate:

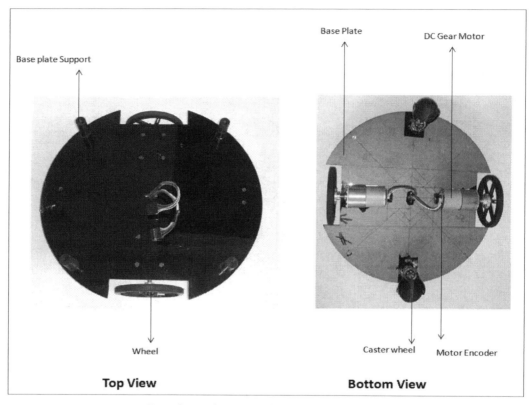

Base plate with motors, wheels, and caster wheels

The base plate has a radius of 15cm and motors with wheels are mounted on the opposite sides of the plate by cutting a section from the base plate. A rubber caster wheel is mounted on the opposite side of the base plate to give the robot good balance and support for the robot. We can either choose ball caster wheels or rubber caster wheels. The wires of the two motors are taken to the top of the base plate through a hole in the center of the base plate. To extend the layers of the robot, we will put base plate supports to connect the next layers. Now, we can see the next layer with the middle plate and connecting tubes. There are hollow tubes, which connect the base plate and the middle plate. A support is provided on the base plate for hollow tubes. The following figure shows the middle plate and connecting tubes:

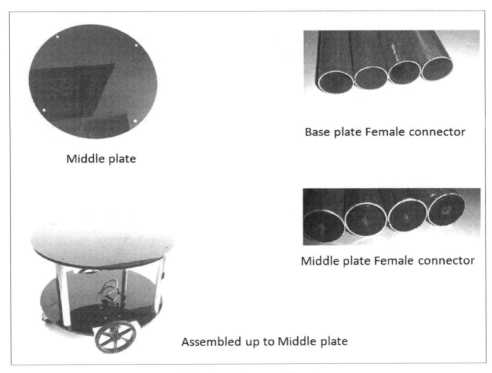

Middle plate

Base plate Female connector

Middle plate Female connector

Assembled up to Middle plate

Middle plate with connecting tubes

The connecting tubes will connect the base plate and the middle plate. There are four hollow tubes that connect the base plate to the middle plate. One end of these tubes is hollow, which can fit in the base plate support, and the other end is inserted with a hard plastic with an option to put a screw in the hole. The middle plate has no support except four holes:

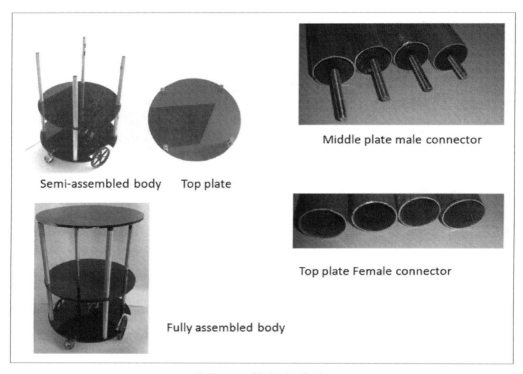

Semi-assembled body   Top plate

Middle plate male connector

Top plate Female connector

Fully assembled body

Fully assembled robot body

The middle plate male connector helps to connect the middle plate and the top of the base plate tubes. At the top of the middle plate tubes, we can fit the top plate, which has four supports on the back. We can insert the top plate female connector into the top plate support and this is how we will get the fully assembled body of the robot.

The bottom layer of the robot can be used to put the **Printed Circuit Board (PCB)** and battery. In the middle layer, we can put Kinect and Intel NUC. We can put a speaker and a mic if needed. We can use the top plate to carry food. The following figure shows the PCB prototype of robot; it consists of Tiva C LaunchPad, a motor driver, level shifters, and provisions to connect two motors, ultrasonic, and IMU:

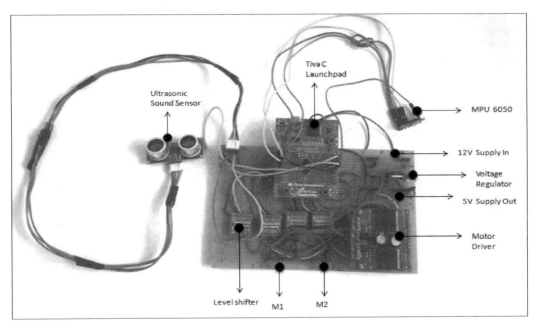

ChefBot PCB prototype

The board is powered with a 12 V battery placed on the base plate. The two motors can be directly connected to the M1 and M2 male connectors. The NUC PC and Kinect are placed on the middle plate. The Launchpad board and Kinect should be connected to the NUC PC via USB. The PC and Kinect are powered using the same 12 V battery itself. We can use a lead-acid or lithium-polymer battery. Here, we are using a lead-acid cell for testing purposes. We will migrate to lithium-polymer for better performance and better backup. The following figure shows the complete assembled diagram of ChefBot:

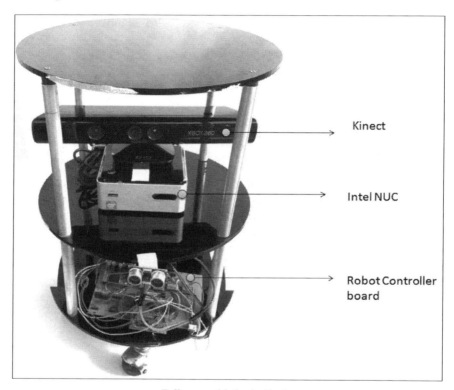

Fully assembled robot body

After assembling all the parts of the robot, we will start working with the robot software. ChefBot's embedded code and ROS packages are available in GitHub. We can clone the code and start working with the software.

Configuring ChefBot PC and setting ChefBot ROS packages

In ChefBot, we are using Intel's NUC PC to handle the robot sensor data and its processing. After procuring the NUC PC, we have to install Ubuntu 14.04.2 or the latest updates of 14.04 LTS. After the installation of Ubuntu, install complete ROS and its packages we mentioned in the previous chapters. We can configure this PC separately, and after the completion of all the settings, we can put this in to the robot. The following are the procedures to install ChefBot packages on the NUC PC.

Clone ChefBot's software packages from GitHub using the following command:

```
$ git clone https://github.com/qboticslabs/Chefbot_ROS_pkg.git
```

We can clone the code in our laptop and copy the chefbot folder to Intel's NUC PC. The chefbot folder consists of the ROS packages of ChefBot. In the NUC PC, create a ROS catkin workspace, copy the chefbot folder and move it inside the src directory of the catkin workspace.

Build and install the source code of ChefBot by simply using the following command This should be executed inside the catkin workspace we created:

```
$ catkin_make
```

If all dependencies are properly installed in NUC, then the ChefBot packages will build and install in this system. After setting the ChefBot packages on the NUC PC, we can switch to the embedded code for ChefBot. Now, we can connect all the sensors in Launchpad. After uploading the code in Launchpad, we can again discuss ROS packages and how to run it. The cloned code from GitHub contains Tiva C LaunchPad code, which is going to be explained in the upcoming section.

Interfacing ChefBot sensors with Tiva C LaunchPad

We have discussed interfacing of individual sensors that we are going to use in ChefBot. In this section, we will discuss how to integrate sensors into the Launchpad board. The Energia code to program Tiva C LaunchPad is available on the cloned files at GitHub. The connection diagram of Tiva C LaunchPad with sensors is as follows. From this figure, we get to know how the sensors are interconnected with Launchpad:

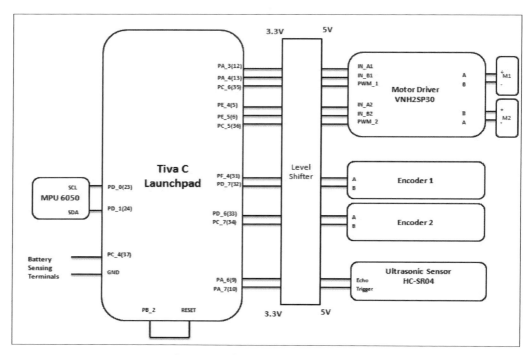

Sensor interfacing diagram of ChefBot

M1 and M2 are two differential drive motors that we are using in this robot. The motors we are going to use here is DC Geared motor with an encoder from Pololu. The motor terminals are connected to the **VNH2SP30** motor driver from Pololu. One of the motors is connected in reverse polarity because in differential steering, one motor rotates opposite to the other. If we send the same control signal to both the motors, each motor will rotate in the opposite direction. To avoid this condition, we will connect it in opposite polarities. The motor driver is connected to Tiva C LaunchPad through a 3.3 V-5 V bidirectional level shifter. One of the level shifter we will use here is available at: https://www.sparkfun.com/products/12009.

The two channels of each encoder are connected to Launchpad via a level shifter. Currently, we are using one ultrasonic distance sensor for obstacle detection. In future, we could expand this number, if required. To get a good odometry estimate, we will put IMU sensor MPU 6050 through an I2C interface. The pins are directly connected to Launchpad because MPU6050 is 3.3 V compatible. To reset Launchpad from ROS nodes, we are allocating one pin as the output and connected to reset pin of Launchpad. When a specific character is sent to Launchpad, it will set the output pin to high and reset the device. In some situations, the error from the calculation may accumulate and it can affect the navigation of the robot. We are resetting Launchpad to clear this error. To monitor the battery level, we are allocating another pin to read the battery value. This feature is not currently implemented in the Energia code.

The code you downloaded from GitHub consists of embedded code. We can see the main section of the code here and there is no need to explain all the sections because we already discussed it.

Embedded code for ChefBot

The main sections of the Launchpad code is discussed here. The following are the header files used in the code:

```
//Library to communicate with I2C devices
#include "Wire.h"
//I2C communication library for MPU6050
#include "I2Cdev.h"
//MPU6050 interfacing library
#include "MPU6050_6Axis_MotionApps20.h"
//Processing incoming serial data
#include <Messenger.h>
//Contain definition of maximum limits of various data type
#include <limits.h>
```

The main libraries used in this code are for the purpose of communicating with MPU 6050 and process the incoming serial data to Launchpad. MPU 6050 can provide the orientation in quaternion or Euler values by using the inbuilt **Digital Motion Processor (DMP)**. The functions to access DMP is written in MPU6050_6Axis_MotionApps20.h. This library has dependencies such as I2Cdev.h and Wire.h; that's why we are including these headers as well. These two libraries are used for I2C communication. The Messenger.h library allows you to handle a stream of text data from any source and helps to extract the data from it. The limits.h header contains definitions of maximum limits of various data types.

After we include the header files, we need to create an object to handle MPU6050 and process the incoming serial data using the `Messenger` class:

```
//Creating MPU6050 Object
MPU6050 accelgyro(0x68);
//Messenger object
Messenger Messenger_Handler = Messenger();
```

After declaring the messenger object, the main section is to assign pins for the motor driver, encoder, ultrasonic sensor, MPU 6050, reset, and battery pins. After assigning the pins, we can see the `setup()` function of the code. The definition of the `setup()` function is given here:

```
//Setup serial, encoders, ultrasonic, MPU6050 and Reset functions
void setup()
{
  //Init Serial port with 115200 baud rate
  Serial.begin(115200);
  //Setup Encoders
  SetupEncoders();
  //Setup Motors
  SetupMotors();
  //Setup Ultrasonic
  SetupUltrasonic();
  //Setup MPU 6050
  Setup_MPU6050();
  //Setup Reset pins
  SetupReset();
  //Set up Messenger object handler
  Messenger_Handler.attach(OnMssageCompleted);
}
```

The preceding function contains custom routine to configure and allocate pins for all the sensors. This function will initialize serial communication with 115,200 baud rate and set pins for the encoder, motor driver, ultrasonic, and MPU6050. The `SetupReset()` function will assign a pin to reset the device, as shown in the connection diagram. We have already seen the setup routines of each sensors in the previous chapters, so there is no need to explain the definition of each functions. The `Messenger` class handler is attached to a function called `OnMssageCompleted()`, which will be called when a data is input to the `Messenger_Handler`.

The following is the main `loop()` function of the code. The main purpose of this function is to read and process serial data and send available sensor values as well:

```
void loop()
{
    //Read from Serial port
    Read_From_Serial();
    //Send time information through serial port
    Update_Time();
    //Send encoders values through serial port
    Update_Encoders();
    //Send ultrasonic values through serial port
    Update_Ultra_Sonic();
    //Update motor speed values with corresponding speed received from
PC and send speed values through serial port
    Update_Motors();
    //Send MPU 6050 values through serial port
    Update_MPU6050();
    //Send battery values through serial port
    Update_Battery();
}
```

The `Read_From_Serial()` function will read serial data from the PC and feed data to the `Messenger_Handler` handler for processing purpose. The `Update_Time()` function will update the time after each operation in the embedded board. We can take this time value to process in the PC or take the PC time for processing.

We can compile the code in Energia IDE and can burn the code in Launchpad. After uploading the code, we can discuss the ROS nodes to handle the Launchpad sensor values.

Writing a ROS Python driver for ChefBot

After uploading the embedded code to Launchpad, the next step is to handle the serial data from Launchpad and convert it to ROS Topics for further processing. The `launchpad_node.py` ROS Python driver node interfaces Tiva C LaunchPad to ROS. The `launchpad_node.py` file is on the `script` folder, which is inside the `chefbot_bringup` package. The following is the explanation of `launchpad_node.py` in important code sections:

```
#ROS Python client
import rospy
import sys
```

```
import time
import math

#This python module helps to receive values from serial port which
execute in a thread
from SerialDataGateway import SerialDataGateway
#Importing required ROS data types for the code
from std_msgs.msg import Int16,Int32, Int64, Float32,
String, Header, UInt64
#Importing ROS data type for IMU
from sensor_msgs.msg import Imu
```

The `launchpad_node.py` file imports the preceding modules. The main modules we can see is `SerialDataGateway`. This is a custom module written to receive serial data from the Launchpad board in a thread. We also need some data types of ROS to handle the sensor data. The main function of the node is given in the following code snippet:

```
if __name__ =='__main__':
  rospy.init_node('launchpad_ros',anonymous=True)
  launchpad = Launchpad_Class()
  try:

    launchpad.Start()
    rospy.spin()
  except rospy.ROSInterruptException:
    rospy.logwarn("Error in main function")

  launchpad.Reset_Launchpad()
  launchpad.Stop()
```

The main class of this node is called `Launchpad_Class()`. This class contains all the methods to start, stop, and convert serial data to ROS Topics. In the main function, we will create an object of `Launchpad_Class()`. After creating the object, we will call the `Start()` method, which will start the serial communication between Tiva C LaunchPad and PC. If we interrupt the driver node by pressing *Ctrl + C*, it will reset the Launchpad and stop the serial communication between the PC and Launchpad.

The following code snippet is from the constructor function of `Launchpad_Class()`. In the following snippet, we will retrieve the port and baud rate of the Launchpad board from ROS parameters and initialize the `SerialDateGateway` object using these parameters. The `SerialDataGateway` object calls the `_HandleReceivedLine()` function inside this class when any incoming serial data arrives on the serial port.

This function will process each line of serial data and extract, convert, and insert it to the appropriate headers of each ROS Topic data type:

```
#Get serial port and baud rate of Tiva C Launchpad
port = rospy.get_param("~port", "/dev/ttyACM0")
baudRate = int(rospy.get_param("~baudRate", 115200))

##################################################################
rospy.loginfo("Starting with serial port:
" + port + ", baud rate: " + str(baudRate))

#Initializing SerialDataGateway object with serial port, baud
 rate and callback function to handle incoming serial data
self._SerialDataGateway = SerialDataGateway(port,
baudRate, self._HandleReceivedLine)
rospy.loginfo("Started serial communication")


##################################################################
##Subscribers and Publishers

#Publisher for left and right wheel encoder values
self._Left_Encoder = rospy.Publisher('lwheel',Int64,queue_size
= 10)
self._Right_Encoder = rospy.Publisher('rwheel',Int64,queue_size
= 10)

#Publisher for Battery level(for upgrade purpose)
self._Battery_Level =
rospy.Publisher('battery_level',Float32,queue_size = 10)
#Publisher for Ultrasonic distance sensor
self._Ultrasonic_Value =
rospy.Publisher('ultrasonic_distance',Float32,queue_size = 10)

#Publisher for IMU rotation quaternion values
self._qx_ = rospy.Publisher('qx',Float32,queue_size = 10)
self._qy_ = rospy.Publisher('qy',Float32,queue_size = 10)
self._qz_ = rospy.Publisher('qz',Float32,queue_size = 10)
self._qw_ = rospy.Publisher('qw',Float32,queue_size = 10)

#Publisher for entire serial data
self._SerialPublisher = rospy.Publisher('serial',
String,queue_size=10)
```

We will create the ROS publisher object for sensors such as the encoder, IMU, and ultrasonic sensor as well as for the entire serial data for debugging purpose. We will also subscribe the speed commands for the left-hand side and the right-hand side wheel of the robot. When a speed command arrives on Topic, it calls the respective callbacks to send speed commands to the robot's Launchpad:

```
self._left_motor_speed = rospy.Subscriber('left_wheel_
speed',Float32,self._Update_Left_Speed)
self._right_motor_speed = rospy.Subscriber('right_wheel_
speed',Float32,self._Update_Right_Speed)
```

After setting the ChefBot driver node, we need to interface the robot to a ROS navigation stack in order to perform autonomous navigation. The basic requirement for doing autonomous navigation is that the robot driver nodes, receive velocity command from ROS navigational stack. The robot can be controlled using teleoperation. In addition to these features, the robot must be able to compute its positional or odometry data and generate the tf data for sending into navigational stack. There must be a PID controller to control the robot motor velocity. The following ROS package helps to perform these functions. The `differential_drive` package contains nodes to perform the preceding operation. We are reusing these nodes in our package to implement these functionalities. The following is the link for the `differential_drive` package in ROS:

`http://wiki.ros.org/differential_drive`

The following figure shows how these nodes communicate with each other. We can also discuss the use of other nodes too:

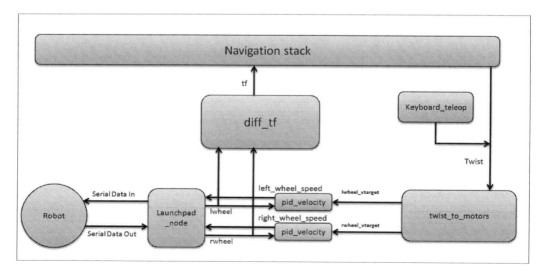

The purpose of each node in the `chefbot_bringup` package is as follows:

- `twist_to_motors.py`: This node will convert the ROS `Twist` command or linear and angular velocity to individual motor velocity target. The target velocities are published at a rate of the ~rate Hertz and the publish `timeout_ticks` times velocity after the `Twist` message stops. The following are the Topics and parameters that will be published and subscribed by this node:
    - Publishing Topics:
        - `lwheel_vtarget` (std_msgs/Float32): This is the the target velocity of the left wheel(m/s).
        - `rwheel_vtarget` (std_msgs/Float32): This is the target velocity of the right wheel(m/s).
    - Subscribing Topics:
        - `Twist` (geometry_msgs/Twist): This is the target `Twist` command for the robot. The linear velocity in the x direction and angular velocity theta of the Twist messages are used in this robot.
    - Important ROS parameters:
        - `~base_width` (float, default: 0.1): This is the distance between the robot's two wheels in meters.
        - `~rate` (int, default: 50): This is the rate at which velocity target is published(Hertz).
        - `~timeout_ticks` (int, default:2): This is the number of the velocity target message published after stopping the Twist messages.
- `pid_velocity.py`: This is a simple PID controller to control the speed of each motors by taking feedback from wheel encoders. In a differential drive system, we need one PID controller for each wheel. It will read the encoder data from each wheels and control the speed of each wheels.
    - Publishing Topics:
        - `motor_cmd` (Float32): This is the final output of the PID controller that goes to the motor. We can change the range of the PID output using the out_min and out_max ROS parameter.
        - `wheel_vel` (Float32): This is the current velocity of the robot wheel in m/s.

- ° Subscribing Topics:
  - ° `wheel` (`Int16`): This Topic is the output of a rotary encoder. There are individual Topics for each encoder of the robot.
  - ° `wheel_vtarget` (`Float32`): This is the target velocity in m/s.
- ° Important parameters:
  - ° `~Kp` (`float` ,`default: 10`): This parameter is the proportional gain of the PID controller.
  - ° `~Ki` (`float, default: 10`): This parameter is the integral gain of the PID controller.
  - ° `~Kd` (`float, default: 0.001`): This parameter is the derivative gain of the PID controller.
  - ° `~out_min` (`float, default: 255`): This is the minimum limit of the velocity value to motor. This parameter limits the velocity value to motor called `wheel_vel` Topic.
  - ° `~out_max` (`float, default: 255`): This is the maximum limit of `wheel_vel` Topic(Hertz).
  - ° `~rate` (`float, default: 20`): This is the rate of publishing `wheel_vel` Topic.
  - ° `ticks_meter` (`float, default: 20`): This is the number of wheel encoder ticks per meter. This is a global parameter because it's used in other nodes too.
  - ° `vel_threshold` (`float, default: 0.001`): If the robot velocity drops below this parameter, we consider the wheel as stopped. If the velocity of the wheel is less than `vel_threshold`, we consider it as zero.
  - ° `encoder_min` (`int, default: 32768`): This is the minimum value of encoder reading.
  - ° `encoder_max` (`int, default: 32768`): This is the maximum value of encoder reading.
  - ° `wheel_low_wrap` (`int, default: 0.3 * (encoder_max - encoder_min) + encoder_min`): These values decide whether the odometry is in negative or positive direction.
  - ° `wheel_high_wrap` (`int, default: 0.7 * (encoder_max - encoder_min) + encoder_min`): These values decide whether the odometry is in the negative or positive direction.

- `diff_tf.py`: This node computes the transformation of odometry and broadcast between the odometry frame and the robot base frame.

  - Publishing Topics:

    - `odom` (`nav_msgs/odometry`): This publishes the odometry (current pose and twist of the robot.

    - `tf`: This provides transformation between the odometry frame and the robot base link.

  - Subscribing Topics:

    - `lwheel` (`std_msgs/Int16`), `rwheel` (`std_msgs/Int16`): These are the output values from the left and right encoder of the robot.

- `chefbot_keyboard_teleop.py`: This node sends the `Twist` command using controls from the keyboard.

  - Publishing Topics:

    - `cmd_vel_mux/input/teleop` (`geometry_msgs/Twist`): This publishes the twist messages using keyboard commands.

After discussing nodes in the `chefbot_bringup` package, we will look at the functions of launch files.

Understanding ChefBot ROS launch files

We will discuss the functions of each launch files of the `chefbot_bringup` package.

- `robot_standalone.launch`: The main function of this launch file is to start nodes such as `launchpad_node`, `pid_velocity`, `diff_tf`, and `twist_to_motor` to get sensor values from the robot and to send command velocity to the robot.

- `keyboard_teleop.launch`: This launch file will start the teleoperation by using the keyboard. This launch starts the `chefbot_keyboard_teleop.py` node to perform the keyboard teleoperation.

- `3dsensor.launch`: This file will launch Kinect OpenNI drivers and start publishing RGB and depth stream. It will also start the depth stream to laser scanner node, which will convert point cloud to laser scan data.

- `gmapping_demo.launch`: This launch file will start SLAM gmapping nodes to map the area surrounding the robot.

- `amcl_demo.launch`: Using AMCL, the robot can localize and predict where it stands on the map. After localizing on the map, we can command the robot to move to a position on the map, then the robot can move autonomously from its current position to the goal position.

- `view_robot.launch`: This launch file displays the robot URDF model in RViz.

- `view_navigation.launch`: This launch file displays all the sensors necessary for the navigation of the robot.

Working with ChefBot Python nodes and launch files

We already set ChefBot ROS packages in Intel's NUC PC and uploaded the embedded code to the Launchpad board. The next step is to put the NUC PC on the robot, configure remote connection from the laptop to the robot, testing each nodes, and working with ChefBot Launch files to perform autonomous navigation.

The main device we should have before working with ChefBot is a good wireless router. The robot and the remote laptop have to connect on the same network. If the robot PC and remote laptop are on the same network, the user can connect from the remote laptop to the robot PC through SSH using its IP. Before putting the robot PC in the robot, we should connect the robot PC in the wireless network, so once it's connected to the wireless network, it will remember the connection details. When the robot powers, the PC should automatically connect to the wireless network. Once the robot PC is connected to the wireless network, we can put it in the actual robot. The following figure shows the connection diagram of the robot and remote PC:

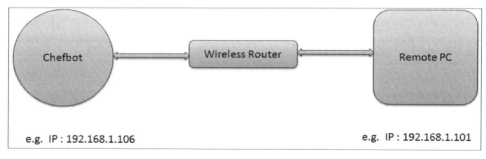

Wireless connection diagram of the robot and remote PC

The preceding figure assumes that the ChefBot IP is **192.168.1.106** and the remote PC IP is **192.168.1.101**.

We can remotely access the ChefBot terminal using SSH. We can use the following command to log in to ChefBot, where `robot` is the username of ChefBot PC:

```
$ ssh robot@192.168.1.106
```

When you log in to ChefBot PC, it will ask for the robot PC password. After entering the password of the robot PC, we can access the robot PC terminal. After logging in to the robot PC, we can start testing the ROS nodes of ChefBot and test whether we can receive the serial values from the Launchpad board inside ChefBot. Note that you should log in again to ChefBot PC through SSH if you are using a new terminal.

If the `Chefbot_bringup` package is properly installed on the PC and if the Launchpad board is connected, then before running the ROS driver node, we can run the `miniterm.py` tool to check whether the serial values come properly to the PC via USB. We can find the serial device name using the `dmesg` command. We can run `miniterm.py` using the following command:

```
$ miniterm.py /dev/ttyACM0 115200
```

If it shows the permission denied message, set the permission of the USB device by writing rules on the `udev` folder as we did in *Chapter 5, Working with Robotic Actuators* and Wheel Encoders of this book or we can temporarily change the permission using the following command. We are assuming `ttyACM0` is the device name of Launchpad. If the device name is different in your PC, then you have to use that name instead of `ttyACM0`:

```
$ sudo chmod 777 /dev/ttyACM0
```

If everything works fine, we will get values like those shown in following screenshot:

The letter b is used to indicate the battery reading of the robot; currently, it's not implemented. The value is set to zero now. The letter t indicates the total time in microseconds after the robot starts running the embedded code. The second value is time in seconds; it's the time taken to complete one entire operation in Launchpad. We can use this value if we are performing real-time calculations of the parameters of the robot. Currently, we are not using this value; we may use this in the future. The letter e indicates values of the left and right encoder respectively. Both the values are zero here because the robot is not moving. The letter u indicates the values from the ultrasonic distance sensor. The distance value we get is in centimeters. The letter s indicates the current robot wheel speed of the robot. This value is for inspection purpose. Actually, speed is a control output from the PC itself.

To convert these serial data to ROS Topics, we have to run the drive node called launchpad_node.py. The following code shows how to execute this node.

First, we have to run roscore before starting any nodes:

```
$ roscore
```

Run launchpad_node.py using the following command:

```
$ rosrun chefbot_bringup launchpad_node.py
```

If everything works fine, we will get the following output in the node running terminal:

```
robot@robot-desktop:~$ rosrun chefbot_bringup launchpad_node.py
Initializing Launchpad Class
[INFO] [WallTime: 1424097603.219564] Starting with serial port: /dev/ttyACM0, bau
d rate: 115200
[INFO] [WallTime: 1424097603.220825] Started serial communication
```

After running launchpad_node.py, we will see the following Topics generated, as given in the following screenshot:

```
robot@robot-desktop:~$ rostopic list
/battery_level
/imu/data
/left_wheel_speed
/lwheel
/qw
/qx
/qy
/qz
/right_wheel_speed
/rosout
/rosout_agg
/rwheel
/serial
/ultrasonic_distance
```

We can view the serial data received by driver node by subscribing /serial Topic. We can use it for debug purposes. If the serial Topic shows the same data as we saw on miniterm.py, then we can confirm that the nodes are working fine. The following screenshot is the output of /serial Topic:

```
---
data: 16266, in:  e     1        -1
---
data: 16267, in:  u     10
---
data: 16268, in:  s     0.00     0.00
---
```

After setting the chefbot_bringup package, we can start working with the autonomous navigation of ChefBot. Currently, we are accessing only the ChefBot PC's terminal. To visualize the robot model, sensor data, maps, and so on, we have to use RViz in the user's PC. We have to do some configuration in the robot and user PC to perform this operation. It should be noted that the user's PC should have the same software setup as in the ChefBot PC.

The first thing we have to do is, set the ChefBot PC as a ROS master. We can set the ChefBot PC as the ROS master by setting the ROS_MASTER_URI value. ROS_MASTER_URI is a required setting, It informs the nodes about the **Uniform Resource Identifier (URI)** of the ROS master. When you set the same ROS_MASTER_URI for the ChefBot PC and the remote PC, we can access the Topics of the ChefBot PC in the remote PC. So, if we run RViz locally, then it will visualize the Topics generated in the ChefBot PC.

Assume that the ChefBot PC IP is **192.168.1.106** and the remote PC IP is **192.168.1.101**. To set ROS_MASTER_URI in each system, the following command should include the .bashrc file in the home folder. The following figure shows the setup needed to include .bashrc in each system:

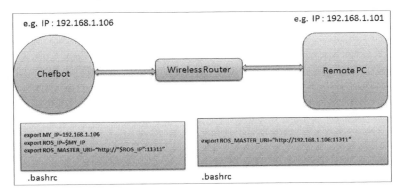

Add these lines at the bottom of `.bashrc` on each PC and change the IP address according to your network.

After we perform these settings, we can just start `roscore` on the ChefBot PC terminal and execute command `rostopic list` on the remote PC.

If you see any Topics, you are done with the settings. We can first run the robot using the keyboard teleoperation to check the robot's functioning and confirm whether we get the sensor values.

We can start the robot driver and other nodes using the following command. Note that this should execute in the ChefBot terminal after login, using SSH:

```
$ roslaunch chefbot_bringup robot_standalone.launch
```

After launching the robot driver and nodes, start the keyboard teleoperation using the following command. This also has to be done on the new terminal of the ChefBot PC:

```
$ roslaunch chefbot_bringup keyboard_teleop.launch
```

To activate Kinect, execute the following command. This command is also executed on the ChefBot terminal:

```
$roslaunch chefbot_bringup 3dsensor.launch
```

To view sensor data, we can execute the following command. This will view the robot model in RViz and should be executed in the remote PC. If we set up the `chefbot_bringup` package in the remote PC, we can access the following command and visualize the robot model and sensor data from ChefBot PC:

```
$ roslaunch chefbot_bringup view_robot.launch
```

The following screenshot is the output of RViz. We can see **LaserScan** and **PointCloud** in the screenshots:

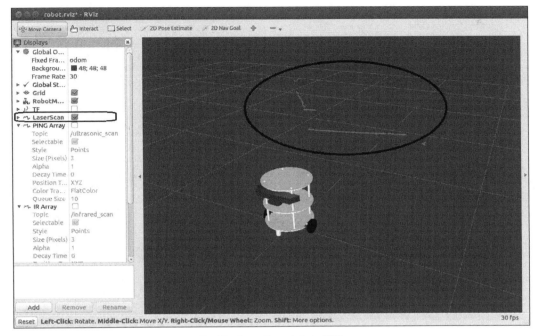

ChefBot LaserScan data in RViz

The preceding screenshot shows **LaserScan** in RViz. We need to tick **LaserScan** Topic from the left-hand side section of RViz to enable the laser scan data. The laser scan data is marked on the viewport. If you want to watch the Point Cloud data from Kinect, click on the **Add** button on the left-hand side of RViz and select **PointCloud2** from the pop up window.

Select **Topic** /camera/depth_registered from the list and you will see the following screenshot:

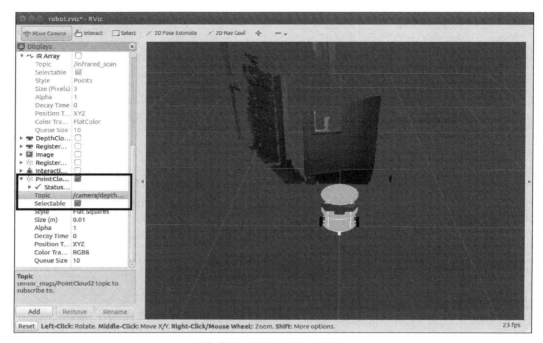

ChefBot with Point Cloud data

After working with sensors, we can perform SLAM to map the room. The following procedure helps to start SLAM on this robot.

Working with SLAM on ROS to build the map of the room

To perform gmapping, we have to execute the following commands:

Starting the robot driver in the ChefBot terminal:

```
$ roslaunch chefbot_bringup robot_standalone.launch
```

Execute the following command to start the gmapping process. Note that it should be executed on the ChefBot terminal:

```
$ roslaunch chefbot_bringup gmapping_demo.launch
```

Gmapping will only work if the odometry value received is proper. If the odometry value is received from the robot, we will receive the following message for the preceding command. If we get this message, we can confirm that gmapping will work fine:

```
[ INFO] [1422618733.585407153]: Created local_planner dwa_local_planner/DWAPlanner
ROS
[ INFO] [1422618733.604762090]: Sim period is set to 0.20
[ INFO] [1422618735.208493249]: odom received!
```

To start the keyboard teleoperation, use the following command:

```
$ roslaunch chefbot_bringup keyboard_teleop.launch
```

To view the map being created, we need to start RViz in the remote system using the following command:

```
$ roslaunch chefbot_bringup view_navigation.launch
```

After viewing the robot in RViz, you can move the robot using the keyboard and see the map being created. When it maps the entire area, we can save the map using the following command on the ChefBot PC terminal:

```
$rosrun map_server map_saver -f ~/test_map
```

where `test_map` is the name of the map being stored on the `home` folder. The following screenshot shows the map of a room created by the robot:

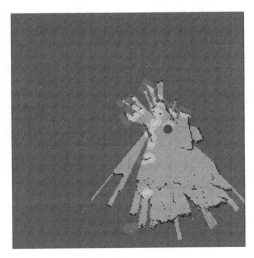

Mapping a room

After the map is stored, we can work with the localization and autonomous navigation using ROS.

Working with ROS localization and navigation

After building the map, close all the applications and rerun the robot driver using the following command:

```
$ roslaunch chefbot_bringup robot_standalone.launch
```

Start localization and navigation on the stored map using the following command:

```
$ roslaunch chefbot_bringup amcl_demo.launch map_file:=~/test_map.yaml
```

Start viewing the robot using the following command in the remote PC:

```
$ roslaunch chefbot_bringup view_navigation.launch
```

In RViz, we may need to specify the initial pose of the robot using the **2D Pose Estimate** button. We can change the robot pose on the map using this button. If the robot is able to locate the map, then we can use the **2D Nav Goal** button to command the robot to move to the desired position. When we start localization, we can see the particle cloud by the AMCL algorithm around the robot:

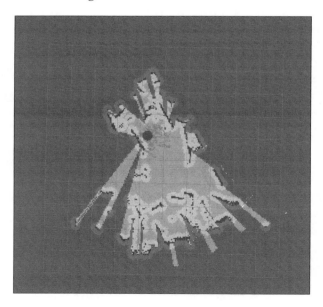

The following is a screenshot of the robot that navigates autonomously from the current position to the goal position. The goal position is marked as a black dot:

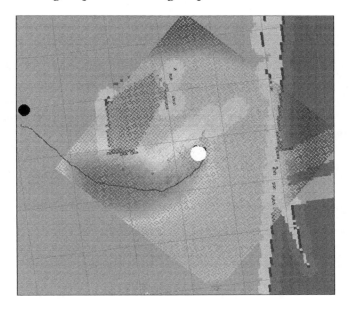

The black line from the robot to the black dot is the robot's planned path to reach the goal position. If the robot is not able to locate the map, we might need to fine-tune the parameter files in the `Chefbot_bringup param` folder. For more fine tuning details, you can go through the AMCL package on ROS. You can visit the following link:

`http://wiki.ros.org/amcl?distro=indigo`

Questions

1. What is use of the robot ROS driver node?
2. What is the role of the PID controller in navigation?
3. How to convert the encoder data to odometry data?
4. What is role of SLAM in robot navigation?
5. What is role of AMCL in robot navigation?

Summary

This chapter was about assembling the hardware of ChefBot and integrating the embedded and ROS code into the robot to perform autonomous navigation. We saw the robot hardware parts that were manufactured using the design from *Chapter 5, Working with Robotic Actuators and Wheel Encoders*. We assembled individual sections of the robot and connected the prototype PCB that we designed for the robot. This consists of the Launchpad board, motor driver, left shifter, ultrasonic, and IMU. The Launchpad board was flashed with the new embedded code, which can interface all sensors in the robot and can send or receive data from the PC. After discussing the embedded code, we wrote the ROS Python driver node to interface the serial data from the Launchpad board. After interfacing the Launchpad board, we computed the odometry data and differential drive controlling using nodes from the `differential_drive` package that existed in the ROS repository. We interfaced the robot to ROS navigation stack. This enables to perform SLAM and AMCL for autonomous navigation. We also discussed SLAM, AMCL, created map, and executed autonomous navigation on the robot.

11
Designing a GUI for a Robot Using Qt and Python

In the last chapter, we discussed the integration of robotic hardware components and software packages for performing autonomous navigation. After the integration, the next step is to build a GUI to control the robot. We are building a GUI that can act as a trigger for the underlying ROS commands. Instead of running all the commands on the terminal, the user can work with the GUI buttons. The GUI we are going to design is for a typical hotel room with nine tables. The user can set a table position in the map of the hotel room and command the robot to go to a particular table to deliver food. After delivering the food, the user can command the robot to go to its home position.

Some of the most popular GUI frameworks currently available are Qt (`http://qt.digia.com`) and GTK+ (`http://www.gtk.org/`), Qt and GTK+ are open source, cross-platform user interface toolkits and development platforms. These two software frameworks are widely used in Linux desktop environments, like GNOME and KDE.

In this chapter, we will be using Python binding of the Qt framework to implement the GUI because Python binding of Qt is more stable than other UI Python bindings. We can see how to develop a GUI from scratch and program it using Python. After discussing basic Python and Qt programming, we will discuss ROS interfaces of Qt, which are already available in ROS. We will first look at what is the Qt UI framework is and how to install it on our PC.

Installing Qt on Ubuntu 14.04.2 LTS

Qt is a cross-platform application framework that is widely used to develop application software with a GUI interface as well as command line tools. Qt is available on almost all operating systems, like Windows, Mac OS X, Android, and so on. The main programming language used for developing Qt applications is C++ but there are bindings available for languages such as Python, Ruby, Java, and so on. Let's take a look at how to install Qt SDK on Ubuntu 14.04.2. We will install Qt from the **Advance Packaging Tool** (**APT**) in Ubuntu. The APT already comes with the Ubuntu installation. So for installing Qt/Qt SDK, we can simply use the following command, which will install Qt SDK and its required dependencies from the Ubuntu package repository. We can install Qt version 4 using the following command:

```
$ sudo apt-get install qt-sdk
```

This command will install the entire Qt SDK and its libraries required for our project. The packages available on Ubuntu repositories may not be the latest versions. To get the latest version of Qt, we can download the online or offline installer of Qt for various OS platforms from the following link:

http://qt-project.org/downloads

After installing Qt on our system, we can see how we can develop a GUI using Qt and interface with Python.

Working with Python bindings of Qt

Let's see how we can interface Python and Qt. In general, there are two modules available in Python for connecting to the Qt user interface. The two most popular frameworks are:

- PyQt
- PySide

PyQt

PyQt is one of the popular most Python bindings for Qt cross-platform. PyQt is developed and maintained by Riverbank Computing Limited. It provides binding for Qt version 4 and Qt version 5, and comes with GPL (version 2 or 3) along with a commercial license. PyQt is available for Qt version 4 and 5, called PyQt4 and PyQt5, respectively. These two modules are compatible with Python versions 2 and 3. PyQt contains more than 620 classes that cover user interface, XML, network communication, web, and so on.

PyQt is available on Windows, Linux, and Mac OS X. It is a prerequisite to install Qt SDK and Python in order to install PyQt. The binaries for Windows and Mac OS X are available on the following link:

```
http://www.riverbankcomputing.com/software/pyqt/download
```

We can see how to install PyQt4 on Ubuntu 14.04.2 using Python 2.7.

Installing PyQt on Ubuntu 14.04.2 LTS

If you want to install PyQt on Ubuntu/Linux, use the following command. This command will install the PyQt library, its dependencies, and some Qt tools:

```
$ sudo apt-get install python-qt4 pyqt4-dev-tools
```

PySide

PySide is an open source software project that provides Python binding for the Qt framework. The PySide project was initiated by Nokia, and offers a full set of Qt binding for multiple platforms. The technique used in PySide to wrap the Qt library is different from PyQt, but the API of both is similar. PySide is currently not supported on Qt 5. PySide is available for Windows, Linux, and Mac OS X. The following link will guide you to set up PySide on Windows and Mac OS X:

```
http://qt-project.org/wiki/Category:LanguageBindings::PySide::Downloads
```

The prerequisites of PySide are the same as PyQt. Let's see how we can install PySide on Ubuntu 14.04.2 LTS.

Installing PySide on Ubuntu 14.04.2 LTS

The PySide package is available on the Ubuntu package repository. The following command will install the PySide module and Qt tools on Ubuntu:

```
$ sudo apt-get install python-pyside pyside-tools
```

Let's work with both modules and see the differences between both.

Working with PyQt and PySide

After installing the PyQt and PySide packages, we can see how to write a **Hello World** GUI using PyQt and PySide. The main difference between PyQt and PySide is only in some commands; most of the steps are the same. Let's see how to make a Qt GUI and convert it into Python code.

Introducing Qt Designer

Qt Designer is the tool for designing and inserting control into Qt GUI. Qt GUI is basically an XML file that contains the information of its components and controls. The first step to work with GUI is its designing. The Qt Designer tool provides various options to make excellent GUIs.

Start Qt Designer by entering the command `designer-qt4` in the terminal. The following image shows what you will be able to see after running this command:

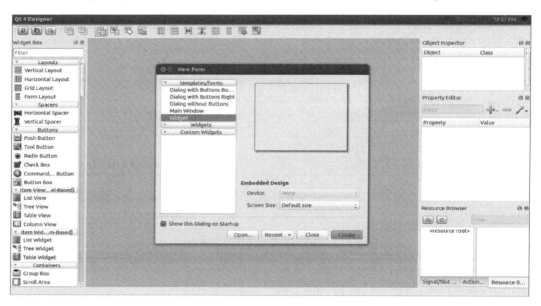

The preceding image shows the Qt designer interface. Select the **Widget** option from the **New Form** window and click on the **Create** button. This will create an empty widget; we can drag various GUI controls from the left-hand side of Qt 4 designer to the empty widget. Qt widgets are the basic building blocks of Qt GUI.

The following image shows a form with a **PushButton** dragged from the left-hand side window of Qt Designer:

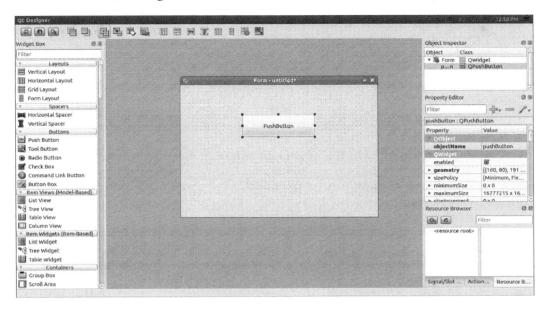

The **Hello World** application that we are going to build has a **PushButton**, when we click on the **PushButton**, a **Hello World** message will be printed on the terminal. Before building the **Hello World** application, we need to understand what Qt signals and slots are, because we have to use these features for building the **Hello World** application.

Qt signals and slots

In Qt, GUI events are handled using the signals and slots features. A signal is emitted from the GUI when an event occurs. Qt Widgets have many predefined signals, and users can add custom signals for GUI events. A slot is a function that is called in response to a particular signal. In this example, we are using the `clicked()` signal of **PushButton** and creating a custom slot for this signal. We can write our own code on this custom function. Let's see how we can create a button, connect a signal to a slot, and convert the entire GUI to Python.

Here are the steps involved in creating the **Hello World** GUI application:

1. Drag and create a **PushButton** from Qt Designer to the empty **Form**.
2. Assign a slot for the button clicked event, which emits a signal called `clicked()`.
3. Save the designed UI file in the `.ui` extension.
4. Convert UI files to Python.
5. Write the definition of the custom slot.
6. Print the **Hello World** message inside the defined slot/function.

We have already dragged a button from Qt Designer to an empty **Form**. Press the *F4* key to insert a slot on the button. When we press *F4*, the **PushButton** turns red, and we can drag a line from the button and place the ground symbol($\perp$) in the main window. This is shown in the following screenshot:

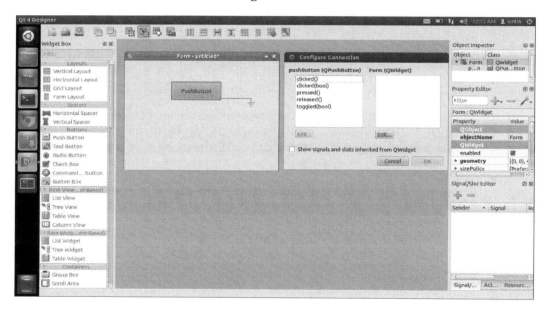

Select the **clicked()** signal from the left-hand side and click on the **Edit..** button to create a new custom slot. When we click on the **Edit..** button, another window will pop up to create a custom function. You can create a custom function by clicking on the + symbol.

We created a custom slot called **message()**, as shown in the screenshot below:

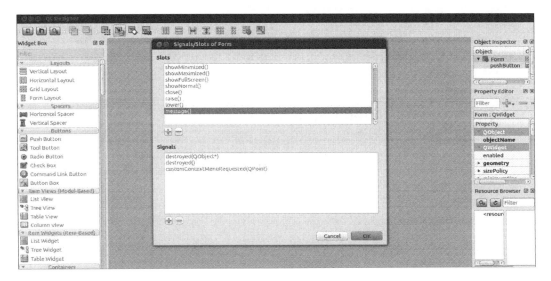

Click on the **OK** button and save the UI file as `hello_world.ui`, and quit the Qt designer. After saving the UI file, let's see how we can convert a Qt UI file into a Python file.

Converting a UI file into Python code

After designing the UI file, we can convert the UI file into its equivalent Python code. The conversion is done using a `pyuic` compiler. We have already installed this tool while installing PyQt/PySide. The following are the commands to convert a Qt UI file into a Python file.

We have to use different commands for PyQt and PySide. The following command is to convert UI into its PyQt equivalent file:

```
$ pyuic4 -x hello_world.ui -o hello_world.py
```

The `pyuic4` is a UI compiler to convert a UI file into its equivalent Python code. We need to mention the UI filename after the `-x` argument and mention the output filename after the `-o` argument.

There are not many changes for the PySide command, instead of `pyuic4`, PySide uses `pyside-uic` to convert UI files into Python files. The remaining arguments are the same:

```
$ pyside-uic -x hello_world.ui -o hello_world.py
```

The preceding command will generate an equivalent Python code for the UI file. If we run this Python code, the UI designed in Qt Designer will pop up. The generated script will not have the definition of the custom function `message()`. We should add this custom function to generate the code. The following procedure will guide you through adding the custom function; so when you click on the button, the custom function `message()` will be executed.

Adding a slot definition to PyQt code

The generated Python code from PyQt is given here. The code generated by `pyuic4` and `pyside-uic` are the same, except in importing module names. All other parts are the same. The explanation of the code generated using PyQt is also applicable to PySide code . The code generated from the above conversion is as follows. The code structure and parameters can change according to the UI file that you have designed:

```python
from PyQt4 import QtCore, QtGui

try:
    _fromUtf8 = QtCore.QString.fromUtf8
except AttributeError:
    _fromUtf8 = lambda s: s

class Ui_Form(object):

    def setupUi(self, Form):
        Form.setObjectName(_fromUtf8("Form"))
        Form.resize(514, 355)

        self.pushButton = QtGui.QPushButton(Form)
        self.pushButton.setGeometry(QtCore.QRect(150, 80, 191, 61))
        self.pushButton.setObjectName(_fromUtf8("pushButton"))

        self.retranslateUi(Form)
        QtCore.QObject.connect(self.pushButton, QtCore.SIGNAL(_
fromUtf8("clicked()")), Form.message)
        QtCore.QMetaObject.connectSlotsByName(Form)


    def retranslateUi(self, Form):
        Form.setWindowTitle(QtGui.QApplication.translate("Form",
"Form", None, QtGui.QApplication.UnicodeUTF8))
```

```
        self.pushButton.setText( QtGui.QApplication.translate("Form",
"Press", None, QtGui.QApplication.UnicodeUTF8))

if __name__ == "__main__":
    import sys
    app = QtGui.QApplication(sys.argv)
    Form = QtGui.QWidget()
    ui = Ui_Form()
    ui.setupUi(Form)
    Form.show()
    sys.exit(app.exec_())
```

The preceding code is the equivalent Python script of the Qt UI file that we designed in the Qt designer application. Here is the step-by-step procedure of the working of this code:

1. The code will start executing from if __name__ == "__main__":. The first thing in a PyQt code is to create a QApplication object. A QApplication class manages the GUI application's control flow and main settings. The QApplication class contains the main event loop, where all events from the Windows system and other sources are processed and dispatched. It also handles initialization and finalization of an application. The QApplication class is inside the QtGui module. This code creates an object of QApplication called app.

2. The Form = QtGui.QWidget() line creates an object called Form from the QWidget class that is present inside the QtGui module. The QWidget class is the base class of all the user interface objects of Qt. It can receive the mouse and keyboard event from the main Windows system.

3. The ui = Ui_Form() line creates an object called ui from the Ui_Form() class defined in the code. The Ui_Form() object can accept the QWidget class that we created in the previous line and it can add buttons, text, button control, and other UI components into this QWidget object. The Ui_Form() class contains two functions: setupUi() and retranslateUi(). We can pass the QWidget object to the function called setupUi(). This function will add UI components on this widget object such as buttons, assigning slots for signals, and so on. The retranslateUi() function will translate the language of the UI to other languages if needed, for example, if we need translation from English to Spanish, we can mention the corresponding Spanish word in this function.

4. The Form.show() line displays the final window with buttons and text.

The next thing is to create the slot function, which prints the **Hello World** message. The slot definition is created inside the `Ui_Form()` class. The following steps insert the slot called `message()` into the `Ui_Form()` class.

The `message()` function definition is as follows:

```
def message(self):
print "Hello World"
```

This should be inserted as a function inside the `Ui_Form()` class. Also, change the following line in the `setupUi()` function inside the `Ui_Form()` class:

```
QtCore.QObject.connect(self.pushButton, QtCore.SIGNAL(_
fromUtf8("clicked()")), Form.message)
```

The `Form.message` parameter should be replaced with the `self.message` parameter. The preceding line connects the **PushBbutton** signal `clicked()` to the `self.message()` slot that we already inserted in the `Ui_Form()` class.

Up and running of Hello World GUI application

After replacing the `Form.message` parameter with the `self.message` parameter, we can execute the code and the output will look like this:

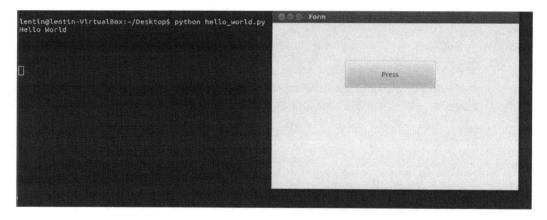

When we click on the **Press** button, it will print the **Hello world** message. This is all about setting a custom GUI with Python and Qt.

In the next section, we will see the actual GUI that we are designing for the robot.

Working with ChefBot's control GUI

After completing the **Hello World** application in PyQt, next we can discuss a GUI for controlling ChefBot. The main use of building a GUI is to create an easier way to control the robot, for example, if the robot is deployed in a hotel to serve food, the person who controls this robot need not have knowledge about the complex commands to start and stop this robot; so building a GUI for ChefBot can reduce the complexity and make it easier for the user. We are planning to build a GUI using PyQt, ROS and Python interface. The ChefBot ROS package is available on GitHub on the following link:

```
https://github.com/qboticslabs/Chefbot_ROS_pkg.git
```

If you haven't cloned the code yet, you can do it now using following command:

```
$ git clone https://github.com/qboticslabs/Chefbot_ROS_pkg.git
```

The GUI code named `robot_gui.py` is placed in the `scripts` folder, which is inside the `chefbot_bringup` package.

The following screenshot shows the GUI that we have designed for ChefBot:

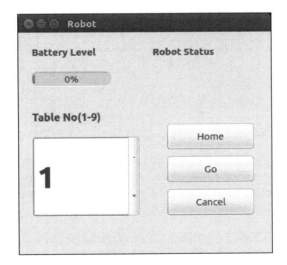

The GUI has the following features:

- It can monitor robot battery status and robot status. Robot status indicates the working status of the robot, for example, if the robot encounters an error, it will indicate the error on this GUI.

- It can command the robot to move into a table position for delivering food. There is a spin box widget on the GUI to input the table position. Currently, we are planning this GUI for a nine table room, but we may expand it into any number according to requirement. After inputting the table number, we can command the robot to go to that table by clicking on the **Go** button; the robot will get into that position. If we want to return the robot to the initial position, we can click on the **Home** button. If we want to cancel the current robot movement, click on **Cancel** to stop the robot. The working of this GUI application is as follows:

When we have to deploy ChefBot in a hotel, the first procedure that we have to do is to create a map of the room. After mapping the entire room properly, we have to save the map on the robot's PC. The robot does the mapping only once, after mapping we can run the localization and navigation routines, and command the robot to get into a position on the map. The ChefBot ROS package comes with a map and simulation model of a hotel-like environment. We can run this simulation and localization now for testing the GUI and in the next chapter, we can discuss how to control the hardware using the GUI. If you install ChefBot ROS packages on your local system, we can simulate a hotel environment and test the GUI.

Start the ChefBot simulation in a hotel-like arrangement using the following command:

```
$roslaunch chefbot_gazebo chefbot_hotel_world.launch
```

After starting the ChefBot simulation, we can run the localization and navigation routines using an already built map. The map is placed on the chefbot_bringup package. We can see a map folder inside this package. Here, we will use this map for performing this test. We can load the localization and navigation routine using the following command:

```
$ roslaunch chefbot_gazebo amcl_demo.launch
map_file:=/home/lentin/catkin_ws/src/chefbot/chefbot_bringup/map/hotel1.
yaml
```

The path of the map file can change in a different system, so use the path in your system instead of this path.

If the path mentioned is correct, it will start running the ROS navigation stack. If we want to see the robot position on the map or manually set the initial position of robot, we can use RViz using the following command:

```
$ roslaunch chefbot_bringup view_navigation.launch
```

In RViz, we can command the robot to go to any map coordinates using the **2D Nav Goal** button.

We can command the robot to go to any map coordinates using programming too. The ROS navigation stack is working using the ROS actionlib library. The ROS actionlib library is for performing preemptable tasks, it is similar to ROS Services. An advantage over ROS services is that we can cancel the request if we don't want it at that time.

In the GUI, we can command the robot to go to a map coordinate using Python actionlib library. We can get the table position on the map using the following technique.

After starting the simulator and AMCL nodes, launch the keyboard teleoperation and move the robot near each table. Use the following command to get the translation and rotation of the robot:

```
$ rosrun tf tf_echo /map /base_link
```

When we click on the **Go** button, that position is fed to the navigation stack and the robot plans its path and reaches its goal. We can even cancel the task at anytime. So the ChefBot GUI acts as an actionlib client, which sends map coordinates to the actionlib server, that is, the navigation stack.

We can run the robot GUI now to control the robot using the following command:

```
$ rosrun chefbot_bringup robot_gui.py
```

We can select a table number and click on the **Go** button for moving robot to each table.

Assuming that you cloned the files and got the robot_gui.py file, we can discuss the main slots we added into the Ui_Form() class for the actionlib client and to get values of battery level and robot status.

We need to import the following Python modules for this GUI application:

```
import rospy
import actionlib
from move_base_msgs.msg import *
import time
from PyQt4 import QtCore, QtGui
```

The additional modules we require are ROS Python client `rospy`, and the `actionlib` module to send values to the navigation stack. The `move_base_msgs` module contains the message definition of the goal that needs to be sent to the navigation stack.

The robot position near each table is mentioned in a Python dictionary. The following code shows hardcode values of the robot's position near each table:

```
table_position = dict()
table_position[0] = (-0.465, 0.37, 0.010, 0, 0, 0.998, 0.069)
table_position[1] = (0.599, 1.03, 0.010, 0, 0, 1.00, -0.020)
table_position[2] = (4.415, 0.645, 0.010, 0, 0, -0.034, 0.999)
table_position[3] = (7.409, 0.812, 0.010, 0, 0, -0.119, 0.993)
table_position[4] = (1.757, 4.377, 0.010, 0, 0, -0.040, 0.999)
table_position[5] = (1.757, 4.377, 0.010, 0, 0, -0.040, 0.999)
table_position[6] = (1.757, 4.377, 0.010, 0, 0, -0.040, 0.999)
table_position[7] = (1.757, 4.377, 0.010, 0, 0, -0.040, 0.999)
table_position[8] = (1.757, 4.377, 0.010, 0, 0, -0.040, 0.999)
table_position[9] = (1.757, 4.377, 0.010, 0, 0, -0.040, 0.999)
```

We can access the position of the robot near each table by accessing this dictionary.

Currently, we have inserted only four values for a demonstration purpose. You can add more values by finding the position of other tables.

We are assigning some variables to handle the table number, the position of robot and the `actionlib` client inside the `Ui_Form()` class.

```
#Handle table number from spin box
self.table_no = 0
#Stores current table robot position
self.current_table_position = 0
#Creating Actionlib client
self.client = actionlib.SimpleActionClient('move_base',MoveBaseAction)
#Creating goal message definition
self.goal = MoveBaseGoal()
#Start this function for updating battery and robot status
self.update_values()
```

The following code shows the signals and slots assignment in this code for buttons and spin box widgets:

```
#Handle spinbox signal and assign to slot set_table_number()
QtCore.QObject.connect(self.spinBox, QtCore.SIGNAL(_
fromUtf8("valueChanged(int)")), self.set_table_number)
```

```
#Handle Home button signal and assign to slot Home()
QtCore.QObject.connect(self.pushButton_3, QtCore.SIGNAL(_
fromUtf8("clicked()")), self.Home)

#Handle Go button signal and assign to slot Go()
QtCore.QObject.connect(self.pushButton, QtCore.SIGNAL(_
fromUtf8("clicked()")), self.Go)

#Handle Cancel button signal and assign to slot Cancel()
QtCore.QObject.connect(self.pushButton_2, QtCore.SIGNAL(_
fromUtf8("clicked()")), self.Cancel)
```

The following slot handles the spin box value from the UI and assigns a table number. Also, it converts the table number to the corresponding robot position:

```
def set_table_number(self):
    self.table_no = self.spinBox.value()
    self.current_table_position = table_position[self.table_no]
```

Here is the definition of the **Go** slot for the **Go** button. This function will insert into the robot position of the selected table in a goal message header and send it to the navigation stack:

```
def Go(self):

    #Assigning x,y,z pose and orientation to target_pose message
    self.goal.target_pose.pose.position.x=float(self.current_table_
position[0])

    self.goal.target_pose.pose.position.y=float(self.current_table_
position[1])
    self.goal.target_pose.pose.position.z=float(self.current_table_
position[2])

    self.goal.target_pose.pose.orientation.x =    float(self.current_
table_position[3])
    self.goal.target_pose.pose.orientation.y=    float(self.current_
table_position[4])
    self.goal.target_pose.pose.orientation.z=    float(self.current_
table_position[5])

    #Frame id
    self.goal.target_pose.header.frame_id= 'map'
```

```
#Time stamp
self.goal.target_pose.header.stamp = rospy.Time.now()

#Sending goal to navigation stack
self.client.send_goal(self.goal)
```

The following code is the `Cancel()` slot definition. This will cancel all the robot paths that it was planning to perform at that time.

```
def Cancel(self):
    self.client.cancel_all_goals()
```

The following code is the definition of `Home()`. This will set the table position to zero, and call the `Go()` function. The table at position zero is the home position of the robot:

```
def Home(self):
    self.current_table_position = table_position[0]
    self.Go()
```

The following definitions are for the `update_values()` and `add()` functions. The `update_values()` method will start updating the battery level and robot status in a thread. The `add()` function will retrieve the ROS parameters of the battery status and robot status, and set them to the progress bar and label, respectively:

```
def update_values(self):
    self.thread = WorkThread()
    QtCore.QObject.connect( self.thread,    QtCore.
SIGNAL("update(QString)"), self.add )
    self.thread.start()
def add(self,text):
  battery_value = rospy.get_param("battery_value")
  robot_status = rospy.get_param("robot_status")
    self.progressBar.setProperty("value", battery_value)
      self.label_4.setText(_fromUtf8(robot_status))
```

The `WorkThread()` class used in the preceding function is given here. The `WorkThread()` class is inherited from `QThread` provided by Qt for threading. The thread simply emits the signal `update(Qstring)` with a particular delay. In the preceding function `update_values()`, the `update(QString)` signal is connected to the `self.add()` slot; so when a signal `update(QString)` is emitted from thread, it will call the `add()` slot and update the battery and status value:

```
class WorkThread(QtCore.QThread):
  def __init__(self):
```

```
    QtCore.QThread.__init__(self)
def __del__(self):
 self.wait()
def run(self):
 while True:
    time.sleep(0.3) # artificial time delay
    self.emit( QtCore.SIGNAL('update(QString)'), " " )
    return
```

We have discussed how to make a GUI for ChefBot, but this GUI is only for the user who controls ChefBot. If someone wants to debug and inspect the robot data, we may have to go for other tools. ROS provides an excellent debugging tool to visualize data from the robot.

The rqt tool is one of the most popular ROS tools, which is based on a Qt-based framework for GUI development for ROS. Let's discuss the rqt tool, installation procedure, and how we can inspect the sensor data from the robot.

Installing and working with rqt in Ubuntu 14.04.2 LTS

rqt is a software framework in ROS, which implements various GUI tools in the form of plugins. We can add plugins as dockable windows in rqt.

Installing rqt in Ubuntu 14.04.2 can be done using the following command. Before installing, ensure that you have the full installation of ROS Indigo.

```
$ sudo apt-get install ros-indigo-rqt
```

After installing the rqt packages, we can access the GUI implementation of rqt called rqt_gui, in which we can dock rqt plugins in a single window.

Let's start using rqt_gui.

Run the roscore command before running rqt_gui:

```
$ roscore
```

Run the following command to start rqt_gui:

```
$ rosrun rqt_gui rqt_gui
```

We will get the following window if the commands work fine:

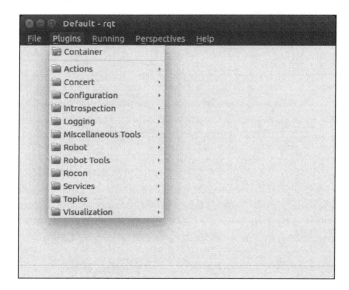

We can load and unload plugins at run time. To analyze the ROS message log, we can load the **Console** plugin from **Plugins | Logging | Console**. In the following example, we load the **Console** plugin and run a talker node inside `rospy_tutorials`, which will send a **Hello World** message to a Topic called `/chatter`.

Run the following command to start the node `talker.py`:

```
$rosrun rospy_tutorials talker.py
```

In the following screenshot, `rqt_gui` is loaded with two plugins named **Console** and **Topic Monitor**. The **Topic Monitor** plugin can be loaded from **Plugins | Topics | Topic Monitor**. The **Console** plugin monitors the messages printing on each nodes and their severity. It is very useful for debugging purposes. In the following figure, the left section of `rqt_gui` is loaded with the **Console** plugin and the right side is loaded with **Topic Monitor**. **Topic Monitor** will list the topics available and will monitor their values.

In the following figure, the **Console** plugin monitors the `talker.py` node's messages and their severity level whereas **Topic Monitor** monitors the value inside the `/chatter` Topic.

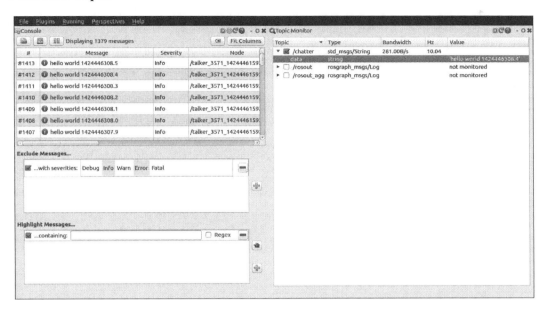

We can also visualize data such as images and plot graphs on `rqt_gui`. For robot navigation and its inspection, there are plugins for embedding RViz in `rqt_gui`. The **Navigation viewer** plugin views the from `/map` Topic. The visualization plugins are available in **Plugin | Visualization**.

Questions

1. What are the popular UI toolkits available on the Linux platform?

2. What are the differences between PyQt and PySide Qt bindings?

3. How do you convert a Qt UI file into Python script?

4. What are Qt signals and slots?

5. What is rqt and what are its main applications?

Summary

In this chapter, we discussed creating a GUI for ChefBot that can be used by an ordinary user who doesn't have any idea about the internal working of a robot. We used Python binding of Qt called PyQt to create this GUI. Before we go to the main GUI design, we saw a **Hello World** application to get an easier understanding of PyQt. The UI design was done using the Qt Designer tool and the UI file was converted into its equivalent Python script using Python UI compiler. After designing the main GUI in Qt Designer, we converted the UI file into Python script and inserted the necessary slots in the generated script. The ChefBot GUI can start the robot, select a table number, and command the robot to get into that position. The position of each table is acquired from the generated map we hardcoded the positions in this Python script for testing. When a table is selected, we set a goal position on the map, and when we click on the **Go** button, the robot will move into the goal position. The user can cancel the operation at any time and command the robot to come to the home position. The GUI can also receive the real-time status of the robot and its battery status. After discussing the robot GUI, we saw the debugging GUI tool in ROS called rqt. We saw some plugins used for debugging the data from the robot. In the next chapter, we will see the complete testing and calibration of the robot.

12
The Calibration and Testing of ChefBot

In this chapter, we will discuss the calibration and testing of ChefBot that is necessary before deploying the robot in the work place. The testing can be done using the GUI that we built in the previous chapter. Before the test run, we can calibrate the sensors and address the issues in the ChefBot hardware and software. In the testing procedure, we can build a map of a hotel kind of arrangement and navigate on the map using ROS on ChefBot. We can also see ways to improve accuracy and upgrade the ChefBot prototype in future.

First, we will look at the calibration of sensors such as Kinect, Quadrature encoder, and IMU to improve the accuracy of the robot.

The Calibration of Xbox Kinect using ROS

Kinect calibration is required to improve the accuracy of the Kinect data. In this robot, Kinect is used instead of a laser scanner. We can generate data equivalent to that provided by laser scanner by converting Point Cloud data, using a depth image to laser scanner converter package in ROS. This converted data may not be as precise as an actual laser scanner, so in effect, the error from the converted laser scanner can affect robot mapping, navigation, and localization. To reduce the errors to some extent, we can do a calibration prior to our application. Kinect can even work on factory settings without being calibrated, each device has its own camera parameters and these can change from device to device. Some of the camera parameters are focal length, format size principle point, and lens distortion. When we perform camera calibration, we are able to adjust these values.

One of the calibrations used in Kinect is intrinsic calibration. Some of the intrinsic parameters are focal length and distortion model. Using intrinsic calibration, we can correct these values of IR (depth) and RGB camera intrinsic parameters.

Let's see how to perform Kinect intrinsic calibration using ROS and Python.

Calibrating the Kinect RGB camera

Before calibrating Kinect using ROS, ensure that the OpenNI driver packages and camera calibration packages of ROS are installed. If they are not installed, we can install them using the following command:

```
$ sudo apt-get install ros-indigo-openni-launch ros-indigo-camera-calibration
```

Before the calibration, print an 8 x 6 checkerboard of 0.108 meter in length. We will get a standard 8 x 6 checkerboard file from the following link:

```
http://wiki.ros.org/camera_calibration/Tutorials/MonocularCalibration
```

Follow the procedure to calibrate the RGB camera in Kinect:

1. Start the OpenNI driver using the following command. This will start Kinect RGB and depth stream images:

    ```
    $ roslaunch openni_launch openni.launch
    ```

2. After launching drivers, run the calibrator code available on the camera_calibration package. The cameracalibrator.py file is the node that performs camera calibration. We have to specify the RGB raw image topic, camera topic, size of the checkerboard and size of the square that we are using. Simply run the calibrator node by using following command:

    ```
    $ rosrun camera_calibration cameracalibrator.py image:=/camera/rgb/image_raw camera:=/camera/rgb --size 8x6 --square 0.108
    ```

3. The above command will open the following window:

4. Assuming that you have a printed checkerboard and you hold it in your hand and show it on the Kinect RGB camera, you can see patterns getting detected, as in the preceeding figure. If it is detected properly, then move the checkerboard to the left, right, top, and bottom of the camera view, as shown in the following figure. There are four bars on the right; the **X** and **Y** bar indicate the amount of data collected in the x and y direction and the **Size** and **Skew** bars indicate the samples of images, that are, towards/away from the camera and tilted up/down respectively.

5. At each step, hold the checkerboard still until the image gets highlighted by the detection pattern in the calibration window. The necessary checkerboard position is shown as follows:

6. When we move the checkerboard around the RGB camera, the size of the bars increase and when the calibration program gets enough samples for calibration, the **CALIBRATE** button will become active.

7. We click on the **CALIBRATE** button to start calibration. The calibration process can take about a minute. The calibration window may be non-responsive for some time, but it will be ready eventually.

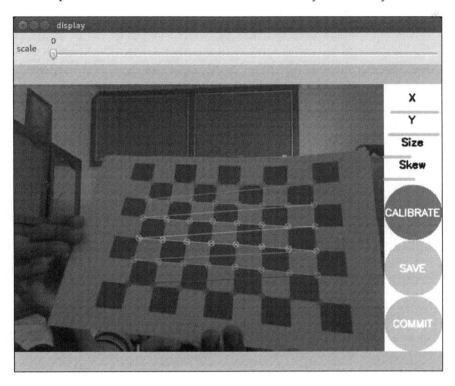

After the calibration process is complete, we can see the calibration results in the terminal and the corrected image will be shown in the calibration window.

A successful calibration will result in a rectified image and a failed calibration usually results in a blank or unrecognizable image.

After calibration, we can use the slider on the top of the calibration window to adjust the size of the rectified image. The scale value will show as zero the rectified image, and some pixels in the original image will be discarded. A scale of 1.0 means we can see the original image and the rectified image has black borders where there are no input pixels in the original image.

If you are satisfied with the calibration, click on the **COMMIT** button to send the calibration parameters to the camera for permanent storage. The GUI exits and you should see `writing calibration data to ...` in the console.

Calibrating the Kinect IR camera

Kinect can detect the depth of the environment using an IR camera and an IR speckle projector, which can perform the same function as a stereo camera. We can calibrate the depth image that we got from Kinect using the checkerboard that we used for the RGB camera calibration.

The difficulty in calibrating a depth image is that the speckle pattern on the depth image can block the accurate detection of the corners of the checkerboard. One possible solution is to cover the IR projector and illuminate it with another IR source such as sunlight, incandescent lamp, and so on. The first figure shows the checkerboard with the speckle pattern and the second figure shows the depth image illuminated by an incandescent lamp and covering the speckle IR projector.

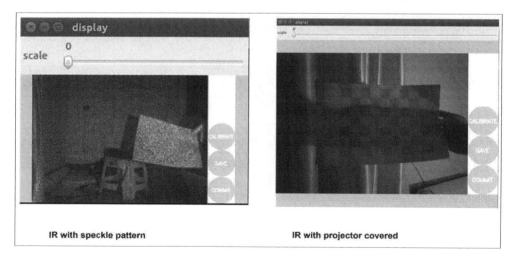

IR with speckle pattern   IR with projector covered

The Python script used for the RGB camera can be used for depth calibration. The following command is used to calibrate the IR camera. Run the calibrator node using the depth image topic; we are using the **8 x 6** checkerboard with a size of 0.108 meter, as shown in the following example:

```
$ rosrun camera_calibration cameracalibrator.py image:=/camera/ir/image_
raw camera:=/camera/ir --size 8x6 --square 0.108
```

The ROS driver for Kinect cannot stream both IR and RGB images. It will decide which of the two to stream, based on the amount of subscribers. It is best to not run any ROS nodes during the calibration of the depth image, which subscribe RGB frames.

Repeat the same movements of the RGB camera calibration in depth camera too. After calibration, we can press the **COMMIT** button to save the calibration values to a file. When we press the **COMMIT** button, the values will be sent to the openni_camera driver package in a form of ROS service call. When openni_camera receives the camera parameters, it will store them to a file with the help of an ROS package called camera_info_manager. The camera_info_manager package can handle these parameters and store them in some location. The default location of intrinsic parameters is $HOME/.ros/camera_info/NAME.yaml and the name of file contains the camera name and device serial number. This file can be moved to any public location we want. The name of the files of RGB and depth calibration will look like rgb_A00362903124106A.yaml and depth_A00362903124106A.yaml.

The content of the RGB camera calibration file is given as follows:

```
image_width: 640
image_height: 480
camera_name: rgb_A00362903124106A
camera_matrix:
  rows: 3
  cols: 3
  data: [543.275251827696, 0, 286.5024846235134, 0,
544.9622371717294, 270.5536535568697, 0, 0, 1]
distortion_model: plumb_bob
distortion_coefficients:
  rows: 1
  cols: 5
  data: [0.1236660642773772, -0.2974236496563437,
0.008147821573873778, -0.03185623828978901, 0]
rectification_matrix:
```

```
    rows: 3
    cols: 3
    data: [1, 0, 0, 0, 1, 0, 0, 0, 1]
projection_matrix:
    rows: 3
    cols: 4
    data: [531.7443237304688, 0, 263.0477918357592, 0, 0,
559.802490234375, 274.1133349321171, 0, 0, 0, 1, 0]
```

If the files are placed in the default location, the OpenNI driver can automatically take the calibration files from this location. If we want to save them in some other location, we have to use the launch file section given in the following code and mention the path of the camera calibration files as arguments of openni.launch:

```
<launch>
<!-- Include official launch file and specify camera_info urls -->
  <include file="$(find openni_launch)/launch/openni.launch">
    <!-- provide arguments to that launch file -->
    <arg name="rgb_camera_info_url"
        value="file:///public/path/rgb_ A00362903124106A.yaml" />
    <arg name="depth_camera_info_url"
        value="file:///public/path/depth_ A00362903124106A.yaml" />
  </include>
</launch>
```

Wheel odometry calibration

Calibration is required in odometry to reduce navigational errors. The main parameter needed to calibrate this is the measure of **Distance per encoder ticks of the wheels**. It is the distance traversed by the robot wheel after during each encoder tick.

The wheel base is the distance between the two differential drive wheels. Distance per encoder ticks is the distance traversed by the wheel on each encoder count. We can calibrate the robot by monitoring encoder counts of each wheel by driving for a fixed distance. The average of these counts is divided by the total distance traveled to get a starting value for the encoder click, which happens per millimeter. The encoder manufacturer may mention an encoder count in one revolution, but in a practical scenario, there will be changes in it.

To calibrate the robot, drive the robot for a fixed distance and note down the encoder counts in the left and right motor. The following equation can give an average count per millimeter:

Counts per millimeter = (left counts + right counts)/2)/ total millimeter traveled

Error analysis of wheel odometry

An error from the wheel odometry can result in accumulation of errors in the position of the robot. The odometry value can change when the wheel slips on the ground or moves on an uneven terrain. The odometry error generated while the robot rotates can cause severe errors in the robot's final position. For example, in a 10 meter trip of robot, if both wheels slip by 1 centimeter, it can cause 0.1 percent errors in the total distance and the robot will arrive 1 cm short of its destination.

However, if the slip between two wheels is 1 centimeter, it can cause more errors than the first case that we discussed. This can result in a large error in both X and Y coordinates.

Assume that the robot wheel base is 10 centimeter and a slip of 1 centimeter between two wheels can result in 0.1 radian error, which is about 5.72 degrees. Given here is the equation to find the heading error:

$$\text{heading error} = (\text{left - right}) \, / \, \text{Wheel base}$$

$$= (0.01 \, / \, 0.1)$$

$$= 0.1 \text{ radians} * (180 \, / \, PI) = \sim 5.72 \text{ degrees}$$

We can find the final position of the robot after 10 meters with a heading error of 0.1 radian, as shown here:

$$X' = 10 * \sin(5.72) = \sim 1 \text{ meter}$$

$$Y' = 10 * \cos(5.72) = 9.9 \text{ meter}$$

From these calculations, we know that a heading error of 0.1 radian causes a shift of 1 meter in the x direction from the destination position. The illustration of this error is given as follows:

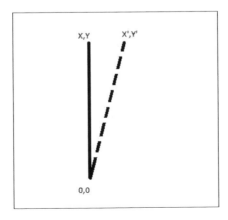

From this analysis, we understood that a small error in θ produces large errors in X and Y. The main error affects the orientation of the robot rather than the distance traveled. There are some methods to reduce this error. These are mentioned in the following section.

Error correction

From the above analysis, it can be seen that the most important error in the robot's position calculation is the error in heading, the θ calculation. Some of the methods to reduce θ errors are as follows:

- **Digital compass**: We can deploy a digital compass in the robot to get the heading of the robot and thereby reduce the robot heading error. Digital compass can be used alone but it may encounter problems such as if there is any local magnetic anomaly, it can make a big noise in the reading. Also, the compass must be perfectly inclined to the robot's surface; if the surface is uneven, there will be errors in the compass readings.

- **Digital gyroscope**: The digital gyroscope provides the rate of change of the angle or angular velocity. If we know the angular velocity, we can find the angle by integrating the values over a period of time. We can find the angular velocity of the robot using gyro; but the gyro value can make errors too. If a robot has to cover a great distance, the error computing from gyro will increase, so gyro can only be used if the robot covers a short distance. If the robot covers a great distance, we can use the combination of a gyroscope and a compass.

- **Gyro-corrected compass**: In this method, we incorporate the gyro and compass in to a single unit, so that one sensor can correct the other. Combining these sensor values using a Kalman filter can give better heading values for the robot.

In the ChefBot prototype, we are using Gyro alone. In future upgrades, we will replace gyro with the combination of gyro and compass.

We are using an IMU called MPU-6050 by Invense to get the heading of the robot. The following section explains a simple calibration method to reduce the offset of MPU 6050. Here are the procedures to calibrate the sensor.

Calibrating the MPU 6050

MPU 6050 calibration can be done using the Energia code, which is used to display the raw values of the sensor mentioned in *Chapter 6, Working with Robotic Sensors*. This example is already available in Energia examples. You will get this code by navigating to `File/Examples/MPU 6050/Examples/MPU 6050_raw`. Load this sketch into Energia and follow the procedure given here:

1. Place the MPU 6050 breakout board on a flat surface. We can use an inclinometer to check the inclination of the surface.

2. Modify the current program by setting the offset to zero. We can set the offset of three axes values of gyroscope to 0 using the following function:

   ```
   ("setXGyroOffset , setYGyroOffset , setZGyroOffset"  =0)
   ```

3. Upload the raw code to Launchpad and take the Energia serial monitor to confirm whether the serial data is coming from the Launchpad. Leave the breakout for 5 to 10 minutes to allow the temperature to stabilize and read the gyro values and note down the values.

4. Set the offset values to the readings noted and upload the code again to the Launchpad.

5. Repeat this procedure until we get a reading of 0 from each gyro axis.

6. After achieving the goal, we finally get the offsets that can be used for future purposes.

These are the necessary procedures to calibrate MPU6050. After sensor calibration, we can test the robot hardware using the GUI.

Testing of the robot using GUI

We have already discussed how to build a map of the environment using the robot simulation and robot hardware. In this section, we discuss how to command the robot to go into a particular place of the map. A better way to find the position of the robot in each table is to manually drive the robot using teleoperation.

Assuming that ChefBot packages are configured in both the robot's PC and the user's PC, there should be Wi-Fi networks to which both the robot and user PCs can connect and communicate using the IP assigned to each PC. It should be noted that we have to set `ROS_MASTER_URI` and `ROS_IP`, as mentioned in *Chapter 10, Integration of ChefBot Hardware and Interfacing it into ROS, Using Python*.

The following procedure can be used to test the robots that are working in a hotel environment:

1. Remote login to the robot PC from the user PC using the `ssh` command. The command is given as follows:

   ```
   $ ssh <robot_pc_ip_address>
   ```

2. If the room is not mapped yet, we can map it using the following commands in the robot terminal. Start the robot sensors and the odometry handling nodes using the following command:

   ```
   $ roslaunch chefbot_bringup robot_standalone.launch
   ```

3. After starting the nodes, we can start the gmapping nodes using the following command:

   ```
   $ roslaunch chefbot_bringup gmapping_demo.launch
   ```

4. After starting gmapping, we can start the keyboard teleoperation nodes to move the robot using the keyboard:

   ```
   $ roslaunch chefbot_bringup keyboard_telop.launch
   ```

5. After launching the teleoperation, run RViz in the user system to view the map generated:

   ```
   $ roslaunch chefbot_bringup view_navigation.launch
   ```

6. A typical map is given in the preceding figure. It can vary according to the environment. After generating the map, we have to run the following command to save the generated map in the home folder:

```
$ rosrun map_server map_saver -f ~/<name_of_the_map>
```

7. After saving the map, we can start the AMCL node for autonomous navigation:

```
$ roslaunch chefbot_bringup amcl_demo.launch map_file:=~/<map_
name.yaml>
```

8. The robot on the map after starting AMCL is shown in the figure. After running AMCL, start the keyboard teleoperation and move to each table referring the map.

9. Check whether the robot's position is the same in map and in the actual environment. If there is a huge difference, then we need to remap the room. If there is less difference, we can retrieve and view robot's position near each table with respect to the map, using the following command:

```
$rosrun tf tf_echo /map /base_link
```

We will get the translation and rotation value of the robot in each position, as shown in the following screenshot:

```
Frame chefbot_caster_front_link exists with parent base_link.
Frame chefbot_caster_back_link exists with parent base_link.
Frame cliff_sensor_front_link exists with parent base_link.
Frame cliff_sensor_left_link exists with parent base_link.
Frame cliff_sensor_right_link exists with parent base_link.
Frame gyro_link exists with parent base_link.

At time 1024.033
- Translation: [0.058, 0.033, 0.010]
- Rotation: in Quaternion [0.000, 0.000, -0.005, 1.000]
            in RPY [0.000, 0.000, -0.009]
At time 1024.438
- Translation: [0.058, 0.033, 0.010]
- Rotation: in Quaternion [0.000, 0.000, -0.005, 1.000]
            in RPY [0.000, 0.000, -0.009]
At time 1024.830
- Translation: [0.058, 0.033, 0.010]
- Rotation: in Quaternion [0.000, 0.000, -0.005, 1.000]
            in RPY [0.000, 0.000, -0.009]
At time 1025.228
- Translation: [0.058, 0.033, 0.010]
- Rotation: in Quaternion [0.000, 0.000, -0.005, 1.000]
            in RPY [0.000, 0.000, -0.009]
```

Note the corresponding position of the robot near each table and feed it to the GUI code. The editing GUI code must be on the user PC. After inserting the position of the robot in each table on the GUI code, run the GUI node using the following command on the user system:

```
$ rosrun chefbot_bringup robot_gui.py
```

The following GUI will pop up and we can control the robot using this GUI.

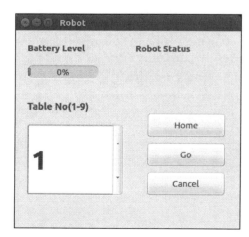

We can command the robot to go into a particular table by giving the table number on the GUI and pressing the **Go** button. When we press the **Go** button, the corresponding goal position is sent to the navigation stack. After testing the GUI, we can deploy the robot on the current environment.

We can see the advantages and disadvantages of this navigation method. The navigation method mainly depends on the ROS framework and programming using Python.

Pros and cons of the ROS navigation

The main highlight of the ROS navigation is that the code is open and reusable. Also, it is simple to understand, even if the handling technology is complex. People with minimal computer knowledge can program an autonomous robot.

The cons of this method are: this is not yet stable and is still in the testing stage, we can't expect high accuracy from this method, and the code may not be of industrial standards.

Questions

1. What is the main use of the intrinsic calibration of Kinect?
2. How we can calibrate MPU 6050 values?
3. How we can calibrate the wheel odometry parameters?
4. What are the possible errors in wheel odometry?
5. What are the pros and cons of this robot design?

Summary

In this chapter, we have discussed all the possible errors and calibrations required before starting the robot. The calibration is required to reduce errors from the sensors. We also saw all the steps to do before working with robot GUI that we have designed. We also have seen the pros and cons of this method. The area we are handling is still being researched so we can't expect high accuracy from the current prototype.

Index

Symbols

B

bags 57
baudRate variable 134
BeagleBone
  URL 106
binaries, for Windows and Mac OS X
  URL 259
Blender
  about 22
  installing 23
  URL 21
  URL, for documentation 23
  URL, for downloading 23
  URL, for Python scripting 34
  URL, for tutorials 33
Blender Python APIs 34
block diagram, robot
  about 94
  Central Processing Unit 106, 107
  embedded controller board 101
  encoder 95
  Inertial Measurement Unit (IMU) 104
  Kinect 105, 106
  motor 95
  motor driver 97, 98
  power supply/battery 108
  speakers/mic 108
  ultrasonic sensors 102
block diagram, speech recognition system
  about 188
  acoustic model 189
  feature extraction 189
  language model 189
  lexicon 189
  recognized words 189
  search algorithm 189
Bootstrap method
  used, for loading A.L.I.C.E. AIML files 220
  used, for loading brain files 220
bpy module
  about 34
  Context Access 34

Data Access 34
Operators 34
brain file
  A.L.I.C.E. AIML files, saving in 219, 220
  loading, Bootstrap method used 220
breakout board
  URL, for purchasing 105
Bullet
  URL 66

C

CAD tools
  AutoCAD 22
  Blender 22
  Google SketchUp 22
  Inventor 22
  LibreCAD 22
  Maya 22
  SolidWorks 22
calibration
  URL 278
Carmine
  about 167
  URL, for purchasing 167
caster wheels
  reference link 30
catkin
  defining 61
  URL 61
Central Processing Unit 106
ChefBot
  ROS Python driver, writing for 239-245
ChefBot description ROS package
  chefbot_base_gazebo.urdf.xacro 80-82
  chefbot_base.urdf.xacro 83, 84
  creating 77-80
  kinect.urdf.xacro 83
ChefBot hardware
  building 230-234
  specifications 94
  working 110, 111

Thank you for buying
Learning Robotics Using Python

About Packt Publishing

Packt, pronounced 'packed', published its first book, *Mastering phpMyAdmin for Effective MySQL Management*, in April 2004, and subsequently continued to specialize in publishing highly focused books on specific technologies and solutions.

Our books and publications share the experiences of your fellow IT professionals in adapting and customizing today's systems, applications, and frameworks. Our solution-based books give you the knowledge and power to customize the software and technologies you're using to get the job done. Packt books are more specific and less general than the IT books you have seen in the past. Our unique business model allows us to bring you more focused information, giving you more of what you need to know, and less of what you don't.

Packt is a modern yet unique publishing company that focuses on producing quality, cutting-edge books for communities of developers, administrators, and newbies alike. For more information, please visit our website at www.packtpub.com.

About Packt Open Source

In 2010, Packt launched two new brands, Packt Open Source and Packt Enterprise, in order to continue its focus on specialization. This book is part of the Packt Open Source brand, home to books published on software built around open source licenses, and offering information to anybody from advanced developers to budding web designers. The Open Source brand also runs Packt's Open Source Royalty Scheme, by which Packt gives a royalty to each open source project about whose software a book is sold.

Writing for Packt

We welcome all inquiries from people who are interested in authoring. Book proposals should be sent to author@packtpub.com. If your book idea is still at an early stage and you would like to discuss it first before writing a formal book proposal, then please contact us; one of our commissioning editors will get in touch with you.

We're not just looking for published authors; if you have strong technical skills but no writing experience, our experienced editors can help you develop a writing career, or simply get some additional reward for your expertise.

Building Machine Learning Systems with Python

ISBN: 978-1-78216-140-0   Paperback: 290 pages

Master the art of machine learning with Python and build effective machine learning systems with this intensive hands-on-guide

1. Master Machine Learning using a broad set of Python libraries and start building your own Python-based ML systems.

2. Covers classification, regression, feature engineering, and much more guided by practical examples.

3. A scenario-based tutorial to get into the right mind-set of a machine learner (data exploration) and successfully implement this in your new or existing projects.

Raspberry Pi Robotic Projects

ISBN: 978-1-84969-432-2   Paperback: 278 pages

Create amazing robotic projects on a shoestring budget

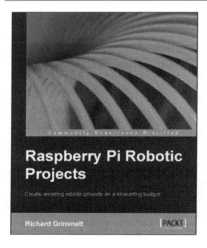

1. Make your projects talk and understand speech with Raspberry Pi.

2. Use standard webcam to make your projects see and enhance vision capabilities.

3. Full of simple, easy-to-understand instructions to bring your Raspberry Pi online for developing robotics projects.

Please check **www.PacktPub.com** for information on our titles

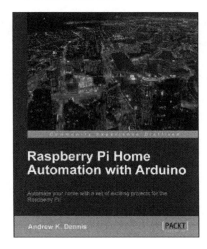

Raspberry Pi Home Automation with Arduino

ISBN: 978-1-84969-586-2   Paperback: 176 pages

Automate your home with a set of exciting projects for the Raspberry Pi!

1. Learn how to dynamically adjust your living environment with detailed step-by-step examples.

2. Discover how you can utilize the combined power of the Raspberry Pi and Arduino for your own projects.

3. Revolutionize the way you interact with your home on a daily basis.

BeagleBone Robotic Projects

ISBN: 978-1-78355-932-9   Paperback: 244 pages

Create complex and exciting robotic projects with the BeagleBone Black

1. Get to grips with robotic systems.

2. Communicate with your robot and teach it to detect and respond to its environment.

3. Develop walking, rolling, swimming, and flying robots.

Please check **www.PacktPub.com** for information on our titles

59215223R00183